LOUIS BOURGAIN

HALIFAX FOR LIBERTÉ !

4 Group's Gallant Frenchmen
at Elvington
1944-45

'They were my friends.'

À Madame DUBLOC et à mon ami Alfred son époux en regrettant simplement de ne pas nous y rencontrer plus souvent

Très affectueusement

le 4 Mai 1999

Bourgain

Published in the United Kingdom by Compaid Graphics
Little Ash, Street Lane, Lower Whitley, Warrington, Cheshire.
WA4 4EN

COPYRIGHT All rights reserved. No part of this publication may be reproduced, or transmitted in any form without the permission of Compaid Graphics (Publishers) and the Author.

Copyright material included in this book is reproduced with permission received on behalf of The Yorkshire Air Museum and other sources.

ISBN 1 900604 07 8

LOUIS BOURGAIN

HALIFAX FOR LIBERTÉ !

4 Group's Gallant Frenchmen
at Elvington
1944-45

Originally published in France as *Sarabande Nocturne*
Translated from the French by Peter Hinchliffe OBE MIL

Foreword by Jules Roy
Foreword to the English edition by The Lord Deramore
Illustrations by Lucien Broque

This book is dedicated
to all the former members of the
Groupes *"Guyenne* and *Tunisie"*

"They were my friends"

The Author

Louis Bourgain

Former student of the *École Polytechnique*;

Lieutenant-Colonel of the Reserve;

Completed a tour of operations as a pilot with the *Groupe de Bombardement Lourd Guyenne* (No. 346 Squadron, Bomber Command);

Officer of the *Légion d'Honneur;*

Croix de Guerre (four citations);

Commandeur de l'Ordre du Mérite;

DFC (Distinguished Flying Cross);

Honorary Vice-President of the *Amicale des Anciens des Groupes Lourds*;

Co-President of the Yorkshire Air Museum.

General de Gaulle conferring on *Lieutenant-Colonel* Louis Bourgain the cross of a Commander of the Order of Merit.

Previous Publications

1951: *"Sarabande Nocturne"*, First Edition (Out of Print);

1988: *"Machines Tournantes et Circuits Pulsés"*, *Éditions Dunod;*

1991: *"Nuits de feu sur l'Allemagne"* (Out of Print);

1994: *"La Victoire après l'Enfer"*.

1997 *"Sarabande Nocturne"*, second edition.

Louis Bourgain as a young *Lieutenant*.

My thanks are due to:

My friend **Jules Roy** for his kind foreword;

Lucien Broque, who applied his talent to the production of the illustrations;

Gisèle, my wife, for her unfailing support throughout;

André Hautot, for the help he gave me, and for so many of the photographs;

I should like to express my additional thanks to people closely involved with the English edition of this book, particularly:

Peter Hinchliffe, who translated this book into English, flew operationally with Bomber Command during the war. He served with the French at Elvington from March 1945 until just before *Groupes Lourds* returned to France the following October.

The Lord Deramore for his kind and perceptive Foreword to the English edition;

Derek Reed, a Trustee of the Yorkshire Air Museum, for his advice and help, not least for recommending Peter Hinchliffe and for involving The Lord Deramore;

Colonel Robert Nicaise, the *Premier Vice-Président* of *L'Amicale des Anciens des Groupes Lourds* (the Association of the Heavy Bomber Groups), for his support and help.

The Trustees of the Yorkshire Air Museum wish to go on record to express their appreciation for the tremendously hard work of the editorial team, **Cath. and Eric Humphrey** and **Brian Gaunt**, who in their turn wish to thank **Mike Mansfield** of Compaid Graphics for all his help.

The author's royalties from the English edition of this work will be shared between the Yorkshire Air Museum and the *Amicale des Anciens des Groupes Lourds*.

This book consists mainly of a narrative about war-time events during the days of 'Little France' at Elvington, near York, but this has been set 'in context' with surrounding historical events.

Contents

Foreword to the French Edition 1
Foreword to the English Edition 3
Author's Note. 5
PART ONE 8

    The French Heavy-Bomber Squadrons on operations

Section 1 9

    The History of the *Groupes Lourds Français* in Great Britain from 1943 to 1945.

Section 2 22

    The Halifax

PART TWO 24

    On Course for all the Perils

Chapter 1 25

    In which the author decides that it is better not to wait until the end of his book before introducing the hero of the story to his readers.

Chapter 2 28

    In which the reader, thrown in at the deep end, may form an impression of the difficulties associated with a bombing mission over the Ruhr.

Chapter 3 36

    From which it may be seen that aircrew know how to use their leisure time in a sensible way.

Chapter 4 38

> In which P.O. Jules gives a lecture on how various commands are used at Elvington.

Chapter 5 41

> In which P.O. Jules discovers the secret of the Normandy operations.

Chapter 6 47

> From which the reader may understand R/T as used on board a Halifax.

Chapter 7 53

> In which P.O. Jules puts the reader in the picture on culinary matters at Elvington.

Chapter 8 55

> In which, for the first time, the reader catches a glimpse of the intimate life of P.O. Jules

Chapter 9 58

> In which flying activity redoubles in intensity and one sees P.O. Jules in action.

Chapter 10 66

> From which one might note the dire consequences that can come from a typographical error.

Chapter 11 70

> In which the reader is put more fully in the picture on the subject of bicycles.

Chapter 12 72

    In which the reader once again enters into the atmosphere of the mess.

Chapter 13 76

    In which one may see the inexorability of Fate at Elvington.

Chapter 14 82

    In which one sees how P.O. Jules always keeps ahead of the game.

Chapter 15 85

    In which the reader will observe that certain aspects of life on camp are more eventful than might appear at first sight.

Chapter 16 89

    From which the reader will understand what is meant by a day on Stand-by.

Chapter 17 92

    In which the reader joins P.O. Jules in deploring the state of apparent oblivion that the Heavy Bomber *Groupes* live in.

Chapter 18 94

    In which it is a matter of improving on the ordinary.

Chapter 19 97

    In which the reader is made aware of the misfortunes of P.O. Jules.

Chapter 20 99

> In which the question of recommendation for promotion rebounds and leads to the formation of an FFI cell at Elvington.

Chapter 21 102

> In which the reader discovers the importance of Gremlins at Elvington.

Chapter 22 108

> From which one may note that contact with Headquarters is not indispensable for keeping up the morale of those who are doing the fighting.

Chapter 23 113

> In which the reader is present when the crew comes back from an operation.

Chapter 24 117

> From which the reader may form an idea of what a bombing mission to the Ruhr means.

Chapter 25 124

> From which the reader will note that No. 346 Squadron, not completely forgotten, attracts the attention of certain personalities in London and in North Africa.

Chapter 26 127

> An account of two consecutive raids on Cologne, from which it will become apparent to the reader that meteorology is anything but an exact science.

Chapter 27 131

> The tale of a dog

Chapter 28 133

> In which the reader learns how P.O. Jules passes the long winter evenings.

Chapter 29 136

> From which the reader may see how things keep piling up.

Chapter 30 141

> From which the reader will note that in many ways Elvington resembles the Tower of Babel.

Chapter 31 145

> When the Pathfinders die at the time of the Breton Legends.

Chapter 32 152

> From which the reader might sense that P.O. Jules' morale sometimes wavers.

Chapter 33 155

> In which the reader is once more confronted with the risk of collision.

Chapter 34 158

> In which the reader is there when P.O. Jules flies his last operation.

Chapter 35 169

> In which the reader rediscovers France at last.

PART THREE 175
In Memoriam

Section 1 176

The human and material losses in the French Groupes Lourds:

Section 2 179

1. Members of Aircrew who became casualties on operations:

2. Ground Personnel killed while preparing for an operation:

3. Aircrew killed in training accidents in Great Britain:

4. Crew members killed or injured on leaving Elvington for France.

PART FOUR 228
The Crews

Section One 229

The crews of Groupe Guyenne

Section Two 232

The crews of Groupe Tunisie

Section Three 235

Some of the crews who survived the war

PART FIVE. 242
> **The End of the War**

PART SIX. 258
> **On Course......:**

Chapter 36 259
> In which the reader meets P.O. Jules again four years later.

PART SEVEN 262
> **When the Past becomes the Present**
>
> The creation of the Yorkshire Air Museum and the Memorial to the Allied Air Forces.

PART EIGHT. 282
> **Epilogue**

If you can fill the unforgiving minute
With sixty seconds' worth of distance run,
Yours is the Earth and everything that's in it,
And – which is more – you'll be a Man, my son!

Rudyard Kipling

Foreword to the French Edition

The author of this book, *'Saraband Nocturne'* [1], is no stranger to me. We met in Great Britain in the early summer of 1944 in a French *Groupe* of heavy bombers. It was wartime. The world was divided into three factions: those fighting against Nazi Germany; those fighting with it; and those doing their best to stay neutral. We belonged to the first faction, which was spread across the whole planet. We came from the French Army that was occupying North Africa when the Allies landed there. Flyers who had no aeroplanes left, we enlisted in the Royal Air Force in 1943, and after nine months of military induction and training in England we arrived at the camp at Elvington, which is near to the city of York but a long way from anywhere else. London was 200 miles to the south, Edinburgh 200 miles to the north. We were flying the Handley Page Halifax with its four Hercules engines that gave a total of 7,200 horsepower and were capable of lifting 32 tonnes of airframe, petrol and bombs. We normally flew operations by night in fleets that sometimes comprised hundreds, sometimes thousands, of aircraft, which called for considerable discipline, rude health and faultless organisation. Each man had to do what he was supposed to do, and nothing more. Above all nothing more, otherwise it could have been catastrophic.

Our aeroplanes flew almost without interruption, except when they had to go in for overhaul or repair. The crews, being less robust, needed rest. Therefore there were two crews to each machine. Each crew took its turn. Louis Bourgain was a pilot and captain of aircraft; I was also captain of aircraft, but I was a bomb aimer. Each crew had, in addition, a navigator, a wireless operator, a flight engineer and two gunners. Bourgain and I belonged to No. 346 Squadron, which had an establishment of a dozen aircraft; No. 347 Squadron had the same number. Operational flights over Germany and the occupied countries varied in their intensity and in the emotions they generated. Losses were cruel. After a certain number of sorties a crew was worn out. In our time the number varied between thirty and forty. After that, those still alive had the right to recognition by the United Nations.

---

[1] *'Saraband Nocturne'* was the French title of *'Halifax for Liberté'*

I have a clear recollection of Pilot Officer Jules, the main character in this work. He was a young *Capitaine* who stood out from the others by reason of an apparent indolence, not of spirit but of character. In the mess, among his contemporaries, in the briefing room or in his flying kit, whatever situation he found himself in, Pilot Officer Jules smiled. Quite rightly, he believed that things could have been worse. In this book P.O. Jules describes his life by day, and by night, without taking it too seriously. He reminds one of André Maurois' famous Major O'Grady. P.O. Jules is a quiet, modest man, full of wisdom and humour. *'The only complicated thing about P.O. Jules is that you never know whether he's being serious or joking,'* as you will read somewhere in this book. P.O. Jules is living in the middle of hell, and he knows it: but he decides not to think about it too much. Maybe he doesn't like everything that happens to him, but he tries to escape from difficult situations without recourse to high-sounding words. For him the exceptional, the exaggerated, the unexpected, the surprising, extreme danger, become his daily bread: nothing to get alarmed about; it's just routine; we'll make it. But at the same time we won't forget the friends we loved and who didn't make it. Where so many others have seen nothing but the tragic and the sublime, he is content to play things down, even though he sometimes makes the best of a situation. One would be wrong to imagine that P.O. Jules did not consistently have in mind the dramatic nature of the Saraband: it contains a great deal of noise, of din, of unrest and even of savagery. Sometimes it is quite hideous. At the time when we were involved in flights over Germany, in military discipline and all that went with it, sometimes the only means of moral escape was by innocence or mockery. P.O. Jules has chosen to tell his own story in a very laid-back way. *'He had a peculiar philosophy, pretending that the life of wartime pilots was entirely peaceful...'*

A hero without knowing he was one, a hero without wanting to be one.

I met P.O. Jules again recently: he hasn't changed.. **Jules Roy**

Fig 1. *The crew of* Commandant Roy

Foreword to the English Edition

by

The Lord Deramore

Lord Deramore's family home, Heslington Hall, now part of York University was, during the Second World War, the Headquarters of 4 Group, of which the French Squadrons, Nos. 346 and 347, were a significant part.

Lord Deramore is the younger brother of S/Ldr. The Lord (Stephen) Deramore, who was a Controller at 4 Group HQ during WW2. Arthur Deramore was a F/Lt. Navigator in the RAFVR and flew 352 operational hours in Blenheims, Marauders and Wellingtons. of No. 14 Squadron in the Mediterranean and UK theatres. He inherited the Barony in December 1964 on the death of Stephen, his brother.

**

This excellent translation of Lt/Col.Louis Bourgain's book *Sarabande Nocturne* makes a very welcome addition to the bookshelves of all who are interested in European history between 1933 and 1946, but especially those concerned with the war in the air. But it is more than a dry-as-dust history. The author's modesty, sense of humour, philosophical insight and poetic gift raise it to the ranks of classical war books. The humour reminds one of *The Good Soldier Schweik*, the descriptions of night bombing raids over Germany have the power of *All Quiet on the Western Front* and the philosophical reflections are reminiscent of much in *Winged Victory*.

The author's French nationality gives added poignancy to his tale, and reminds us how true French patriots were betrayed by their country's corrupt and demoralised politicians in the 1930s. Poorly paid and ill equipped armed forces were in the Spring of 1940 in no state to combat the rebuilt German war machine. The British were forced to evacuation at Dunkirk and the French reeled further and further back till Field Marshal Pétain, the Hero of Verdun in WW1, signed a shameful Armistice to set up a puppet Government in the Southern half of France. The humiliation felt by all patriotic Frenchmen can be imagined.

General de Gaulle, however, escaped to Britain and formed the Free French movement, to which many thousands of French patriots rallied, often against appalling odds, to serve under the banner of *La Croix de Lorraine*. French pilots were flying Spitfires in 1940 and, as early as December 1st., 1941, a twenty-four aircraft bombing attack on the Afrika Korps was composed of six Blenheims each from a French Squadron and RAF Squadrons Nos. 14, 45 & 84.

After the Anglo-American landings in North Africa in November 1942, the Free French Movement was replaced by 'Le Comité Français Libération' and, as Col.Bourgain records, the HQ of the French Air Force moved to Algiers. His story of the English WAAF, whose hand in marriage was sought by an amorous member of the French ground crew of No.346 Squadron, is hilarious.

By 1944/45 there were no less than nine French Squadrons operating with the RAF against the common enemy and for the freedom of all those European countries submerged into Hitler's Greater European State. In addition to fighter and medium bomber squadrons there were the two Halifax Heavy Bomber Squadrons, Nos.346 and 347, which formed part of 4 Group RAF Bomber Command at Heslington, near York. So it came about that come VE Day in 1945, these brave French men had more than vindicated the Honour of France.

Peter Hinchliffe has done us all a service by his hard work and skill in translating *Sarabande Nocturne*. *Halifax for Liberté* is a delightful and most readable book. The Yorkshire Air Museum deserves our thanks for arranging its publication.

Deramore

Author's Note

The first edition of *Sarabande Nocturne* appeared in 1951. In it I attempted to tell the adventures of my friend P.O. Jules during his tour of operations with Bomber Command of the Royal Air Force from June 1944 to January 1945.

At first this book was intended solely for former members of the *Groupes Guyenne* and *Tunisie*. My aim was simply to reproduce the atmosphere on the station at Elvington with its carefree moments and those blemished by absence and by death. Primarily I wanted the book to spotlight the friendship that united me with P.O. Jules and by extension with all the pilots and aircrew who shared my operational life during those long months.

Equally, however, it was written for all those on the ground, mechanics and armourers, who laboured for our safety and who we knew were happy to see us again in the darkness of night or the mists of early morning.

It was intended to be a tribute to all of them.

That first edition did not contain a historical perspective. There seemed to be no point in explaining Bomber Command to those who had experienced it.

This second edition is aimed at a broader public, particularly young people, so that it is necessary to describe, even if only superficially, the aerial offensive in the West from 1939 to 1945. During the four years from 1942 to 1945, whenever the weather conditions over the target were suitable,

Fig 2. *The author in his pilot's parachute harness.*

British and American bombers attacked industrial and military objectives in Nazi Germany every single day: no exception was made for holidays, not even Christmas. (British aircraft had been bombing German targets since 1939.)

The *Groupes Guyenne* and *Tunisie* took part in this vast battle. For twelve months, from June 1944 to May 1945, French crews fought alongside their British comrades.

The French people who, under the Occupation, heard the uninterrupted nightly throbbing of aircraft passing above their heads on their long journey to and from Germany, could not help being aware that a formidable battle was being fought in the skies above Western Europe. But what they did not know, though they might have suspected, was that among those aircraft there were probably some with Tricolour roundels that carried the Cross of Lorraine, those of the *'Guyenne'* and *'Tunisie'* Squadrons. They learned of this officially only after the war, because nothing was done to publicise it at the time.

PART ONE

The French Heavy-Bomber Squadrons on operations
1943 to 1945

"*L'Équipage*" ("The Crew"): painting by Gérard Weygand, aviation artist.

No matter how hard the mission set for them
No one was ever found wanting

Section 1

The History of the *Groupes Lourds Français* in Great Britain from 1943 to 1945.

Nos. 346 and 347 Squadrons, Royal Air Force.

The month of March 1943 marked a decisive turning point in our flying history. Fighting in North Africa was coming to an end. The troops of Field Marshal Rommel, the famous *Afrika Korps,* had retreated from El Alamein in Egypt into Tunisia, where they had moved into the peninsula of Cape Bon, some kilometres south of Tunis.

From the beginning of 1943 the French Bomber *Groupes* 2/23 and 1/25 had been fighting at the side of their allies. With their old *Léo 45* machines they had occupied the airfield at Blida in the south of Algeria. Flying conditions were made difficult by the lack of navigation aids. The airfield was badly furnished with radio direction-finding equipment. Despite this the French bombers carried out a number of harassing raids against the rear of the retreating German troops. In doing so they proved to themselves that they were capable of fighting and that they had the will to do so. Like all their comrades, most of whom had crossed the Mediterranean in May and June 1940 at the time of the collapse, they were ready to go and fly operationally. Their sole wish was to cast out the invader and to liberate their country.

It was at this time that the French Air Ministry decided, in consultation with their allies, upon a fundamental reorganisation of our Air Force. Under the terms of the agreement with the staffs of the Allies it was to be divided into two parts:

- The first part, which was equipped with American equipment, would join the ranks of the United States Air Force.

- The second, equipped with British equipment, would join those of the Royal Air Force.

Among the units with British equipment were two heavy-bomber *Groupes,* destined to be integrated into Bomber Command. *Groupes* 2/23 and 1/25 became a framework for these units. From then on they were known as the *Groupes 'Guyenne'* and *'Tunisie'.*

Once these decisions had been taken, things started to move. At the beginning of August 1943 the first elements of *Groupe Guyenne* were assembled on the beach of Zéralda. A fortnight later they moved to Algiers, where they embarked on the SS 'Orbita', bound for Liverpool. *Groupe Tunisie* took the same route two weeks afterwards.

Fig 3. The insignia of the Groupe Guyenne. *Top section, the badge of the Third Escadrille, representing the Egyptian eagle. Lower section, a small white rabbit carrying a begging bag.*

Fig 4. The insignia of the Groupe Tunisie. *In the top section, the badge of the Groupe, which shows a sand owl. The lower section is the badge of the Second Escadrille, a buffalo.*

Fig 5. "...A small white rabbit..."
- kept as a mascot in "Little France" (Elvington Base).

Training in RAF schools.

Now began for both aircrew and ground personnel the long cycle of training in Royal Air Force schools. The first task was to accustom the pilots to flying in the execrable weather conditions that prevailed over England: low cloud, bad visibility, icing and so on. Then it was necessary to give the crews the cohesion necessary to fly the long and perilous missions that would eventually be their lot when they went into action over Germany.

Air Commodore de Beaumont was the first senior British officer to greet them. He was from the British Air Ministry, where he was in charge of airmen from overseas. In this capacity he was responsible for organising the various steps in forming the squadrons. He was a direct descendant of the Count de Beaumont, one of the most faithful companions of William the Conqueror, who had played a major part in the Battle of Hastings. Without the Air Commodore's ancestor the outcome of the battle might have been different, England might not have become Norman and the flag bearing three golden leopards on a red background[2] might not fly on British buildings today as it flies on the battlements of the Castle of Caen in Normandy.

Air Commodore de Beaumont, who spoke excellent French, enjoyed talking with the French crews. His favourite subject of conversation was the Norman influence on our two countries. One could sense that he was a true friend of France, one of those who believed that the Anglo-French Alliance was the last bastion of liberty.

---

[2] This forms part of the Royal Standard

RAF Station Elvington

In the middle of May 1944, after long months in R.A.F. training schools, the first crews from *Groupe Guyenne* finally arrived at their base, Elvington, situated a few kilometres from the old medieval city of York.

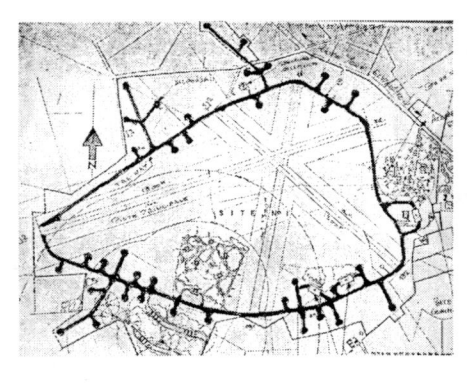

Fig 6. The Elvington Base. In 1944 and 1945 it was the only foreign enclave on British territory, Two thousand French were stationed there. The British and French flags flew side by side at the entrance to the base.

There they were reunited with the ground staff who had taken over the installations a month earlier.

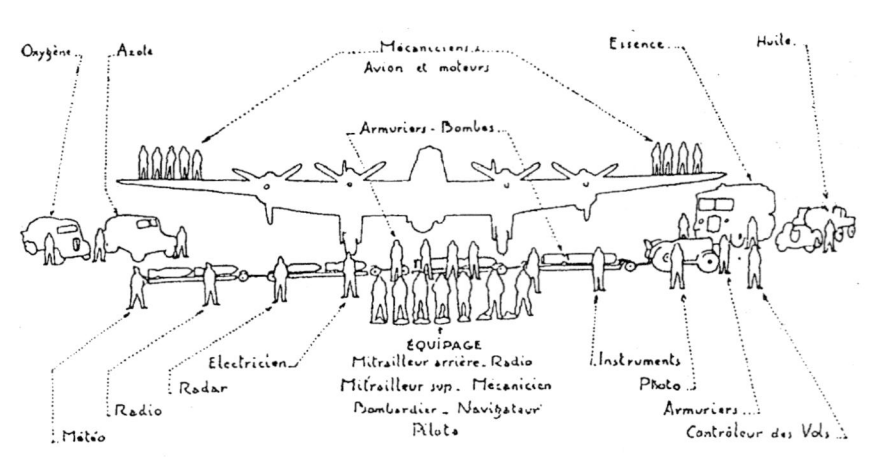

Fig 7. The groundcrew and aircrew needed to put a Halifax to work.

Fig 8. Commandant Churet. The ground crews at Elvington did a wonderful job. No matter what difficulties they encountered they always succeeded in providing the number of serviceable aircraft that Headquarters Bomber Command demanded. Commandant Churet was their boss. He combined firmness with gentleness.

The base was one of the oldest in Bomber Command. In 1940 it only had grass runways. The increased weight of aircraft had made it necessary to replace them with concrete runways. This work and other work concerned with the construction of buildings was carried out in 1941. No. 77 Squadron then took over the base, remaining there until the arrival of the French ground and aircrew personnel.

In due course Elvington became a French base in May 1944. All the personnel there, from the ordinary airman to the Colonel commanding the base, were French. The only exceptions were a number of British officers who acted as interpreters, technicians and administrators, so catering for the necessary liaison with the civilian and military authorities. Both the French and the British flags flew at the entrance to the base on the road leading to the village. Elvington base was a French enclave on British territory. It was the only one of its kind in the United Kingdom.

The Position of the French *Groupes* within Bomber Command

When they arrived at Elvington the *Groupes Guyenne* and *Tunisie* became Nos. 346 and 347 Squadrons, Bomber Command. Within the overall operational plan nothing distinguished them from the British squadrons. They received the same orders, they were subject to the same discipline and they were integrated into the Bomber Command hierarchy. Above the *Colonel* who commanded the base were respectively:

Fig 9. From left to right: Air Commodore Walker, Air Vice-Marshal Carr and Air Chief Marshal Sir Arthur Harris. *This photograph brings together the three senior commanders of the Groupes Lourds when they were operational. For all the veterans this is an emotive memory.*

- **Air Commodore Walker.** He commanded the station in 1943. In 1944 he was the youngest officer of Air rank in the RAF. He had lost an arm when attempting to save the life of a mid-upper gunner trapped in a blazing aircraft on return from an operation. Athletic by nature, he had been a prominent rugby player before the war. He was always there on the touchline when French rugby or football teams were playing.

Fig 10. The Rugby team of Elvington Base, showing, in the centre, Air Commodore Walker and Capitaine Notelle, the manager of the rugby team.

- 15 -

- **Air Vice-Marshal Carr.** He commanded No. 4 Group, which was stationed in Yorkshire and comprised seventeen squadrons.

Fig 11. Although no badge was authorised this represents the insignia of No. 4 Group, to which the Groupes Guyenne and Tunisie were attached, and within which they were known as Nos. 346 and 347 Squadrons respectively.

Further to the north, in the present North Yorkshire and just into County Durham, was No. 6 Group, which was made up entirely of Canadian squadrons.

- **Air Chief Marshal Sir Arthur Harris.** Harris commanded Bomber Command for more than three years without ever taking a day off. He never observed a public holiday, even at Christmas. Every night he waited until the bomber crews were back, anxious about their fate. He received his orders directly from the civil authority, the War Cabinet, which was presided over by Sir Winston Churchill himself and which decided on targets and priorities. Both during hostilities and since, his actions and his controversial methods have been unjustly criticised. For the French who had the honour to serve under him, however, he remains one of the principal architects of victory. He liked the French and the French returned his affection.

At the end of the war Bomber Command had 130 squadrons, fifty equipped with Lancasters, fifty with Halifaxes and thirty with Mosquitos. It could send out 2,000 bombers each night, each capable of dropping five tons of bombs.

The *Groupes Lourds* on operations from June 1944 to May 1945

Aircraft from *Groupe Guyenne* carried out their first operation during the night of 1st/2nd June 1944. The target was a radar station located at a place near Cherbourg called '*La Ferme d'Urville*'. The radar was responsible for the surveillance of the western part of the Channel. It was completely destroyed.

On the night of the 5th/6th June a deception operation by No. 617 Squadron, commanded by Group Captain Leonard Cheshire, neutralised the two radar stations at Douvre la Deliverance and Le Havre.

Fig 12. Group Captain Leonard Cheshire, V.C.: In 1945 he was the youngest and most decorated Group Captain in the Royal Air Force. After the war he dedicated himself almost entirely to charity work, achieving a formidable output. To all those who knew him or had the honour to be in touch with him he was above all a 'good' man, with all the greatness that the adjective can imply.

On the night of the invasion, therefore, the Germans were deprived of all their radars. They were effectively blind and so unable to deploy their defences – gunboats, swift torpedo boats, submarines, surface vessels – against the invasion fleet. The immense Allied armada was able to cross without having to suffer a naval defeat.

This success was without a doubt the greatest victory won by Bomber Command throughout the hostilities.

During the same night crews from *Groupe Guyenne* attacked gun batteries in the Atlantic Wall near to la Pointe du Hoc, where Americans Rangers would earn glory a few hours later.

In the middle of June crews from *Groupe Tunisie* in their turn began operations.

Then together, for a period of eleven months, they plied the skies of Germany and the occupied territories in the course of operations that sometimes exceeded eight-and-a-half hours in the air, in a state of nervous tension that can scarcely be imagined by those who have not experienced it. At any moment of their flight the worst of dangers might assail them. Night fighters, anti-aircraft fire, collision, engine failure, icing, bad weather, returning to base in the fogs of England: these were the fates awaiting them.

They lived in exile, far from their families, far from their homeland, far from everything. In such difficult conditions, and despite the heavy losses they had to suffer, not a single one of them refused to fly.

Beginning from this time the two *Groupes* took part successively in the Battle of Normandy, the Battle of the Secret Weapons and the Battle of Germany.

By day and by night, whenever the weather circumstances allowed it, they took off from the airfield at Elvington for long and perilous raids on Germany. In this way they carried out 123 missions, which represented 2,500 sorties, and they dropped 10,000 tons of bombs.

Compared with the tonnage dropped by the British during the Second World War – 955,000 tons - this is only a small weight of bombs. But the French crews tried to compensate for their numerical inferiority by the quality of their application, as is evidenced by the facts reported in the paragraph below.

A message addressed to the French at Elvington at the end of the war is ample proof. Here it is:

'Please convey to all French personnel who have served or are serving in Bomber Command my admiration and my gratitude for their unfailing cooperation, their outstanding gallantry and efficiency.

'Together we carried the battle into the heart of Germany and taught the enemy a lasting lesson in the full meaning of war, a cruel lesson that the enemy lived through and which will always be remembered. That is their reward.

'To all those brave French airmen who carried on the fight in our ranks, the warmest salutations of Bomber Command.'

The French crews and Air Commodore Walker

On the occasion of the first operations in which the French crews participated Air Commodore Walker was present on the station at Elvington. He attended all the briefings and then went to the Air Traffic Control Tower to watch the take-offs. He waited patiently for the bombers to come back. When the bombers arrived overhead the base he watched the approaches and landings. After the debriefing of the last crew to return Air Commodore Walker turned to *Commandant* Puget and said, 'Now to work !'

Fig 13. Air Commodore 'Gus' Walker & Commandant Puget.

Then one after the other he checked the navigators' logs, taking note of the difference between the route laid down and that actually followed. While this checking process was going on the photographs taken by the crews above the target were developed. Air Commodore Walker himself attempted to measure all the inaccuracies of aim. When this meticulous work was completed he turned back to *Commandant* Puget:

'Good job. Very good job,' he said. 'I won't need to check again in future.'

From then on when he visited the French he behaved more like a friend than a boss. Reciprocal esteem was the basis of the relationship.

In the broader respect the French crews had a deep admiration for their British senior officers. Their task was to prepare the operation in such a way that the enemy remained ignorant as long as possible of that night's principal target. Above all it was important that the German fighters should not succeed in intercepting the bomber stream. That didn't often happen, but one particular example was the night of the 4th/5th November 1944, when the *Groupe Guyenne* lost five crews from sixteen that took part in an operation to Bochum.

Bomber Command – the Balance Sheet

The main aim of this chapter is to give an account of the French squadrons within Bomber Command, but it nevertheless seems appropriate to give an outline sketch of the aerial offensive in the west during World War Two.

Let us note first of all that the principal aim of strategic bombing is the destruction of the military and industrial potential of the enemy.

In the industrial field, the destruction of synthetic fuel plants reduced production to five percent of its original value. The strategic bombing of industrial cities forced the German Minister of Production to divert manufacture into small towns and villages. The items made in this way then had to be transported by rail to the assembly plants. Railway stations and marshalling yards played an important part in industrial production while the items were in transit. Losses in production are difficult to quantify, but they were certainly significant.

In the military domain the *Luftwaffe* was obliged, in order to defend German towns, to withdraw all its fighter units that were stationed in France and on the Italian Front. In the same way at the beginning of 1944, when the Battle of Berlin began, a large part of the German fighter force on the Eastern Front was brought back to the region of the capital of the Third Reich.

From the viewpoint of ethics, it is certain that the aerial bombing helped to reduce the length of the war by several months, possibly by as much as a year.

At the beginning of 1942 Hitler had embarked upon what he called 'the final solution', which consisted of the extermination of Jews, concentration camp inmates, dissidents and so on. The number of people who perished in extermination camps is estimated at ten million. Alongside this slaughter may be put the total of 650,000 German war victims. If the duration of the war had not been reduced, what might have been the comparative figures?

Thus the aerial offensive in the west played a decisive role in the final victory. As the Minister of Armaments, Albert Speer, wrote in his memoirs:

'The bombing from the air was the principal cause of the defeat of Germany and the collapse of the Third Reich.'

Section 2

The Halifax

The Halifax was a metal-skinned, twin-fin monoplane of light alloy construction.

Fig 14. The HALIFAX III

The reader will note that the Halifax did not possess a belly turret. German fighters could therefore attack from below without being detected by the crew. As a result, losses increased. On the other hand the introduction of such a turret would have had a direct adverse effect on the radius of action and the tonnage of bombs carried. To attack a given target it would therefore have been necessary to increase the number of aircraft dispatched, which would have resulted in heavier losses.

The configuration of the aircraft was a result of an evaluation of these two contradictory requirements. In it one sees the principal reason for the solution adopted.

At first the *Groupes Lourds* were equipped with the Halifax III. Towards the end of the war the Halifax Mk.VI replaced the Halifax III in Bomber Command units.

As a result of the increased power of its engines its performance (ceiling, speed, bomb-load) was significantly superior to that of its predecessor.

The Halifax Mk.VI was powered by four Bristol Hercules 100 engines.

- Span: 31.6 metres.
- Length: 21.8 metres.
- Height: 6.1 metres.

Number of crew members: seven, comprising one pilot, one navigator, one bomb aimer, one wireless operator, one flight engineer, one mid-upper gunner, one rear gunner.

Bristol Hercules 100 engines:

- Maximum take-off power: 1,700 horsepower.
- Maximum cruise power: 1,200 horsepower.
- Fourteen cylinders in radial formation, air-cooled.

Performance:

- Maximum all-up weight on take-off: 30.5 tonnes.
- Maximum speed at 10,000 feet: 470 km/hr.
- Operational ceiling with full load: 21,000 feet.
- Duration: 14 hours (4,500 kilometres).
- Average bomb-load: 4 tonnes of bombs for an operation of six to seven hours duration.
- Average fuel consumption at economic cruising speed: 1,000 litres/hr.

PART TWO

On Course for all the Perils

Chapter 1

In which the author decides that it is better not to wait until the end of his book before introducing the hero of the story to his readers.

How did Pilot Officer Jules come to arrive in England? Did he come via Spain? Did he cross the Pyrenees in the depth of winter? Did he leave

Fig 15. Some of the officers of the 2nd. group of the 32nd. Wing at Mediouna (Morocco) after the debacle of June 1940.

From left to right : Aspirant[3] Mezergues, Sous-Lieutenant Hoffman, Lieutenant Goepfert, Lieutenant Bourgain, Lieutenant Benoit, Aspirant[1] Watemberg, Lieutenant Commeau.

They are anticipating revenge.

    3   *Aspirant* - the nearest equivalent RAF rank is Officer Cadet

France in a submarine or an aeroplane? Or did he simply come from North Africa?

It doesn't really matter a great deal. The story that follows starts in June 1944 on the airfield at Elvington, a few miles from York. I had just joined one of the heavy bomber squadrons stationed there. The weather was grey and wet, and when I had taken my raincoat off I went into the mess. There were ten officers at the bar, lieutenants and captains, and among them was one who caught my eye straight away. I went up to him and introduced myself:

'*Capitaine* X,' he answered, 'also known as P. O. Jules.'

He turned to the barman:

'Barman - another whisky. We mustn't neglect the lower orders!

'This,' he said, 'is reserved for friends.'

And that was how, in a most unremarkable way, leaning on a bar and enjoying a whisky, I first made the acquaintance of Pilot Officer Jules. He had an innocent laugh, a high forehead and temples innocent of hair. Whenever he spoke of his advancing baldness he was in the habit of saying,

'I'm nine-tenths cloud cover now, but clear skies are on the way.'

During the months that followed I got to know him better; but I was never able to figure out in what circumstances or by what chance a French aircrew officer with the rank of *Capitaine* came to be "promoted" to Pilot Officer in the Royal Air Force, which equates to *sous-lieutenant*. It was an unusual aberration in the military hierarchy that I was never able to explain. Possibly the rank had been conferred on him because of his likeness to P.O. Prune, whose adventures are famous throughout the Royal Air Force. Like him, he drank his whisky straight because, he said, he was afraid that water might turn his iron stomach rusty. And if you told him, 'Jules, you're slipping!' he'd reply, 'It's the war that's tired me out.'

He embraced a philosophy that was far different from that embraced by professors, based on the thesis that sufficiency was often only the same thing as insufficiency. He would insist that the life of an operational pilot was a wholly peaceful one, and that the more worries that beset you the more you should live a carefree existence. One day someone asked him, 'Jules, what are you fighting for?' He replied, 'To be the same as everyone else.'

Then, when someone else pointed out, 'But everybody in the world isn't fighting,' he contented himself with saying, 'But what if I choose to believe that everybody is?'

His was a healthy philosophy. He was under no illusion as to what it meant to take part in thirty-three night missions over Germany, and from time to time he would give voice to this profound thought: 'The life of an operational pilot is bespattered with real dangers.'

Sometimes he would express himself even more mundanely by commenting to his bomb aimer friend Jules, 'Jules, those who don't take things too seriously usually come out best in the end.'

At other times he would propound the mathematical formula 'Ace aviator = dead aviator,' a formula that neatly expressed the harsh reality of those times, that the only heroes were those who were already dead. And he would go on, 'Please God I'll never be a hero!'

His philosophy did not confine itself to matters to do with the war. It covered vast areas in which his education, both mathematical and literary, enabled him to propound theories that were both fascinating and unexpected. For example he believed that, in politics, the length that governments served was conditioned by the country's institutions and traditions. 'The length that a state lasts,' he would say, 'depends on the strength of its constitution.' And he would go on, oddly enough, to observe that it was the same for pilots. Which was why he attached so much importance to keeping himself in condition.

But all this did not stop him from consulting his panicometer from time to time, a precision instrument that he had designed and constructed in the course of all the years of war. Essentially it consisted of a ball that could move between two moving pointers. In the event of danger, the distance between the two pointers decreased, and the ball jammed. Then the needle on the dial pointed towards zero. He knew that in such an event he needed to redouble his attention.

Be he what he might - republican, traditionalist, experimenter, thinker or philosopher - P.O. Jules could help you to pass a pleasant moment or two.

Which is no more than the author wants.

Chapter 2

In which the reader, thrown in at the deep end, may form an impression of the difficulties associated with a bombing mission over the Ruhr.

A fortnight had passed since I had arrived at Elvington, during which time I had passed my qualification tests. These tests consisted of a series of exercises in bombing and navigation. When a crew had carried them out satisfactorily it was assessed as "fit", and the pilot then flew a familiarisation operation in action with a qualified crew.

Chance decided that on the day in question I would carry out my second-pilot trip with P.O. Jules. He it was who was to give me my baptism of fire over Germany, and deep down I was quite pleased. It seemed to me that his inherent optimism would help me to overcome a certain, should I say, understakable apprehension. And so that evening I called in at his room to pick him up and we went together to the intelligence section or briefing room. Operations were always preceded by an interminable succession of meetings in the course of which all details of the target, navigation, the strength of the enemy defences and so on were presented to us. As we crossed the threshold of the holy of holies, the briefing room, P.O. Jules turned to me:

'And now', he said, 'let's get weaving! Work is good for the health! Long live tuberculosis!'

Then he looked at the target on the map, passed his hand across his forehead, his nose, his mouth; then he scratched his head conscientiously and then, at last, his back slightly bowed, he turned towards the table at which his faithful navigator was waiting for him.

'Dudule, they're playing another dirty trick on us!'

'Not to worry, *mon Capitaine,* they won't catch us!'

Of course they wouldn't catch us, but at the same time a raid on Mainz was not to be taken lightly. For P.O. Jules it represented six hours among barrage balloons, searchlights, anti-aircraft fire and night fighters, to say nothing of the danger of collision and a journey back home in the mists of England. Which is why a trip to Mainz didn't amuse anyone, P.O. Jules included.

The bomb aimer, absorbed in his maps, didn't appear to have noticed him, so P.O. Jules called out,

'Greetings and good fortune, O miserable *bombardier*!'

'*Bonjour, mon Capitaine.*'

Then the bomb aimer immersed himself in his maps again, but after two minutes, with an anxious look on his face and a preoccupied air, he asked:

'*Mon Capitaine*, what do you think of this trip?'

Although P.O. Jules didn't think a great deal of it, he replied:

'*Bombardier*, you should never think ahead, because it only makes you tired. What's more, it doesn't change anything. One of two things will happen: either the mission will be easy, in which case that's fine; or it'll be difficult, in which case hard lines - we'll have to try to sort things out, and then will be time enough to think about it.'

Faced with the power of this logic, the bomb aimer realised that it was pointless to continue with that line of conversation, and changing the subject he went on:

'You realise they've stuck us with a *lessiveuse de merde*, don't you?' A '*lessiveuse de merde*', translated into English, is a 'shit-tub'.

'Certainly,' replied P.O. Jules. 'They're not even as funny as they usually are!'

It was P.O. Jules himself who had given the name 'shit-tub' to the two-thousand pound bomb.

He entertained a profound hatred for this kind of bomb, seeing that it was only used against particularly important and strongly defended targets in Germany. To have one on board told the crews: 'Tonight's going to be a real bastard!'

And, indeed, it was a real bastard right from take-off. There were aircraft in every corner of the sky, with the gunner continuously calling out, 'Aircraft to port - *attention*! - aircraft to starboard - look out! - aircraft above . . .

Fig 16. Lieutenant Gonthier. *Part of his crew with a 2,000 pound bomb. During this phase of the operation ground personnel were responsible for filling the fuel tanks, loading the bombs on the aircraft and the final mechanical checks. The amount of fuel taken on was dependent on the distance to the specific target. The bombs most frequently carried were those of 250 or 500 pounds. Two-thousand pound bombs were used against particularly important and heavily defended targets in Germany.*

During the eleven months during which they flew operationally the French Groupes Lourds carried out about 2,500 sorties and dropped just under 10,000 tons of bombs. This is the equivalent of an average load of four tons per sortie.

Heads turned this way and that way until necks became stiff, and all that P.O. Jules could think of was that when all the aeroplanes switched off their navigation lights he wouldn't be able to see them any longer. Then the 350 aircraft taking part in the attack would be advancing through the night, one after the other, invisible to each other. Nor would the gunners be able to see anything, so they would shut up, but that didn't mean that the danger would be any less.

The moment when you are expected to switch off your navigation lights, moreover, is always a critical one, and you try to delay it as long as possible. That is the moment when you really get to the heart of the matter. Soldiers call it coming under fire, gastronomes say they are going for the main course, but P.O. Jules calls it "getting stuck into the cheese". And just as he has crossed the English coast the fateful moment arrives and the navigator announces to P.O. Jules:

'Hello Jules: this is Dudule. You'd better switch the nav. lights off!'

'Plenty of time,' replies P.O. Jules, 'all the other aircraft have still got theirs on.'

'It's usual,' says the navigator, 'to switch them off right away!'

'*Oui, oui,* I know. I will switch them off right away, but just wait a bit.'

The navigator doesn't argue:

'Do what you want,' he says. 'I couldn't care less. In any case, I'll enter it in my log.'

P.O. Jules cannot but agree with this decision. Besides, he always agrees with his navigator. But if, by any chance, they don't agree with each other, one or other of them will always take the piss, and that puts things into perspective.

Some minutes later, in the middle of the North Sea, the green, red and white lights disappear. The silence on board the aircraft is complete. No one says a word. Except when, now and then, the navigator gives the pilot courses to steer, heights to maintain, speeds to fly at.

Sometimes the navigator gets uptight. Adding eight and three and making eleven doesn't seem to be a big deal, but when you are in an aircraft, when you hear the occasional ominous noise, when the most unexpected might happen to you at any moment, then figures can lose their true value and you can just as well make it fourteen, or eighteen, or twenty-one; and when you discover your mistake you start by cursing and then you do the sum again, with progressively less chance of getting the correct answer.

And that is why P.O. Jules has a great admiration for his navigator, who has always got him to the target spot on time.

This time they are due to arrive there between ten and thirteen minutes past midnight. The outward journey has passed almost without incident. But towards midnight P.O. Jules sees ahead of him two clusters of searchlights, eighty in each, and he says to his navigator,

'Hello, Dudule, I form the impression that we're getting there.'

And indeed, a few seconds later the first markers start going down and the bomb aimer takes over the guidance of the aircraft.

'Hello pilot! Steady, steady; left a bit; a bit more left. Spot on! Steady!'

At times like this minutes seem like centuries, particularly when the most unhealthy portents are making themselves felt on all sides. Then, one after the other, three aircraft go down, and involuntarily P.O. Jules declares - with conviction:

'Oh, the bastards!'

He begins to think that the joke has gone on long enough. So he calls up the bomb aimer:

'*Allô bombardier;* this target - is it ever coming?'

'*Oui, oui.* It's coming. Don't worry! Steady, steady.'

Then, in a more measured voice: 'Steady . . .'

Then, through the earphones, the signal everyone has been waiting for - 'Bombs gone!'

'Phew!' adds an anonymous voice. The aircraft, relieved of its load, leaps a hundred feet, the engineer closes the bomb-doors. As far as P.O. Jules is concerned, he turns on to the heading for home, losing height as he does so because the journey back to base is to be flown at low level.

And because there are enemy fighters in the vicinity, and because that is something he doesn't like, he tells his gunners to be doubly vigilant.

He knows how arduous and difficult a gunner's job is. To stay awake; to peer into the darkness for hours on end; to have nothing to do but to search the blackness for an enemy who is doing everything within his powers to defeat his vigilance; to be alone in his turret without being able to communicate with the other members of the crew except by intercom; not to have, as his comrades have, a precise task that helps him to escape from the fears that fill the night; all this is an intolerable strain on the nerves.

But in return, when a gunner picks up an enemy machine, his rôle becomes fundamental. He has to assess how far the fighter is away and the most favourable moment to give the pilot the order to take evasive action. Then, in the manoeuvres that follow, in the infernal noise of the aircraft, vibrating as it is throughout its complete structure, in the extreme centrifugal forces he is submitted to, he has to open fire with his four machine-guns. And then, when the danger is past and he has given his pilot the order to go back on to his course, the long wait begins again and the trip along the *Boulevard des Vacheries* continues.[4] For the moment, the atmosphere is increasingly unhealthy, and the navigator notes in his log, '0032 hours, one aircraft shot down.'

It is the fourteenth that he has logged. To P.O. Jules, hunched over the controls, ready to react in a fraction of a second to orders from the gunners, time seems interminable. Instinctively he eases forward on the control column to get down nearer the ground, into a zone where the night fighters will hesitate to attack. His manoeuvre is not lost on the navigator:

'Jules,' he says, 'I have the feeling that you're flying a little low.'

'Yes,' Jules replies, 'but I prefer it, because ahead they're going down like flies.'

And all this time the miles are slipping by. We cross the coast again, the North Sea. Little by little our breathing becomes more normal, things get less hectic. I have scarcely said a single word during the entire operation. When we are crossing the English Coast again it comes home to me just what we have been through and I simply say to P.O. Jules, 'I guess that's it.'

'That's not it until our two feet are on the ground,' he replies.

And indeed when we get back to base, almost as if by chance, the weather is foul. When we have carried out the usual approach and landing manoeuvres the aircraft touches down lightly on its wheels and begins to roll, when suddenly we feel it starting to swing more and more. Our speed decreases, but we find it impossible to remain on the runway. We begin to bounce about on the uneven grass, and then the aircraft tilts progressively to the starboard side. Finally, to the accompaniment of a loud noise, we come to a stop. The undercarriage has given way and we are on our belly.

---

4 The British called the Ruhr Valley "Happy Valley", but P.O. Jules, more of a realist, christened it *"Boulevard des Vacheries"* - "Dirty Tricks Boulevard".

Without wasting any time P.O. Jules laconically calls up the control tower:

'Hello Farmwork from E for Easy. My undercarriage is up and consequently my aircraft is down.'

'E for Easy, Roger, Out.' Then, turning towards me, he adds, 'An operation isn't over until one's two feet are on the ground.'

Quite possibly even he doesn't realise just how true his words are, because it has been raining for some time and the airfield has been transformed into a veritable lake, and when we attempt to leave the machine we rapidly realise that it will be impossible to get to the control tower without getting soaked to the skin.

P.O. Jules fears water as much as he fears a heart-attack. So, after consultation with the crew 'Soviet', he decides to take to the inflatable dinghy. We don't raise the sail, but we continue on our way with the help of the oars and by distributing the contents of the pack of emergency rations.

When we reach our point of disembarkation a lorry is waiting for us, and a few moments later we are depositing our flying clothing in the locker-room. Then we exchange impressions.

'Well, Dudule, that's one more!'

'One more that means one less,' replies Dudule.

'And afterwards the fellows from Algeria will tell us it's a piece of cake!' comments the wireless operator.

'A piece of cake with Flak shells for Corinthian currants!' adds Dudule.

'I'd like to see them come along with us to see what it's like.' And a malevolent voice puts in, 'No fear of that!'

Then, as the bomb aimer seems to be dropping behind, P.O. Jules changes the subject.

'*Alors bombardier*, are you coming?'

'*Mon Capitaine*, the problem is that my parachute has opened!'

'Well hard lines - that'll cost you half-a-crown.'

A few minutes later we are being put through the traditional debriefing, including the matter of the accident on landing. The subsequent investigation concluded that the crew were not responsible. A piece of shrapnel in the port tyre was the cause of the swing on landing and the collapse of the undercarriage. After the questioning is over we all go back to the mess to drink a cup of hot chocolate. It is almost daylight when P.O. Jules goes back to his room.

Fatigue does not incite him to profound thoughts. For all of us it gives rise to a curious combination of stupefaction and excitement. Before going to sleep all the bomb aimer can think of is that the operation has cost him two shillings and sixpence, when it might have cost him his life. When you get down to it, he thinks, that's not very expensive, and I'd happily give that much every operation to be certain of getting back with my two arms and my two legs.

The next day the BBC announcer on the one-o'clock news says,

'Last night Royal Air Force Halifax and Lancaster bombers attacked Mainz. Thirty-eight of our aircraft are missing.'

But surprisingly he doesn't mention P.O. Jules, who is already under orders for his next mission.

Chapter 3

From which it may be seen that aircrew know how to use their leisure time in a sensible way.

And so next day, as first briefing wasn't until eight in the evening, P.O. Jules went and found his friend, Jules the bomb aimer.

'I thought we might go and do a bit of fishing,' he said. 'The weather's just right for carp.'

There are some things that one doesn't need to say twice. Without doubt the discerning reader who is not himself an angler might well ask why the two Jules regularly went fishing, given that they equally regularly came back empty-handed. On the other hand the born fisherman, someone who has it in his blood, someone whom nothing can stop, not even the degrading business of having to go to the fish-and-chip shop on the corner for a fried fish when he gets back - he will understand it quite easily.

But back home here everything turned out well, this fine afternoon, P.O. Jules had just hooked a carp before the wondering and astonished eyes of his bomb aimer. He removed it delicately from the hook and slipped it into the camouflage net from his steel helmet that he used as a fishing net, when suddenly he heard his bomb aimer addressing him:

'Jules,' the latter said, 'surely you're not going to let that fish die?'

P.O. Jules, who, like the rest of the human race, looks upon a fish that has been caught as a fish that is no more, didn't understand. He opened his eyes wide:

'Jules,' continued the bomb aimer, 'you've got no right to let fish die when they've done no-one any harm.'

Light began to dawn on P.O. Jules.

'Jules,' the *bombardier* persisted, 'in life one must have the soul of an artist and a noble heart. If you have the slightest bit of humanity and sensitivity in you, you won't let this fish die, even in a camouflage net.'

The author begs forgiveness for not being able to set down all the arguments deployed by the bomb aimer to persuade P.O. Jules to throw his fish back into the water. Forget them! The reader need only know that they ended with:

'Where is your human charity?'

To which P.O. Jules replied:

'Where is there human charity when there is a war on? Take a look at your thumb[5], murderous *bombardier*. It is smeared with the blood of the innocent. What can the life of a fish mean to you? But in any case there is no point in continuing the discussion, because this carp has already been dead a long time!'

And, there being nothing left to fight about, the controversy came to an end.

Before he left that afternoon he made a present of his catch to one of the many female visitors who haunted the banks of the river. But imagine his disillusionment when he gathered from the young lady's expressions of gratitude that that evening the carp would become prey to a cat. On the way back he delivered himself of a long discourse on feminine cruelty which gives cats fish for them to eat. And so, from that day onward, he decided to follow the example of his bomb aimer and throw any fish he caught back into the water. When informing his bomb aimer of his intentions he confided in him:

'And then I will always have an excellent explanation for coming back empty-handed!'

But the bomb aimer, whose mind always reached for the highest summits of philosophy, replied:

'Jules, you are a complete bastard!'

And the discussion continued, but now on the subjects of materialism and spiritualism. After midnight, operations having been cancelled, they reached mutual accord in the discovery that whisky was not at all disagreeable, and when they were going to bed at one o'clock they agreed that the next day they would go on another fishing expedition, just as successful as that day's had been.

---

5   Author's note: the bomb aimer uses his right thumb to press the button that releases the bombs.

Chapter 4

In which P.O. Jules gives a lecture on how various commands are used at Elvington.

'Since we have been in England, circumstances have brought with them various changes: men have evolved, things have evolved, even commands have evolved.'

P.O. Jules is speaking and his listeners are following him attentively.

'Today,' he announces,' I should like to consider this subject. At Elvington there are five important commands.

'The first one is the order *"Au charbon!"*[6] It was used for the first time for a mission to the coal-mining area in the Ruhr Valley. Now it's used for all our operations. It simply means, "Off we go!" On the command *"Au charbon!"* you will get into the lorry. On the command *"Au charbon!"* you will get into the aircraft, and so on . . . In a well-organised crew everything proceeds automatically when this command is used.

'The command *"Au charbon!"* applies to all procedures preliminary to an operation. The executive order itself is the command *"Y faut!"*.[7] It comes from the maxim used by our ancestors very many years ago, "*Y faut c'qui faut, mais faut de l'ordre!*" (What must be, must be: but there must be order!) "*Y faut!*" means everything and anything. It is a command that allows anyone to take the initiative. When a captain of aircraft says, "*Y faut!*" all the crew must, in normal circumstances, jump to obey.

'The third order is the whistle. A whistle just before take-off, a whistle every time you bounce on landing. The purpose of this command is to mark every contact you make with the ground. When you hear a whistle you do not have to do anything except hold on for grim life and expect the worst.

---

6   *"Au charbon"*: "Off to the coal!"

7   *"Y faut!"*: Colloquial form of *"Il faut (que)* - literally, "It is necessary (that)."

'The fourth command is "*Y a qu'á.*"[8] This command is to be used only very rarely. That is, only in very difficult and impossible situations. It is the order that makes it possible to resolve difficulties of command. On hearing this order you will not move, but you will pay extra attention. Further, the executive response is usually, "*C'est le cheese!*"[9]

'None of these commands is included in official regulations, but we hope they soon will be. Finally, the last command is "*Micro!*" or "*Vos gueules!*"[10] Both mean exactly the same. They are clear enough for me not to have to explain them to you. They are generally used by the pilot in the air to make it clear to the rest of the crew just how far his authority stretches. The pilot will usually say "*Micro!*" or "*Vos gueules!*" when he realises he hasn't switched his own intercom off. Have you all understood?'

No-one in his audience replies. But P.O. Jules always likes to know whether he has been listened to and understood. It is a small shortcoming in a man who always attaches considerable importance to anything he says, and who would like others to attach the same importance to it. So P.O. Jules wants to check up. He questions the first man his eyes fall on:

'Corporal Verjus,' he says, 'please repeat to me the various orders and what they mean.'

'The first order,' replies the corporal, 'is "*Au charbon!*" On this command, I do the same as everyone else. On the command, "*Y faut!*" I do as I am ordered. On the command, "*Y a qu'á!*" I do nothing and I acknowledge by saying, "*C'est le cheese!*" When I hear a whistle I cling on tight and pray to heaven that nothing happens. Lastly, on "*Micro!*" or "*Vos gueules!*" I don't acknowledge carrying out the order.'

8   "*Y a qu'á!*": Colloquial, abbreviated form of, "Il n'y a qu'á..." - "The only thing to do is..."

9   "*C'est le cheese!*" "Well hard lines!": an unorthodox expression adopted by the French airmen from the English, "Hard cheese!"

10 "*Micro!*" - "Shut your microphone off!".   "*Vos gueules!*" - "Shut your face!"

P.O. Jules is no little surprised at having been so well understood, and he says with some feeling, 'Corporal, I am well pleased with you!'

Then he thanks those present, lights a cigarette and leaves together with his friend Popaul. The two of them make their way to the mess on their bicycles at a leisurely pace. A few minutes later they are sitting at a table ordering a glass of beer and once more discussing what is going on in the world.

Chapter 5

In which P.O. Jules discovers the secret of the Normandy operations.

And so Popaul and P.O. Jules were in the mess in front of a glass of beer, talking and debating while the fag-ends piled up in the ashtray.

Fig 17. Officers' Mess: Mural of Southern England

It was the period when the Allied armies were concentrating their forces prior to launching the grand offensive. On that subject the magazine *'France'* had this to say:

'In this battle, which is above all a battle of movement, it is essential that nothing should be published that might inform the enemy about the location of units and the direction in which they are advancing. A spokesman for General Montgomery had simply the following to say: "We are advancing across the breadth of the enemy defences, and we are penetrating in a favourable direction."'

Commenting on this article, P.O. Jules remarked:

'Journalists are gossips who endanger the most secret of plans because of their mania for having to have something to say.

'Popaul, old friend, this article reveals to us the whole framework of these operations. Just follow my reasoning: an attack,' he went on, 'is characterised on the one hand by the means that are employed, on the other hand by the direction of movement. Do you follow my argument?'

'Oui,' replies Popaul. 'Please continue.'

'Very well then. From this article you can deduce everything. First of all, the means employed - that's General Montgomery's army. Secondly, the axis of advance (perpendicular to the enemy lines) and finally the direction (the most favourable one.)'

'Let's play *belote* instead,' replies Popaul. What has just gone on hasn't had a particularly beneficial effect on his head.

Belote is a game that is played by the intellectuals at Elvington. La Vaps, le Fils, Captain Renard, Popaul, Henry the Evader and, of course, P.O. Jules are the fiercest enthusiasts. Before I begin my story, I think I should introduce these various characters. La Vaps, short for *'La Vapeur'* - 'The Steam' - is the Willis Cup[11] winner. He is an outstanding navigator, and it is he who keeps the score: and some

---

11   Willis Cup. Each month Bomber Command awarded a cup to the best crew. All squadrons were included in the competition. La Vaps and Popaul were winners on a number of occasions.

bright sparks maintain - quite incorrectly - that that is why he always wins. Le Fils, sometimes also called *'le Pébroque* (which means the umbrella, which is slang for the parachute) finds it hard to keep up with the rapid rhythm of the game. No one holds that against him, because he's usually the one who has to fork out at the end. *Capitaine* Renard, better known in aviation circles as *'Le Barbu'*, which means 'The Beard', brings to the game a calmness that springs from his highly-developed capillary system. Popaul, another Willis Cup winner, a poacher by instinct, is the best friend of P.O. Jules, in collusion with whom he sets the traps and shares the spoils. Henry the Evader is so called because he managed to get back to England following a sensational journey after bailing out over occupied territory. Lastly, P.O. Jules is already well enough known to the reader not to have to be introduced. A graduate of the *École de Guerre*, he is better able than any of the others to appreciate the finer points of the game.

And so on the day in question Popaul, la Vaps and P.O. Jules gather around a table, the light falling precisely and equally across it so that none of the players has an unfair advantage.

The game begins. They cut to decide who has to deal. Fate chooses P.O. Jules, who thus forfeits the right to lead.

'It's a bluff,' he announces. 'I'm setting a trap.'

And so P.O. Jules deals the cards. Everybody passes.

'Le Fils,' he says, ' you have lost the lead. It's your turn to deal.'

Le Fils deals the cards in his turn.

'*Tout atout*[12],' says Popaul, who is P.O. Jules' partner.

'Show no mercy!' adds P.O. Jules.

'It's a philosophical ploy,' replies Popaul.

And he begins. The vocabulary that they use is pretty much as usual. And as usual it's le Fils that they are mainly gunning for.

---

12   *Tout atout:* Popaul had a strong hand, and this bid is equivalent to royal abundance in the game of solo whist.

'Come on, le Fils, play your big 'uns! Spit out your high cards! If you've got an ace, then play it!'

Popaul leads from his long suit. Then he passes the lead back to P.O. Jules. Le Vaps and le Fils are whitewashed.

'Count up your cards,' says P.O. Jules to le Fils, his thumb-nail on a hidden jack. 'Let's see the colour of your money!'

And the game continues, and the rhythm gets faster and faster. Inevitably, it is le Fils who has to pay out. And P.O. Jules leaves together with Popaul. Because his ideas are still buzzing around in his head, he reverts to his discourse on current events. His information is reliable, he says, because he has friends everywhere. He pontificates on the linguistic difficulties that the Americans have experienced since their invasion of England. He speaks of the audience that Mr. Churchill had with His Holiness the Pope, in the course of which Churchill is reported to have said, 'The commandments of God are exceeding broad,' to which His Holiness is said to have replied, 'So is the English Channel!'

And P.O. Jules continues his commentary:

'The British,' he says, 'are making some progress in the Caen sector. This advance is due to the deployment of a secret weapon. This secret weapon consists of dropping a NAAFI van by parachute two or three miles behind enemy lines precisely at tea-time. The British charge, burst through the enemy lines and so achieve the advance reported in the newspaper. The success of the operation is proof positive of the effectiveness of the method used.'

But nevertheless P.O. Jules notes that military operations are indeed making progress despite all sorts of difficulties and that soon, at last, he will be able to see his own people again, and that fills him with joy.

At the same time Dudu, P.O. Jules' navigator, whom the reader has already met once or twice, and Jim, his best friend, who is also a navigator, have decided to celebrate the opening of the Second Front in the West in appropriate fashion. It appears to them that their return to France and to their families is only a matter of months, even, possibly, of days. After some slight deliberation on the choice of restaurant they make their way to the Station Hotel, one of the most select spots in the city of York. Attired in their best French Air Force uniforms they present themselves at about mid-day at the entrance to the dining room.

They are among the first to arrive. With due ceremony the *maître d'hôtel* ushers them towards the centre of the room. They take their places at a table where they can be clearly seen by everyone present. A waiter in tails presents them with the menu.

Combining their meagre knowledge of the English language they decipher the menu and come to a choice that they consider judicious. This difficult task completed, they call for the *maître d'hôtel*.

"Just a moment, please,' the latter replies. Our two comrades agree to wait a moment, for the time being at least.

Meanwhile, the dining room is filling up little by little, but the *maître d'hôtel* still hasn't come back. Our two friends begin to get a little worried. They call him for a second time, but the response is just the same:

'Just a moment, please.'

Several more minutes pass. At neighbouring tables the waiters are carrying out their duties. Plates are being refilled, teeth are functioning. Faced with the absolute bareness of their plates, Jim and Dudu begin to despair. They call the *maître d'hôtel* for the third time. His vocabulary does not vary:

'Just a moment, please,' he says. In these circumstances the two friends conclude that action is necessary. To leave the room would be to admit defeat, which they are unwilling to do. Then they decide to take refuge in a trick that they have performed on a number of occasions: eating glasses. This trick consists of taking one of the glasses that are on the table, breaking it into pieces, chewing it until it is reduced to fine particles, and then swallowing it. Piece by piece the glass ends up disappearing until it is nothing but a memory.

For the first time, as a result of this aperitif of glass, they attract attention. At neighbouring tables the customers seem somewhat surprised. Soon the eyes of the whole room are focused on the two Frenchmen. Just as they are about to turn their attention to the Bordeaux glass, the *maître d'hôtel* comes up to them and ceremoniously asks, 'May I help you?'

Just as ceremoniously, Jim answers him: 'Just a moment, please.' A few laughs erupt from the other diners. Soon everything returns to normal, and our two comrades are served with diligence and respect.

Since that day the French have been looked upon as very special guests at the Station Hotel.

Chapter 6

From which the reader may understand R/T as used on board a Halifax.

It was already a fortnight since the Allies had landed in France; and at the same time the northern summer had also started with its rain, its fogs, its low cloud-ceilings. The bad weather made air operations as good as impossible, and we remained firmly glued to the ground. During this period P.O. Jules suggested an addition to rules and regulations. He proposed quite simply that the wearing of raincoats on rainy days and greatcoats on cold days should be permitted.

And it was during those days that the Germans began to use flying bombs for the first time. P.O. Jules, well known as the President of the Mutual Aid Society for the Preservation of Pilots, had already given thought on numerous occasions to devices that would make it possible to dispense with the services of pilots in aeroplanes. In addition to automatic pilots controlled by radar he had proposed other systems using heat rays - or cold rays – that would kill without fail. He had started carrying out definitive experiments on mice, but when it came to specifics he had been unable to say with any certainty whether the mice had died as a result of the ray or because of the food he had given them, which he had stolen from the mess.

Be that as it might, P.O. Jules, who had also thought of flying bombs but hadn't come up with any means of propulsion, was most surprised. He had immediately asked the competent authorities whether there were any analogous projects in England. But alas he didn't get a positive reply.

'You see,' they had told him, 'the emergence of aircraft without pilots will of necessity bring with it a proliferation of pilots without aircraft. Then the principle of the rational utilisation of pilots will be in jeopardy.'

'Send them on leave,' P.O. Jules had replied, a solution that was perhaps too simple but was at least imaginative. For his own part, P.O. Jules knew only too well that he would have to drain the chalice to the bitter dregs and complete the twenty-three operations he still had to do.

And so it was that on that very day that P.O. Jules had flown his tenth operation. The bombing and the return journey had gone well. Five minutes short of base he switched on his R/T and started to listen in to the chatter. Aerial traffic in the vicinity of a destination airfield was controlled entirely by R/T. Each aircraft would call up the control tower in turn to ask for instructions. Given the large number of aircraft it was necessary to observe very strict R/T discipline, not to hold unnecessary conversations and to use a vocabulary that had been specially developed to ensure that communications were as concise as possible. Everyone observed the requirements of the regulations. The pilot of S-Sugar called up the control tower in conformance with this discipline:

'Hello Farmwork from Listless S-Sugar. Over,' he said.

*Fig 18. **Inside the Control Tower.*** *On the first floor of the control tower was a large room with a good view of the airfield and the runways. This was the base for the director of operations and the radio operators who maintained contact with the crews.*

It was also in this room that the final briefing before a mission was held, at which the pilots received their take-off instructions.

'Hello Listless S-Sugar from Farmwork. Over,' replied Air Traffic Control, thus indicating to S-Sugar that his message had been received and understood.

The drill was that the pilot of S-Sugar should then have responded immediately to ask for landing permission. In the event he did not do so. The pilot of S-Sugar repeated:

'Hello Farmwork from Listless S-Sugar. Over.'

Quite obviously he had not heard the controller's reply. The reason was quite simple. In the Halifax there was a switch which, in the right-hand position, put the R/T in the 'Transmit/Receive' mode, but in the left-hand position the pilot could transmit but could not hear the reply. Why had S-Sugar's pilot left the switch in the latter position? It was one of those instances of forgetfulness that one subsequently talks about and says, 'How could I have been so stupid?' but which isn't apparent at the time. S-Sugar didn't realise his mistake at once. He called up the tower several times, but each time he failed to hear the answer. After making several attempts he began to get agitated, and his comments were spread abroad like the words of the Good Samaritan.

'What a shower of idiots in the tower!' was heard.

'They've got nothing to do, and they're not even capable of doing that properly!'

'So what shall we do?'

'We either land or we wait and see what happens.'

'Yes, but we haven't got clearance to land.'

'That doesn't make any difference. Let's slip in between two aircraft. Perhaps they won't notice!'

As far as not being noticed went they had been particularly successful, because for the past fifteen minutes all R/T traffic had been impossible and Air Traffic Control had been able to meditate on the flattering comments that had been broadcast throughout the atmosphere. Because one shouldn't think that the epithet 'idiot' was the only one with which the personnel in charge of the aerial traffic around the airfield had been graced. To do that would be to underestimate the inventive vocabulary of aircrew. The performance didn't end until the crew of S-Sugar had decided to land, which they did without incident.

Fig 19. A Halifax coming in to land. *The runway is covered in snow. Weather conditions when coming back from an operation were often difficult. Fog and low cloud frequently greeted returning crews.*

In the course of the years Bomber Command brought into service diversion airfields fully equipped for landings in conditions of zero visibility and a cloud-base of zero feet.

When they arrived in the debriefing room they very soon came to realise why their radio-communication had been less than satisfactory. They would have given anything to be able to withdraw some of the unfortunate expressions they had made use of, all the more so because their fellow-aircrew made considerable capital out of the grossness of the epithets they had employed. P.O. Jules, all nonchalance, informs the pilot of S-Sugar:

'Do you know,' he says, 'that you described the Senior Flying Control Officer as simian and foul-smelling?'

The pilot of S-Sugar saw nothing for it but to go and make his apologies, apologies which the officer in charge of Flying Control accepted very readily; he knew well how tense aircrew could be when coming back from an operation and that there was no point in making more of such symptoms than they deserved.   As for P.O. Jules, however, he continued with his observations:

'That reminds me,' he said, 'of a story I heard that happened to a crew whose nationality I will not mention for fear of offending certain susceptibilities. The pilot lines up for his approach and gets a red Very light[13] from the ground. Being a disciplined and conscientious pilot he opens up the throttles and goes round again.

'A few minutes later he is on the approach again: another red light, another overshoot. The pilot is getting rather uptight.

' "Red light or no red light," he says, "they're getting up my nose. Next time I'm landing."

'And so, on the third approach, and despite being warned off by Airfield Control, the pilot lands the aircraft ... on its belly.

'The British are very well-organised people. They begin an enquiry into the accident immediately. The crew is called together in front of the investigating officer, and first of all he questions the pilot:

' "I am extremely sorry for what happened," says the latter.

'Continuing his enquiries the investigating officer asks the gunner: "But you, gunner, couldn't you see from your turret that the undercarriage wasn't down?"

' "Of course I saw it," answered the rear gunner, "I warned the pilot on the intercom. I told him to look out, the undercarriage wasn't down."

'The pilot turned to the rear gunner: "Yes, that's right," he said, "I heard you saying something, but with that bloody horn[14] going how did you expect me to understand?"'

---

13   A red flare is an order to break off the approach and make another circuit before coming in to land again.

14   Author's note: When the undercarriage hadn't been lowered and the pilot throttled back for landing a klaxon in the aircraft sounded a warning.

P.O. Jules ended his story with yet another assurance that it was completely authentic. But no-one would believe him.

'Telling the truth is very unpleasant,' said P.O. Jules. 'I'm going to go to my room.'

It was six o'clock in the morning. It was still raining and P.O. Jules, on his bicycle, set off on the long road back to his billet.

Fig 20. . . . . .***On his bicycle.*** . . .. *Sergent Hautot, who was, in **1944**, the youngest of us. Many of the photographs in this book are from his personal collection.*

Chapter 7

In which P.O. Jules puts the reader in the picture on culinary matters at Elvington.

P.O. Jules continued his peregrinations between the mess, his rooms, the bars in York, fishing and - from time to time - targets in Germany and the occupied territories. He was still in the early stages of his tour of operations, but the fourth crew from the squadron had just failed to come back: four out of twelve. Of course, the squadron was brought back up to strength again immediately. We were always the same number, but the absences made themselves felt in the mess when we played the traditional game of *belotte* and didn't find comrades there to play with whom we had lived together with for several years.

We avoided talking about them, our conversations concentrating more on the food in the mess and its unimaginable variety. In P.O. Jules' opinion the caterer's art consisted of the ability to serve up 'Spam' in a different way each day of the week. Spam was a kind of canned meat which in the course of the war had become the British national dish. He could not help noticing the efforts of the chef, but he was suspicious of his innovations, particularly when they involved seasoning the meat with sulphate of soda. The result of this latter experiment was not a particularly happy one. The day it took place the officers suffered serious gastric embarrassment that made carrying out their bombing mission a very painful business.

Indeed, the smaller details of everyday life frequently seemed to take on more importance than operational flying. The first time that P.O. Jules had entered the mess at Elvington he had noticed that, contrary to the practice at all other RAF stations, the officers were not served by winsome waitresses in skirts but by bewhiskered beings in trousers and big boots. Many times he had tried to work out why this should be, and he had compiled a number of hypotheses. Having rejected *a priori* the sentimental explanation, he always arrived at the same conclusion:

'It's nothing but another rotten trick!'

That encouraged him, and he consoled himself by drinking the glass of wine that constituted the daily ration. As it touched his lips he could sense the country air. This continued until the day on which, suddenly and without any warning, the ration of *pinard*[15] vanished. Calling once more on his Cartesian logic P.O. Jules explained this as follows:

'If the *pinard* has disappeared, that means that it is needed more urgently on another front. Since the beginning of the flying-bomb attack the battle has been most bitter in the heart of London. How could the morale of the General Staff survive without an extra ration of plonk!'

That evening P.O. Jules contented himself with writing the following in his diary:

'The *pinard* has run out. Dry thy tears, oh *Corsaire*!'

Incidentally, P.O. Jules was a noted exponent of succinct expressions such as this. One day, at a General Mess Meeting called to elect members of the Mess Committee, he put forward the proposal that there should be inscribed on the door of the dining room in letters of gold, 'Little, but not good'.

If there was one thing that offended P.O. Jules it was the manner in which mess meetings were conducted. In his opinion they were not conducted with proper Republican legality. When the *Colonel* said, 'Is there anybody who doesn't agree with me?' or 'All those in favour raise their hands,' there were always subdued murmurs, but the voting was always in favour, and all the Mess Secretary, Leblanc, had to do was to enter in the minutes, 'Passed unanimously.'

But, truth to tell, P. O. Jules agreed fully with his bomb aimer, decreeing that such things as these were of no importance and that it was sufficient to dismiss them with contempt in concentrated solution.

Sometimes he would go into York with his friend Tony. There they would buy a good beefsteak and then cook it on the stove in their room in an old pilchard tin. Then, while enjoying a cup of good coffee, they would persuade each other that they were happy.

15   *Pinard*: a rough red wine that the French used to import from French North Africa and which was on free issue in aircrew messes.

Chapter 8

In which, for the first time, the reader catches a glimpse of the intimate life of P.O. Jules

Three months had passed by since my arrival on the *Groupe*, and my friendship with P.O. Jules had increased from day to day. There was about him a sensitivity and a human side that I found pleasing. Beneath his cheerful and humorous exterior he hid, deep down, a certain melancholy, and one discovered surprising contrasts within his personality. He could be exuberant and sad within the same minute. But his natural optimism would always put his gloom to flight.

On the day I am writing about neither of us was on the detail for the expected operation. At eight in the morning at breakfast he came up to me and asked me if I would like to make a trip as far as Driffield, a small village about twenty miles from Elvington. He had heard rumours to the effect that there was a pub in the woods there where, it seemed, one could eat extremely well. The location was pleasant and the road there not too boring.

He showed me a detailed plan of the route and, after fifteen minutes of explanation, said to me:

'If we should get lost after all that, it would be beyond my understanding.'

Two hours later we were dismounting from our bicycles. As we arrived at the pub P.O. Jules expanded his chest with pride.

'You see,' he said, 'a pilot can sometimes have the brain of a navigator.'

And he entered the pub triumphantly. It was a pub just like any other pub, with a sign of the limping duck or the dirty bear, a pub of grey stone with a well-mown lawn in front of it on which were neatly-aligned tables with a red and blue check tablecloth and some flowers on each table. We ate what one eats in all the pubs in England, because in that country, from north to south and from east to west, variety exists solely in monotony and, to illustrate that profound thought, P.O. Jules explained to me how many ways there were of making a cake from toothpaste.

When he had finished his peroration we made our way back to Elvington in spite of the west wind that had arisen and which slowed down our progress. That evening we were saying goodnight at the doors to our bedrooms. P.O. Jules went into his own room and I began to write some letters. After an hour I heard a knock at my door. It was he. He had a sheet of paper in his hand and, passing it to me, he asked; 'What do you think of that?' It was a poem, and here it is:

When first I saw you in your beauty,
Hair in the breath of eve, your body abandoned,
I felt in my arms a frisson
As of a shade that passes on an autumn breeze,
And in the dark I spoke to you half-singing words,
The murmurs of love, the lying of a man.
Words are illusion, but eyes cannot deceive;
You tell me I must go, your eyes say stay,
And as I make to leave I see their light,
But yet I know our time has passed
And I must go. Then in the passing night
One final kiss, and then my fading steps.
And sweet it is to lie awake and think:
I gather thoughts, I gather spring-time flowers,
And kisses too, and leaves I pluck as well,
And of all these I make a sun-bouquet
And press it to my pillow with my head,
And dream insanely of a wondrous world.

Though all desire ebbs,
No matter what one will,
I call you sweetheart once again
And feel you are less tired
Of life.

'Jules!' I said, 'I knew you were a lover, but I didn't know you were a poet as well!'

He replied:

'Don't you find that in this country you're still on the outside looking in?'

And he turned to go. As he closed the door he added, quite simply:

'When you write to your wife, don't forget to give her a big kiss from me. Good night, sleep well. *Salut et prospérité.*'

And P.O. Jules went back to his room. He stayed awake for a long time. As I was dozing I heard him light a fresh cigarette. The next morning we met in the mess, and the first thing he said to me was this:

'It's our turn for ops. today. No more poetry!'

Chapter 9

In which flying activity redoubles in intensity and one sees P.O. Jules in action.

And so the next day P.O. Jules featured on the Battle Order. It was the beginning of August 1944 and the weather was particularly favourable: Headquarters Bomber Command seemed disposed to take advantage of such an unusual period to increase the intensity of its operations. Targets were of all sorts, sometimes Germany, sometimes airfields in the occupied territories, sometimes flying-bomb sites. There was one target in particular that seemed to have a special place in the hearts of the competent authorities - the *Forêt de Nieppe* in Northern France.

If you asked P.O. Jules where he was going, he would invariably answer, to the tune of the 'Song of the Volga Boatmen', *'Dans la forêt de Nieppe, Nieppe, Nieppe.'*

And if anyone asked him where he had just been, he would reply, *'Je viens de m'enniepper* - I've just been ni-epping!'

No-one had ever been able to tell us what was hidden in that forest. Aerial photography had shown that a great deal went into it while nothing came out. This struck P.O. Jules as unusual as indeed it did the Intelligence Officer who, always hungry for information, asked him when once he came back from an attack;

'What is your opinion of this target?'

'My opinion,' replied P.O. Jules, 'is that in that forest there is a great deal of wood.'

However, the target on the day in question was once again the Forest of Nieppe. The Intelligence Officer began his briefing with this most unusual sentence:

'Today it is your task to bomb a particularly important target.'

'Which just goes to prove,' added P.O. Jules for the information of his crew, 'that targets aren't always important.'

While the briefing officer was continuing his exposé, P.O. Jules attention was suddenly attracted to a large, ungainly man with the big ears of a brachycephalic, typical of the journalistic profession, whose eyes seemed to be scanning the whole room. P.O. Jules knew that he was fighting in a war and he did so with the closest attention, calculating the risks and trying to make sure he had as many trumps in his hand as possible. He had a horror of one thing - that people wouldn't leave him alone to get on with it. He was happy to fly on operations, but in return he expected that there should not be publicity of any kind.

'*Bombardier* Berlin,' he said. 'It isn't funny. They shouldn't be allowed to annoy people in this way. In any case,' he went on, ' a journalist is not capable of forming a precise idea of our work. Whatever he writes is of necessity subject to constraints. I should be very interested to see what he produces.'

He found out a few days later when he read in the French-language press an article that began as follows:

'With our fliers at 18,000 feet in the shadow of the Crosses of Lorraine. By Allied War Correspondent Roland Duchnoch. When I arrived on the 5th of August 1944 my first visit was to *Colonel* B..., the commanding officer of the *Groupe de Bombardement No. 1*, the base of which is, in accordance with the official formula, somewhere in England. *Colonel* B..., *Légion d'Honneur, Croix de Guerre,* dislikes talking about himself. He is not concerned with words. Results, facts - anything else, he says, is nothing but fine-sounding verbiage.'

P.O. Jules doesn't read very far into this article. All the rest, he concludes, is nothing but fine-sounding verbiage. Let's leave it like that.

P.O. Jules, distracted for a moment by the journalist, refocuses his attention. He makes notes of the important points, and while doing so he lights one cigarette after the other. The atmosphere gets more and more smoke-laden as briefing officer succeeds briefing officer on the platform.

After the Intelligence Officer comes the Met. Officer: then comes the briefing on the technical aspects of the target. Finally the Colonel takes over to emphasise once again a number of important details, in particular the necessity to set course directly above the runway. At last the briefing was over. And not before time, because the smoke from the cigarettes had grown so dense that the air had become unbreathable, and it was with a sensation of joy that P.O. Jules found himself outside again.

Fig 21. Main Briefing. *It was during Main Briefing that the crews were given details of their mission: routes to and from the target; courses to fly; airspeeds and altitudes; the nature of the target; enemy defences; weather conditions etc.*

On the photograph to the left can be seen the backs of the crews and, on the podium, Commandant de Fontréaux, the Station Intelligence Officer, explaining all the markings on the large-scale map of Northern Europe.

As usual he went to the locker room, where he changed his clothes completely, and then he made for the control tower. By this time all these operations had become commonplace to him. He checked his watch, because everything was timed to the split second. He knew that at 1803 hours he would have to start up, that at 1813 hours, when the engines had warmed up, he would run them up to full revs., that at 1820 hours he would start taxying, and that 1828 hours he would take off. He knew that in company with all the other aircraft of the *Groupe* he would be overhead the runway at 1847 hours, and that 2 hours 35 minutes later he would have the target in sight. And indeed everything turned out as planned. A few minutes before his time on target P.O. Jules, seated well forward in his seat, had uncoupled the automatic pilot while the bomb aimer, stretched out prone like a rifleman, was scanning the ground and the sky to make out the target indicators, a kind of brilliant flare used to mark the aiming-point. The first markers were due to go down at 2117 hours, and indeed, precisely to the minute, a vast white light lit up the sky and then, almost immediately afterwards, a magnificent red firework burst. It was time to start bombing, and P.O. Jules called up his bomb aimer:

'Hello bomb aimer. Can you see the markers?'

'*Oui, mon Capitaine*, I can see them. Right,' he ordered, 'just a bit to the right. O.K.'

P.O. Jules held his aircraft on course, making the necessary correction as he passed through the wake of another machine. He obeyed his instruments while keeping his eyes on the sky in order to avoid a collision. The entire mission depended on these few minutes, particularly in view of the fact that enemy fighters had a fondness for the target area. The directional instructions continued:

'Left - left a bit - straight ahead.'

P.O. Jules was turning on to his heading when suddenly the mid-upper gunner announced:

'Pilot! *Attention!* Ju 88, range 1,000 metres, seven o'clock! Don't budge!'

And P.O. Jules didn't budge. He kept on his course. He knew that the enemy fighter wouldn't open fire at a range of more than 300 metres, and so he could maintain his heading for a few more moments. Would this breathing space allow him to release his bombs before he was forced to break off? He hoped so, because if the contrary were the case he would have to begin all over again - the bombing run, the aiming, the dropping of the bombs, with all the risks that were involved in that inferno in which every minute lasted an eternity. He hoped he had time, but the gunner continued to talk, imperturbable.

'Fighter 800 metres! Don't budge, pilot!'

P.O. Jules held his course. It seemed to him that they should have passed the target long ago. He called up the bomb aimer:

'Hallo, *bombardier*, are we far from the target?'

'No, not far. Steady as you go!'

P.O. Jules could quite clearly feel behind him the machine-guns and the cannon that the pilot of the fighter was lining up on him to shoot him down. The following seconds passed in a deathly silence, which the gunner broke by shouting,

'Fighter 600 metres! Prepare to break off!' There was another silence, then:

'Fighter 500 metres! *Attention* pilot! Break off!'

P.O. Jules kicked the rudder-bar hard to the left, at the same time pushing with all his strength to put the aircraft into a dive. None too soon! A hail of shells from the fighter passed over the machine. Instinctively P.O. Jules pulled his head down into his shoulders. The aircraft's speed increased, increased, increased.

At 300 m.p.h. P.O. Jules began to pull back on the control column, at the same time altering course to the opposite direction. After three manoeuvres like this the mid-upper gunner announced:

'Fighter disappeared! Resume heading!'

Alas, they had overshot the target and would have to do an orbit. That meant a 360-degree turn in order to approach the target again, and that in the midst of hundreds of aircraft. It was a dangerous exercise, and no one liked it. When the markers were ahead once more P.O. Jules called up the bomb aimer:

'Hello bomb aimer, you can start the bombing run again.'

'O.K. Skipper!'

The same procedure started once more. The flight engineer reset the throttles. The wireless operator and the navigator, instinctively checking their parachutes, waited to see what would happen. The gunners peered into the darkness, while the bomb aimer guided the pilot.

'Steady - steady - steady!'

Then, at last, the two words they had all been waiting for were heard:

'Bombs gone!'

Fig 22.   The Bombing.
When the markers dropped by the Pathfinders coincided with the crossed wires on the graticule of the bombsight the bomb-aimer pressed the button that released the bombs. The pilot then maintained the same heading for about forty seconds in order to take a photograph of the impact of the bombs.

Immediately after landing the negatives were developed by the Photographic Section and the error in bombing was measured. If clouds obscured the target, as in this photograph, the bomb-aimer sighted on slowly-descending parachute flares. Just as with markers, these flares were dropped by Pathfinders. The men took great risks in conditions of extreme danger in order to ensure the success of operations.

Then, rather quickly, the bomb aimer counted off the 22 seconds during which they were supposed to fly straight and level for the photographs to be taken. If minutes seemed to last centuries over the target it is surprising, on the other hand, how remarkably quickly a bomb aimer can count up to twenty-two seconds. At last, P.O. Jules turned on to the course for home.

Throughout the remainder of the mission he was haunted by the memory of that burst of tracer bullets. Like a song you can't get out of your mind, he kept repeating the same sentence:

'Jules, you are no cleverer than the next man, you're no thicker than the next man, but if he'd got you in his sights, would you have had the same chance as the next man?'

But as it turned out the journey home passed quite normally, the aircraft came to a stop at the dispersal. Cut engines! P.O. Jules wiped the perspiration from his forehead.

'Only twenty more to do!' he said to his navigator.

They went together to the briefing room. There were smiles on their tired faces again. Immediately they entered the intelligence section they saw General Eisenhower's latest order of the day, from which P.O. Jules immediately picked out this sentence:

'In the battle that is now taking place it is important that not a single bomb is wasted.'

P.O. Jules gave it as his opinion that given the scatter and the built-in errors common to all aerial bombing the best way to carry out that order would be to leave the bombs in the bomb-bays. What was more, in his capacity as President of the Mutual Aid Society for the Preservation of Pilots, he had to point out that he could see nothing but advantage in that solution.

It was striking three o'clock in the morning when P.O. Jules got back to his room. He didn't feel tired, a result of his state of overexcitement. He undressed, put on his pyjamas and dressing-gown, and then entered the following impressions in his logbook:

Twenty more to do, twenty more times to go to the *charbon* and to stroll along the *Boulevard des Vacheries*. Twenty more times to listen to the same words - 'Steady - Steady - Left a bit - Steady - Bombs Gone!' Twenty more times saying to yourself that human beings must be mad to get a kick out of dropping bombs on other humans, twenty more times before you'll be back home again, your backside nicely jammed in a comfortable armchair with your toes spread out. Twenty more times before you can have a bit of peace!'

Then P.O. Jules went to bed. At eight o'clock in the morning he headed for the mess. Once with his good friend Popaul he rediscovered his good spirits and his yarns:

'Did you know,' he said, 'that the Colonel has given his permission for a nude woman to be painted on the wall of the mess, as long as she's wearing a slip?'

'The generous action of a superior spirit,' replied Popaul.

As for us, we had to keep our feet firmly on the ground, go to our rooms, get our fishing tackle ready and go to the river bank.

In the sky the sun was shining radiantly.

Fig 23. French Crews at Elvington. YAM

Chapter 10

From which one might note the dire consequences that can come from a typographical error.

The following Sunday the sun was shining brilliantly and singing on the roof-tops as P.O. Jules was making his phlegmatic way to the mess.

Having parked his bicycle in a 'Park no Cycles' area - because there wasn't anywhere else free - he went into the ante-room, where thirty or so officers were chatting and conversing. Having wound his way through these small groups, P.O. Jules came to the sideboard where the mail was sorted, where he looked to see if there were any letters for him. There was, indeed, a telegram awaiting him: that didn't surprise him, because he knew that surprise was the secret weapon of the armed forces.

Taking the telegram from its envelope, he was astonished to read, 'Delighted to love you, Mary.'

It is a source of pleasure to know that someone is delighted to love you, but P.O. Jules was not expecting anything of that nature. And so he was perplexed. He asked himself who might have sent him the telegram, and it occurred to him that it could only have been the Signals Officer, who was in a good position to carry out a practical joke of this nature. He thought a moment and decided to reply by the same procedure. And so he composed the following telegram:

Fig 24. 'Park no Cycles'

'F/O. CREAMWORTH, R.A.F. ELVINGTON. Baby boy twelve pounds arrived today. Both well. PAT.'

That same evening Flying Officer Creamworth, mildly astonished at the premature arrival, was drinking solemnly to the happy event.

That is the first part of the story. Here is the second:

The following morning the sun was once again shining just as brightly when P.O. Jules arrived at the mess and found the confirmation of the first message in his pigeon-hole: 'Delighted to have you, Mary.'

The people at whose home he was going to spend his coming leave had sent him this charming telegram. P.O. Jules found himself in something of a fix. He realised that he had made a rather stupid mistake. He decided to put things right by sending the following telegram:

'F/O CREAMWORTH, R.A.F. ELVINGTON. Sorry cancel previous telegram. Baby not yours. Love PAT'

P.O. Jules preferred not to know what F.O. Creamworth's reaction was on receiving this second telegram. He did not even dare to imagine what it might have been.

He went quietly back to his room, sat at his table, and there his thoughts began to wander. He thought of past years, of more recent years in exile. He picked up the telegram he had just written and stopped at the last word - 'Love'.

Then he lit a cigarette, closed his eyes for a few seconds. And opening his diary he wrote down, without pausing, the following:

Separation

I would have liked to write a poem to you today,
From which at ev'ry moment you could sense
Just what you are to me, and what I feel
Without once saying, 'I love you.'

But that is not possible,
No, that is not possible.
I search in vain for words you do not know,
For phrases new, sighs that are weary, sad,
Words you will repeat in peaceful dreams.
For you alone, for me, tenderly but low.

I love you,
That is my sweetest, endless song,
Like winter's rain that sings its changeless melody
Hours long upon the roof.
These words come ever back into my heart, so full of you.

I love you,
So speaks with joy a newly opened flower,
And so repeats, so low, and says again
The flower I keep in tender memory,
The little summer bloom you sent to me -
Sunlit smiles gathered at your window
I love you, I love your kiss,
I love you, and that is all I have.

I love you,
And that is all my poem.

When he had finished, he turned towards the window.

The night was one of stars, as the nights so often are in the north, and the sky had the sweetness of a breeze, and the breeze was making the trees sway gently, and in their leaves the trees were singing a sweet, poetic song.

How restful it all was, the monotone of solitary nights, long moments when one's thoughts linger on those whom one loves.

Chapter 11

In which the reader is put more fully in the picture on the subject of bicycles.

In the course of his long military career P.O. Jules had noticed that on every station there was always one particular thing that had to be avoided. On the base at Chateauroux before the war, woe be to him who smoked a cigarette near to the hangars. On the base at Mèknes the first thing they told you, even before bidding you welcome, was, 'Make sure you don't put your hands in your pockets. The Colonel doesn't like it.' On the British base at Milltown the C.O. wouldn't tolerate the presence of even one officer in the mess after 0815 hours

On the base at Lyons the *Colonel* deplored the lack of respect shown by the men for the flower-beds. Despite innumerable notices many of the men continued to find the lawns more attractive than the paths. It was then that it occurred to the Colonel that they were walking on the grass because the paths were not in the most favourable positions, so he conscientiously had all the lawns and the paths ploughed up. At the end of a week he marked out all the tracks that had been most used and had them made into paths. They say that from that moment on the lawns were no longer sullied.

On the Elvington base the sensitive question was that of bicycles. They came in all sorts and sizes. Pilot Officer Jules had a woman's bike, and for a very sensible reason: being a convinced believer of the intermingling of the sexes, he considered a bicycle park without women's cycles to be unattractive and boring.

P.O. Jules' cycle was also characterised by having two red lights. In his defence, however, it must be added that neither of them worked. If he had two red lights, it was simply a matter of his love of symmetry. One red light by itself, even if it works, is incapable of satisfying the soul of a mathematician and artist.

Stories about bicycles are not individual stories. They sometimes have a collective character. The principal problem that they posed on the airfield at Elvington was that of where to keep them.

It is true that a shed was provided, but the number of places in it was insufficient. Those who came first made use of it. The rest had to leave their cycles wherever they could, mainly against the wall of the mess, which was however strictly forbidden.

But, faced with the force of circumstances, the majority of the officers yielded to that force and did things they would normally be reluctant to do. The *Commandant* did not see the problem from the same angle and considered their behaviour to be a matter of indiscipline.

Things had reached a critical point the previous day when a fatigue party complete with a lorry arrived to collect all cycles that were not properly parked. And at two o'clock in the afternoon, in the sultry heat of August that the sun was favouring us with, a large number of officers might have been seen proceeding on foot, an example of both military might and servitude.

P.O. Jules, however, is always capable of retaining his spirit of decision and initiative. In the mess he delivered a long speech that began along the following lines: 'Unforeseen events oblige us to take draconian decisions...' and which ended, 'We will do so in the interests of Republican order!'

In between he had put forward the following two solutions:

The first one involved an increase in pay that would enable every officer to buy a car and so be relieved of all the worries connected with cycle-parking. The second suggestion was that officers would be authorised to carry somebody on their crossbar, which would result in a fifty-percent reduction in the number of bicycles necessary and would thus allow the cycle park to operate normally. He was careful to point out that as he himself had a lady's bike the second solution was entirely free from self-interest.

The *Commandant* took a careful note of these ideas, but in the short term P.O. Jules decided that he would go to the mess on foot on every second day.

Chapter 12

In which the reader once again enters into the atmosphere of the mess.

Beginning the following morning P.O. Jules put into effect the provisional solution he had come up with. He was walking along the road at a leisurely pace, watching the crows flying, the greying sky and the big, sad trees, when his friend Tony, on his way to the mess, overtook him. He stopped, dismounted from his bicycle, and the conversation began:

'So,' said Tony, 'you're sticking to your principles?'

'If one has principles,' replied P.O. Jules, 'one has to abide by them, right up to and including the bitter end. But let's talk about something else instead. This bicycle business is beginning to get on my nerves.'

And that is how they came to talk about pay.

'Did you know,' said P.O. Jules, 'that the allowance paid to a serviceman on leave is well above the operational flying pay, and what is more it's additional to his basic pay. Doesn't that make you wish you could spend your life a long way from this bloody station, Elvington?'

'Certainly,' replied Tony, 'but if you apply for special leave you can bet your life it won't be granted.'

'It's a pity,' went on P.O. Jules, 'that we're in this country. If we were in France I think I'd feel up to having a close relative die every week, like the airman I had on my squadron before the war. There would frequently be telegrams from Toulouse informing him of the death of his uncle, *Monsieur* Nablat; of his aunt, *Madame* Folbergère; or of his grandmother, *Madame* Ecartitefigues. As you might imagine, after a certain time the entire business seemed to us to be somewhat unnatural. We therefore asked the *gendarmerie* in Toulouse to investigate. The results of the investigation were satisfactory. M. Nablat, Mme. Folbergère and Mme. Ecartitefigues had indeed died on the dates in the telegrams. The whole matter was therefore laid to rest, just as all the poor people in question had been. And our airman went on in a regular manner having a member of his family die every week or every fortnight. The poor man was dogged by unhappiness.

Fig 25. 'Madame Pancake': Mrs. Plunkett, known as "Ginette"

'Some long time afterwards someone or other noticed that the gendarmerie's investigation had focused on the deaths themselves and not on the family relationships. This is how our soldier had gone about things: one of his pals in Toulouse would extract from the morning papers there the name of a man or woman who featured in the "Deaths" column. That pal would then, depending on the whim of the moment, attribute to that individual some family relationship or other and go to the post office and send off a telegram, for instance: "Cousin Mélanie Chasseclou died suddenly. Your presence indispensable."

'This subterfuge lasted a whole year, and it wasn't until the end of his military service that the trick was discovered. It was simple, but it had to be thought of first. It's a pity,' concluded P.O. Jules, 'that we can't do something of the sort in this country.'

While they were still talking, Tony and P.O. Jules had arrived at the mess, where there seemed to be an air of excitement, an unusual thing at that time of the morning.

What had happened? Our two friends found out quickly enough. The one responsible for the excitement was the amiable *Madame* Pancake.

These are the facts:

It was two o'clock in the morning when *Madame* Pancake, the intelligence officer on the base at Elvington and in general quite well informed, began, little by little, to feel doubts invading her mind. She could no longer remember what time the briefing for the next operation was, when both operation and briefing had been cancelled the previous evening because of the weather conditions. Mme. Pancake was, then, unaware of this small item of detail, and not for anything in the world would she have missed the operational take-off: she decided therefore to take her courage in both her hands and telephone *Colonel* V.G.X.

All the senior officers at Elvington were accommodated in one hut with a common telephone, and they all got out of their beds in perfect unison. They rapidly came to appreciate that they would have done better not to bother. And so they went their separate ways, but not without having made judicious comments to themselves about the elegance of the others' pyjamas.

Then, however, at about 0800 hours, Mme. Pancake realised her error. So she decided to ring *Colonel* V.G.X. again. The call arrived just as the latter was brushing his teeth. He hurried to the phone, forgetting to spit out the toothpaste. When he realised it, it was too late, and he could find no other way of answering the phone except by swallowing a hefty portion of dentrifice. Quite understandably, that did not put him in the best of humours. And I would prefer not to record here the reply he gave to poor Mme. Pancake.

As for P.O. Jules, he could not avoid paying homage to the good qualities of Mme. Pancake, the only woman on the Elvington base, and that

Fig 26. From left to right: Lieutenant-Colonel Vigouroux (V.G.X), Air Vice-Marshal Whitley (Chief of Staff), unknown and Colonel Bailly. (Yorkshire Air Museum Collection).

among 2,000 Frenchmen. He appreciated quite clearly that the job was frequently thankless, and he admired her for always being so pleasant and ready to be his indispensable partner in the somewhat unconventional last waltz that usually marked the end of evening sessions in the mess. He appreciated her too for her kindness.

As the story made its way from table to table, P.O. Jules had finished his breakfast. And so he went into the anteroom to lend a hand in the preparations for the Elvington base's grand party.

Chapter 13

In which one may see the inexorability of Fate at Elvington.

And so a few days later, on the 26th of August, the Grand Elvington Base Party was due to take place. All the officers and the mess staff had surpassed themselves to make the party a success.

Alas, however, life in the armed forces is such that one never knows what one will be doing the next moment. It was plain to see that everyone feared the worst. And for us the worst that could happen was that an operation would be laid on for that very day. Because from the very moment that operations were announced neither civilians nor any unauthorised persons were permitted to enter the camp area. It therefore followed that if we were on operations the party would have to be cancelled.

And that is just what happened: No. 346 and No. 347 Squadrons were on the order of battle. The party couldn't take place. It had to be postponed until the following day. All the effort that had been put in was a complete loss. And the officers were furious. As for P.O. Jules, he went to his room and, in an attempt to modify his thoughts, wrote this poem, a parody of *'Brise'*:

Gremlins, who imperceptibly
Stir the wisteria in the old vine tree
Gate-crashed a party, as I know well -
That day my joyous spirits fell.
One day while walking there had come to me the thought:
We'd throw a party of a very special sort,
A party French, as only that could be,
Délicieuse et belle et si gentille.

So willingly the French all rallied round
To do such jobs as could be found.
Gallois, who had artistic flair,
Was pleased to use unsung his talents there,
So each day in the Mess, without delay,
The magic of his paintbrush he'd display.
He'd rack his brain to find ideas new,
New images and better concepts too,
To help to make this party très unique,
A masterpiece of French taste, so to speak,
To make this simple party something swell -
Si gentille, si délicieuse, si belle.

Spirits were high, the day was here at last,
And all had seen, appearing fast,
A chaste boudoir, Moroccan scene by night,
Paris in the Seine's bright rippling light.
And all was ambience, the atmosphere of France,
And not the slightest thing still left to chance.
Now all the work put in, the thought, the care,
Were ripe to bloom, like flowers when sun is there.
But then a frisson chill occurred,
And heavy was the air: the fateful word:
Was spoken: 'Ops. tonight.'
And dashed were all our prospects bright.
For regulations said when ops. were on,
No stranger was allowed at Elvington.

And so our hopes in ruins fell,
Of our fine party si gentille, si belle.
Had we, we wondered, missed a chance to save the day,
Was there something we had missed, some other way?
No, there was not. As spoke the Greek:
'Against the whims of Fate, mere man is weak.'
The words resound, straight to the point they hit.
To put it vulgarly, 'Le Cheese!' - Hard Sh..!

Paintings by Capitaine (now Général) Pierre Gallois in the Officers' Mess: Figs 29,31,32,33 & 34

Fig 27. *The River Seine from the top of one of the two main towers of the Cathédral Notre Dame.*

Fig 28. *Stage-set of a famous café in the Place du Tertre, Montmartre.*

Fig 29. A street in Montmartre, just behind the Sacré-Coeur Basilic**a**

Fig 30. The Opéra. In the left corner, the 'Café de la Paix'

Fig 31. Place Vendôme and its column.

Figs 32. Place de la Concorde. The obelisk and the fountains. In the background Hotel Crillon and the Ministry of the Navy.

Chapter 14

In which one sees how P.O. Jules always keeps ahead of the game.

And so on Saturday the 26th of August the Grand Party at Elvington had to be postponed until the following day because of an operation that was, as it turned out, cancelled at seven o'clock in the evening. (Which just goes to show that the moral is that you should always wait for counter-orders to be issued).

This gave rise to the following varied consequences:

When numerous trains arrived from London, from Edinburgh, from all over the place, that were bringing the prettiest girls in England, smiles vanished and there were unhappy faces. Tears of disappointment poured down like the native rain of Yorkshire.

Those officers who couldn't leave the airfield because of the operation entrusted their comrades with the task of meeting and looking after the girls they had invited. Drama erupted when, the operation having been cancelled, they went into York and discovered, with varying degrees of pleasure, that their comrades had made the best use of the time at their disposal. Disputes erupted, but no blows were struck, which just goes to show that in the presence of the feminine sex men are sometimes capable of behaving with magnanimity.

At last, on the camp, those officers who had not invited guests or who hadn't been introduced to guests gathered together to have a good argument in conversations in which the point at issue was a matter of millimetres, centimetres and even metres. Then the atmosphere became more relaxed. Songs were sung, and the evening ended on approaching a note of gaiety. The morale of the personnel at Elvington could never be completely suppressed. And the party therefore took place on Sunday the 27th of August. The gateaux had suffered to some degree. The tiered cake was sweating copiously. The chicken was, perhaps, past its prime. Only the Spam sandwiches had retained their original identity, revolting as that was.

I do not propose to describe here the success of the party, which falls outside the modest framework of this work. I will confine myself to recording a few incidents.

By eleven o'clock the temperature had become, one might say, 'ambient'. The thermometer was showing a dizzy rise in individuals' brains, which didn't in any way have the effect of making them more clear. P.O. Jules, however, showed that he was in control of both circumstances and thermometer.

He addressed himself to Colonel V. G. X. along these lines:

'*Mon Colonel,* if you weren't a Colonel I would talk to you as if you were a dear friend and call you "*Colon*"[16]'

Towards midnight, wearing a bowler hat and standing on a chair, he began haranguing the gathering violently, starting something like this:

'Rustics, *bourgeois*, villagers and peasants, rogues, vile bastards and scoundrels!'

The Air Commodore chose this very moment to come over to say goodnight.

'Wait a minute,' said P.O. Jules, jamming the bowler hat down over his superior officer's ears.

At one o'clock in the morning the orchestra began to play old-fashioned waltzes and rather silly popular dances, which reflected both the ambience and the level of the temperature.

Fig 33. *Commandant Vigouroux and the proprietress of Betty's Tea Room in York, a favourite spot for the French.*

---

16   '*Colon*' is a slang expression for '*Colonel*'.

Sadly the party came to a close at two in the morning. It is said that more than one individual found the night very dark, the road very narrow and the way very long. Some even maintained that during the night unfriendly spirits had set traps that led them straight into the ditch.

The following morning all the young ladies were smiling happily, though slightly woozy.

Fig 34. Sergent Dugardin, wireless operator of Sous-Lieutenant Terrien's crew. An excellent violinist, he was the undisputed leader of the orchestra.

Chapter 15

In which the reader will observe that certain aspects of life on camp are more eventful than might appear at first sight.

Roofs with smoking chimneys, a breeze moaning in the trees, bicycles moving along the roads, barracks hidden in woodland, will often give rise to a feeling of calm, but often, too, that feeling is misleading. The roofs hide dramas, the breeze hides storms, and the barrack-huts hide rooms that will have to be cleared out in the early hours of the morning[17]. In just the same way smiles often hide tears.

This duality of sentiments, this feeling of something hidden, all this was encapsulated in the particular sign that everyone at Elvington repeated in the course of days of joy or of anguish. And the sign was that of the raised thumb and the clenched fist.

When P.O. Jules had had the chocks taken away and was about to leave on an operation, he made this sign to the mechanics. That signified both hope and confidence. And when, the operation concluded, he returned to his dispersal, he would cut the engines, open the cockpit window and make the same gesture to the men who would be servicing the aircraft while he was sleeping. And that meant to them the joy he felt at being back on *terra firma*.

In the mess, in the barracks, on the roads, it was always with the thumb that we greeted one another. That saved us the trouble of having to say

---

17   Author's note: If an aircraft failed to come back, the room of each member of the crew was cleared out first thing the following morning and his personal possessions were taken into store by a special section, whose responsibility it was to return them to his family.

Fig 35. "Thumbs Up".

Lieutenant Gonthier with members of Lieutenant Santi's crew. From left to right: Lieutenant Santi (pilot), Sergent Descousis (rear gunner), Lieutenant Barrois (bomb-aimer), Lieutenant Gonthier, Sergeant Cadeau (radio operator).

Despite constant danger, despite losses, there was always an atmosphere of cameraderie – or, better, of friendship - at Elvington. It is nicely captured in this photograph.

anything. On one occasion, for example, P.O. Jules met his boss, Colonel Puget, and as the latter was disturbed about something or other, he didn't feel the need to go into a long explanation. He simply gave a 'thumbs-up' and immediately changed the subject.

He began to talk about the Archimedes Principle. He had - let's admit it - a curious way of expounding the theory:

'A body immersed in liquid,' he said, 'may be considered to be a complete write-off.'

And he went on to mention a course conducted by an Air Force Warrant Officer on the subject of the lighter-than-air balloon. P.O. Jules repeated the words of this Warrant Officer:

'The lighter-than-air balloon is based on the Archimedes Principle. When the weight is heavier than the volume, the balloon will remain on the ground. If, on the other hand, the volume is heavier than the weight, the balloon will rise into the air.'

Colonel Puget smiled, called him an idiot, and left him alone with his friend Popaul, the poacher.

After the traditional game of *belote*, in the course of which P.O. Jules had to invoke his seniority in order to resolve points of disagreement, our two friends left the mess together.

That very same day Popaul said, 'I've had a letter from my girlfriend. You'll have to come with me to write a reply.'

To this P.O. Jules replied, 'O.K., I'll be with you.' This was because his command

Fig 36. On the right is Commandant Puget, who succeeded Colonel Venot as Commander of No. 346 Squadron in September **1944** after the latter's accident.

*On the left, Lieutenant Delaunay, a former pilot of Aéropostale and Air France, who had **10,000** flying hours to his credit and who held the record for the number of South-Atlantic crossings. Despite serious burns to his hands that caused him considerable suffering on cold nights, burns contracted during service with South American Airlines, he insisted, against all advice, in carrying out a tour of operations. In particular, he refused to join Transport Command.*

of the English language meant that he used to write on average two love letters a day for his comrades.

He went on, 'What will it be today - do you want it sentimental or non-sentimental?'

'Today,' replied Popaul, 'I'd like a real "lerve" letter.'

So the two of them went to their barrack-hut and they composed the letter. About four o'clock they went out to collect hazelnuts and see how their snares were.

At eight o'clock, after a heavy drinking session in the mess, in which the number of bottles consumed was impressive and which resulted in a state of euphoria in some of the officers, an unusually wild party developed. *Commandant* de Fonreaux, in a state of distraction, lost a game of shove-halfpenny which, he maintained, he would not have lost otherwise. A little later, well into the night, the party came to a close with the traditional last waltz with Madame Pancake. It was even said that on leaving certain officers removed the official photograph of the Commanding Officer of the base, and that the photograph was later placed at the head of the bed of the Commander of the Third *Escadrille* (so called because there was neither a First nor a Second), and that all night the latter had dreams of fame, basking in reflected glory.

As far as P.O. Jules was concerned, he was incapable of dreaming of anything except whisky.

Chapter 16

From which the reader will understand what is meant by a day on Stand-by.

At one o'clock in the morning someone came to wake P.O. Jules up. The rain was rattling on the roof of his room and making a sinister noise. It had even managed to penetrate through the numerous cracks in the roof and was spreading out in unpleasant puddles on the table, the chairs and the floor. P.O. Jules had been forced to spread his raincoat over the bed to prevent himself getting wet through while he slept.

The section responsible for accommodation had decreed that when winter came the woodland, which had grown smaller during the summer, would expand once more and soon become waterproof again when the weather was bad.

Even as he woke up P.O. Jules said to himself, 'It'll be postponed. The operation won't take place.' And he groaned silently. As a pilot he was permitted to sleep an hour longer than his navigator, because his briefing started later. And so he dozed off sweetly again, took advantage for a few more minutes of the warmth of the blankets, and forgot that he would soon have to wake up again and this time get out of bed.

And, indeed, an hour later Bébert, a comrade who was also on stand-by, came into P.O. Jules' room. Immediately Jules began to complain:

'It'll be postponed!' he said.

It's surprising what one can find to moan about when one is awakened at such an hour of the night. You moan because the fuses have blown and you have to get dressed in the dark. You moan because it never stops raining in this bloody country. You moan because as far as you are concerned this is no time for Christians to be woken up. You moan about anything and everything: it's a kind of safety-valve.

Nevertheless you have to get up and go to the mess for the fried egg and bacon that is waiting for the crews. It is traditional. And on No. 346 Squadron everyone is attached to tradition, just as they are attached to eggs and bacon and meals at any time of the day or night.

By now P.O. Jules is warming himself at the fireside in the big dining room in the Sergeants' Mess, chatting and smoking a cigarette while waiting for briefing to begin.

*Fig 37. **The Officers' Mess:** a map of France: a bas-relief with local small paintings typical of the regions.   YAM*

Right up to the very last moment he is hoping that the mission will be scrubbed so that he won't have to go out into the rain that is still coming down over the whole of the country. But at five minutes to five he leaves the mess and makes his way to the briefing room, where he finds his navigator bad-tempered because he hasn't had enough sleep. He says to him:

'The operation's certain to be scrubbed.'

To which the navigator replies in a surly tone, 'Now we've begun we might as well get it over and done with!'

If instead of saying, 'It's bound to be scrubbed,' P.O. Jules had said, 'It's sure to go ahead,' his navigator would have answered, 'They can't be daft enough to expect us to fly in weather like this.' Men who have slept badly frequently display contrariness of this nature. By now the main briefing is over. The crews go to the parachute section, put on their Mae Wests and parachute-harnesses.

His feet made heavy by his flying boots, the pilot goes to Flying Control, where he receives his final instructions before take-off. He has to make sure that his earphones don't get wet, he has to pick his way round mud and puddles, and once again P.O. Jules can't help complaining.

Time for taxying out and for take-off are given. The crews board the lorries, only to be told that the operation has been postponed. It is 0615 hours, and they have to report back at Flying Control again at 0915. Everybody goes back to bed in order to take the advantage of another two or three hours of sleep.

At 0900 hours the same ceremony, the same nonsense, starts all over again. They have to get up, face the rain again, freeze because they are shivery after a sleepless night, only to learn at about 1015 hours that the operation will not now take place. Such are the joys of stand-by.

And on the fourth day the operation took place. The aircraft took off on the raid, couldn't find their target, and came back with their bombs. P.O. Jules had another moan, but it occurred to him that at least it had provided some distraction for the ground personnel, who did not know the great joys of operational flying. And that was when he remembered the words of his good schoolmaster - 'God willed it thus so that no one should go without.'

Chapter 17

In which the reader joins P.O. Jules in deploring the state of apparent oblivion that the Heavy Bomber *Groupes* live in.

The September issue of the Bulletin of the French Air Forces in Great Britain arrived here today. P.O. Jules noted that his name did not figure in the chapter dealing with citations and awards. He was not in the least surprised, and he consoled himself with the thought that merit is all the greater when it remains hidden or unsung.

On the other hand he took pleasure in the prowess of his comrades in the Fighter *Groupes*. But, in agreement with *Général* B....., he considered that variety in the texts was pointless, that it only caused confusion in people's minds, and that identical citations should reflect identical merit.

He searched for a general formula and formed the opinion that the following citation would be appropriate in the majority of cases:

'A well-proven fighter pilot possessing abundant professional technique, indefatigable, full of drive, courage, willingness and modesty, he has always drawn on the better aspects of his exceptional qualities and has shown in all circumstances ability, enthusiasm and a spirit of self-sacrifice worthy of the highest praise.

'In particular, in the course of one very difficult operation in support of bombers over the Ruhr Valley, he did not hesitate to climb to 36,000 feet and observe, for a period of five minutes, the fleet of bombers 10,000 feet below him flying through an intense anti-aircraft barrage.'

Against the possibility that someone should ever consider mentioning the Heavy Bomber *Groupes*, P.O. Jules suggested the following citation:

'This crew has always carried out orders conscientiously. Has taken part in a number of bombing operations and had achieved good results, as is confirmed by aerial photography. No previous citation.'

P.O. Jules recognised that all crews were of equal worth, and that it was incumbent on them to remain small cogs in the bigger machine. P.O. Jules consoled himself with the knowledge that formulas such as, 'Twice attacked by fighters, hit three times by flak, successful on ten occasions in landing on diversion airfields despite fog and low cloud,' were not sufficiently general in their character to justify a mention in a citation, but then facts are not always what one would like them to be. He expected that everyone would recognise the true merit that was behind the modest phrasing of his suggested citation.

Lest the citation should be considered too long or not precise enough, P.O. Jules suggested the following form of words, which in his view would quite certainly incorporate the desired characteristics of generality and precision:

'A bomber pilot who has a good future behind him.'

At about this time a man named Jules, Inspector General of Supplies, was arrested in Paris. P.O. Jules made a point of commenting that he had nothing in common with this sinister, grey-coloured individual of evil expression and vicious personality. He even spoke of taking legal action against this infamous collaborator who had brought dishonour on a name to which P.O. Jules and his bomb aimer had brought renown, although it had not so far been recognised in citations.

Chapter 18

In which it is a matter of improving on the ordinary.

At this time of the year mushrooms abound in commercial quantities. Is it the humidity, is it the fog? Or is it just the time of the year? I have no idea. The fact is that you can find them everywhere, in the woods, in the meadows and in the fields. We gather them, and when we go back to our billets in the evening we prepare a fine meal that smells good, that simmers gently, the aroma of which you can savour, a fine meal that helps one to forget the cares of the moment.

In general, the British don't like fungi. If you ask their advice of particular species of fungus they always answer, 'Poison!' The English dentist on the camp was the sole exception. He knew good spots where you could pick them by the basketful in less time than it takes to say it. But because he was a connoisseur he always went and picked them very early in the morning, thus feeling confident that he wouldn't be followed and that he could keep the locations secret.

But one day the French medical staff decided to discover his wonderful field. They followed the dentist's tracks, and they found the location. At first light the following morning the entire staff of Sick Quarters set out on an expedition and reaped a massive harvest, but so that there would be no doubt about who was behind the raid a small French flag was planted at the exact spot of each mushroom gathered.

On another occasion the French Medical Officer kindly offered to cook the dentist's mushrooms for him.

A strong smell of garlic rapidly spread throughout the Sick Quarters. When the meal arrived on the table, and when the French medics were tucking in with gusto, the poor dentist, who had been looking forward to consuming his share, muttered:

'I don't like garlic! I don't like garlic!' In that he resembled all Englishmen.

Fig 38. Capitaine Cantoni, medical officer of Elvington Base.

On another occasion, Dudu had gathered a formidable harvest from some small woods, but as it happened there was one type among them that he wasn't too certain about. In looking for an expert he thought of the doctor. The latter looked at them and said, 'They're excellent. You can go ahead.'

Dudu, somewhat reassured, asked him, 'Would you like a few?'

When the doctor accepted, Dudu, this time completely reassured, went back to his quarters and, together with his room-mates, began conscientiously to wash and peel his crop. At about nine o'clock in the evening someone gave a timid knock on the door. It was the doctor, and he said,

'Have you eaten the mushrooms yet? I cooked mine with a silver coin in with them. The coin didn't go black, but I still can't guarantee that they're safe.'

The doctor made his excuses and left. As for the others, doubt had entered their minds. It was impossible to sort out the mushrooms that were definitely OK from those one couldn't be certain about, because nothing looks more like a peeled mushroom than another peeled mushroom, even though it might in fact be of a different species. The question, therefore, was whether to eat them or not to eat them. A discussion began.

First of all Dudu gave it as his opinion that the worst catastrophe that could occur would be a good dose of bellyache. Someone else said that in the world of aviation one had to be seen to be courageous and audacious, and that nothing would prevent him from enjoying the mushrooms, even at the risk of his life. A third, Bichette, didn't venture a personal opinion but said he would do what everyone else did. The last one, Chitan, who is a devil's advocate and was in charge of all matters dealing with supply, said it wasn't a good idea. He pointed out wisely that he had a wife and two children. Nevertheless, he didn't want to chicken out, and by 2230 hours the entire bag of mushrooms had been consumed.

The following morning the doctor, who had spent a disturbed night, asked after our three mushroom-eaters (I write 'three' by analogy to the Three Musketeers, who were in reality four). He was pleased to learn that everything had gone off well, but he added:

'But listen to me. Sometimes acute stomach trouble doesn't appear until three or four days later.'

And all that is why you can go into someone's room on a fine autumn evening, smell the aroma of a good dish of mushrooms, savour their perfume and think, perhaps, that therein lies the essence of life on camp.

Chapter 19
In which the reader is made aware of the misfortunes of P.O. Jules.

P.O. Jules has just been made *Commandant* - the equivalent of Squadron Leader.

This news, like a bombshell, reached Elvington through the intermediary of a particularly well-informed officer. His name was well up on the most recent list of promotions. P.O. Jules saw that he had been elevated to the rank of *Commandant*. He was on the list pinned up on the notice board.

His impeccable execution of the various tasks with which he had been entrusted had come to the notice of higher echelons, and in that way merit had finally been rewarded and P.O. Jules, to his surprise, saw himself 'hanging on the wall', which was the vernacular for being on the promotions list.

Commenting on the news, P.O. Jules, modest as always, contented himself with observing, 'Justice at last!'

But alas, P.O. Jules didn't remain hanging on the wall for long. The authorities in London do not approve of such rapid promotion, which is normally the prerogative of Headquarters personnel. His name was simply crossed off the list.

On experiencing this cruel blow of fate, P.O. Jules was indignant. In vain did he suggest a compromise solution. In vain did he submit his logbook as evidence, in vain did he attempt to get members of his family to intervene, because unfortunately the only relatives P.O. Jules had were factory-workers. The simple truth was that there was nothing that could be done, and the decision remained, and that was that. But all the same it didn't break P.O. Jules' morale.

'I'll show them!' he said.

Which meant that he intended, some day or other, to become a senior officer. When he discussed the matter with his navigator, the latter asked him, 'How can you hope to become a *Commandant* when no one takes you seriously?'

This argument had a profound effect on P.O. Jules.

'What do I have to do to be taken seriously? I certainly don't want to grow a beard like politicians do. Without their beards people would take them for clowns. It's quite obvious. But in any case that's not a precedent, because I'm clean-shaven.'

He concluded: 'I intend to think it over, in any event. In the meanwhile, let's have a drink.'

That evening P.O. Jules went back to his room and wrote simply,

'It would be a good thing if there were no promotion in the forces. All they do is kindle jealousy and show cases of injustice every three months.'

Fig 39. Polishing Buttons. YAM

Chapter 20

In which the question of recommendation for promotion rebounds and leads to the formation of an FFI cell at Elvington.

Unimportant events are sometimes events that have the most serious of consequences. A remarkable example of this is provided by the forming of a *Maquis* group at Elvington.

Whether recommendations for promotion be official, semi-official or entirely unofficial, they inevitably result in a drinking session which, although itself unofficial, is nevertheless of a serious character. (Serious, that is, in terms of the amount of liquid consumed).

Such a drinking session was taking placed in the Officers' Mess, where a considerable number of glasses had already been drunk. At a late hour of the night Flight Lieutenant Ben, the Station Meteorological Officer at Elvington, came into the mess.

Flight Lieutenant Ben is a man of principles. After he has finished his work he never fails to come and drink a glass of beer. And so, on the night in question, he was carrying out this sacrosanct rite of principle when, to his great surprise, he discovered an unusual degree of animation. With no little curiosity he asked P.O. Jules the reason.

The latter told him that he had just been made a *Commandant* in the FFI[18], a Pilot Officer in the RAF, a substantive *Lieutenant* in the French Army, an Acting *Capitaine* in the New Army, P.O. Jules now found himself quite unexpectedly promoted to the rank of *Commandant*. Flight Lieutenant Ben extended his warm congratulations to P.O. Jules, who thanked him and said:

'If you want to join the FFI, nothing could be more simple. We accept all men of good faith into the FFI, regardless of nationality.'

Flight Lieutenant Ben was most interested, and he asked to be enrolled. He was accepted on the spot, and everyone was delighted with the new recruit, who had just brought an international dimension to

---

18   FFI - *Forces Françaises de l'Intérieur*. 'French Forces of the Interior', more generally known as 'The Resistance'.

the Elvington *Maquis* and endowed it with almost world-wide importance.

From then on things snowballed. The Elvington FFI became a society organised into cells, ready to unleash within moments the most unexpected guerrilla action. What is more, Flight Lieutenant Ben became an influential member - as P.O. Jules' adjutant-in-chief he assured continuity when P.O. Jules was on leave. He organised two raids on York on which it is pointless to dwell, because they were both failures. He also received P.O. Jules' permission to style himself *'Colonel'*. When P.O. Jules returned he confirmed the appointment while himself resuming command, Flight Lieutenant Ben having been appointed on the Foreign List.

It would take far too long to relate to the reader the various circumstances that led to the Elvington FFI throwing a smoke-bomb into the Met. Office. Nor is the modest nature of this book capable of recounting the magnificence of the ceremony in which Flight Lieutenant Ben was decorated with the QFE and the QBI with millibar[19]. Suffice it to say that at the end of the ceremony a tear could be seen glinting on the cheek of the old soldier.

Finally, on the occasion of the arrival of a son and heir, Andrew Graham, in the Ben family, a great celebration was organised, during which P.O. Jules, in the name of his comrades, warmly congratulated the Met. Officer.

'In my view,' he said, 'this young Ben arrives like a ray of sunshine and as a light of life among those who spread destruction and death. I thank our friend for having offered an act of birth to those who proliferate acts of death.'

He went on to enlarge on his theme. He explained that aerial bombardment resulted in a loss of balance in the relationship between births and mortality, and that it was necessary to redress that imbalance by means of a considerable increase in acts of love. He therefore

---

[19] QFE and QBI are items from the so-called 'Q-Code', Morse abbreviations for requests and instructions, Both are relevant to meteorology, 'QFE' meaning the atmospheric pressure at ground level, QBI indicating poor visibility. A millibar is a unit of measurement of pressure.

called upon the aircrew of Nos. 346 and 347 Squadrons to give of their best from then on, not only in their professional sphere but also in the peaceful struggle that would lead to the blossoming of womanhood and the prosperity of the country.

Chapter 21

In which the reader discovers the importance of Gremlins at Elvington.

'Do you believe in Gremlins?'

That is generally one of the first questions you are asked when you arrive on an RAF station. Like everybody, P.O. Jules didn't believe in them at first. It was only on the day following the great party that he acknowledged their existence. How else could you explain that the walls danced that evening, that the roads were no longer straight, and the fact that someone had dug the ditches he fell into? But above all that evening he remembered a little man, the size of Tom Thumb, wearing a jacket and with tangled eyebrows, sparkling eyes and a long, pointed beard, coming out of a bottle and then, after dancing on the shelves and the mantelpiece, coming up to him, shaking him energetically by the hand and saying to him, *'Bonjour* Jules!'

To which P.O. Jules replied, *'Bonsoir*, Gremlin!'

P.O. Jules was fond of telling people about this first meeting. And the more he told it the more details he added. As time passed, the external appearance of the Gremlin became more precise, to a degree that was well nigh unbelievable. By now P.O. Jules was even able to tell you the colour of his socks. When I commented to this effect one day he replied quite simply,

'Gremlins are like true friends. They don't form relationships easily, but from the very first moment that you enter their sphere of activity they arrange it so that they take up all of your time.

And then, perhaps, you get to know them as I do, you get to be able to call them by their first name and surname, and sometimes even by their nickname. You get to know all their little whims and their little tricks.

'You will find out,' he went on, 'that one of their favourite jokes is to make you arrive late at briefing or at the wrong place for an important meeting. But, as in all things, one has to learn how to defend one's self. In order to avoid the delays and disappointments that are caused I made myself a wooden clock that always shows five-to. Since I've been using it I've never had any difficulty with the time.'

I smiled, but he was intent on convincing me.

'I can see,' he said, 'that you only half believe me. How can you explain,' he went on, 'all the incidents of engine trouble and snags that always occur at the strangest of moments, if it isn't Gremlins? For myself, I have never had any cause to complain about them, which is thanks to a kind Gremlin who told me one day that nothing would ever happen to me if I took care to dust the engines and the throttles with a rabbit's foot before taking off. And that is why I always have that secret weapon in my pocket: it has become as necessary and indispensable to me as the best of navigational instruments.'

I said that all his arguments were worthless. When he realised that he wasn't going to convince me he decided to use *force majeure* and to call upon all his talents of persuasion. So he took a piece of paper out of his pocket.

'Look,' he said, 'here's a poem a nice little Gremlin recited to me yesterday evening. The poem is entitled 'Twilight'. Here it is:

'A bird flew away as the day turned to night,
He had sung to us of our young dream;
While low in the valley a wandering stream
Mirrored eve's soft, fading light.

Reflections of gold, like the gold of your hair,
A moment exquisite of happiness deep,
And of love, and of caring, of mem'ries to keep,
And of vows ever new that we share.

Yet as night's mantle spreads the stream fades from sight,
 As shadows will fade, and sadness and tears,
 And kisses will fade, a caress disappears,
  And glances, and secret delight.

As darkness advances and light flees and dies -
 No more life, no more sound, silence deep -
And I walk by myself, as a man walks in sleep,
 And I dream, and there's hope in my eyes.

Yet my eyes cannot see you, your image has gone,
 And my thoughts ponder man and deceit,
And I peer in the mist, but our eyes do not meet,
 I walk on, and walk on, and walk on.

 And my heart, which adores you anew,
 Seeks for something of you in the sky,
Your smile or your voice, your perfume, your sigh,
 Seeks for something, the spirit of you.

But nothing is there, and my sadness persists,
And dreams of my thoughts, and thoughts of our dream,
 Just darkness there is, and no sunlight gleams.
  I am lost in a grey world of mists.'

When I had finished reading the poem I tried to make him admit that it had been inspired by someone he loved. He persisted that the contrary was the case. He reverted in some detail to his Gremlin theory. Then he started on the theory of the atom. Then he moved on to the chains of cells that ensure reproduction in the human race. Then we went back to our rooms and to bed, and once again Gremlins good and kind lulled us off to sleep.

   . . . .

The following morning, aware that he hadn't convinced me, P.O. Jules returned to the charge. He decided to tell me the latest story of a certain bomb aimer, Aured, which, he said, could only be explained by the intervention supernatural forces - why not Gremlins? He asked me to judge from the facts.

'So, at about half-past-eleven last Saturday, our bomb aimer was just downing his last whisky in the last pub of what he called his "tour of the grand duchies". Leaving the smoke-filled atmosphere he mounted his bicycle and set out along the road leading to Elvington - at least, he hoped it was. What he didn't know, however, was that that night the Gremlins were even more present than usual. They were waiting for him at every bend in the road. Even when the road was straight he found it difficult to keep in a straight line. In the face of so many accumulated ambushes he decided to stop a while to regain his composure.

'At that very moment a WAAF Police vehicle came alongside. In the front seat two Waafs of impressive stature occupied the pilot's and co-pilot's seats. They swiftly became aware of the critical situation in which our bomb aimer found himself. Without hesitation they decided to come to his aid. In less time than it takes to tell the bomb aimer found himself on the front seat, while his bicycle flew through the air into the rear of the truck.

'As they were on their way to Elvington the twelve strokes of midnight sounded from the Minster. It was time for them to go back to their station. They did not have the time necessary to go to Elvington and back. In such a situation the only solution was to find the bomb aimer a bed for the night. A few moments later they passed the guardroom without any trouble. When they got to their barrack-block they took hold of the bomb aimer and put him on an unoccupied bed in an empty room. Then they went back to their own room. Tomorrow, they thought, will be early enough to decide what to do with him.

'Alas, at about three o'clock in the morning, there was the noise of a night inspection, which hadn't been announced in advance. At once our two Waafs went to the bomb aimer's room, seized him by his head and shoulders and pushed him under the bed. It was a wasted effort. A few moments later the presence of two fur boots sticking out from under the bed did not defeat the wisdom of the inspecting party. Scandal erupted. The judiciary machine went into action.

'The Commission of Inquiry that was rapidly convened reconstructed the course of events. They took no account of the altruism that had motivated our two Waafs, and punished them by posting them, as a disciplinary measure, to an RAF station on the Continent.

'For his part our bomb aimer went back to Elvington. Then the report of the Commission of Inquiry passed through all the stages of the British bureaucracy, then gravitated through those of the French hierarchy, finally arriving on the desk of *Capitaine* Goepfert, Commander of the Fourth Flight.

Fig 40. *This is one of the rare photographs showing aircrew and groundcrew together.*

Front row: the groundcrew.
Back row, from left to right:
Mid-upper Gunner : Sergent Leroy
Flight Engineer : Adjudant-chef Bonhomme
Pilot and Captain of the aircraft : Capitaine Goepfert
Bomb-aimer : Sergent-chef Tolu
Wireless Operator : Adjudant Sprauel
Navigator : Capitaine Aubert

Rear gunner : Sergent Lafon;

Goepfert was an airline pilot. He had escaped from France via Spain and was a longstanding friend of P.O. Jules. He completed a tour of operations and ended the war as commander of the 4th Flight of 346 (Guyenne) Squadron.

'The latter took note of the contents and of the fact that it concluded by asking what action had been taken against the bomb aimer.

'Looking on the file, Goepfert discovered that no action had been taken.

'As it is never too late to do good, he suggested that the bomb aimer should be posted to the same RAF station on the Continent as our two Waafs. Alas, in the meanwhile our bomb aimer had completed his tour of operations and left Elvington. Goepfert sent his file along after him and it began its progress through the echelons of the hierarchy.

'God alone knows where it is now.'

Fig 41. *Capitaine Goepfert with a Halifax.*

After each mission, the groundcrew painted a bomb on the nose of the aircraft. The large yellow bombs (which look dark in this photograph) represented night missions over Germany. The large white bombs represented daylight missions over Germany. The small yellow and white bombs represented night and daylight missions over the occupied territories.

*Missions over Germany counted four points whereas missions over the occupied territories counted three. A tour of operations was finished when a crew's total points reached **120**. From January **1945** the total was progressively increased to **140**.*

It was in this aircraft that Lieutenant Gonthier would be killed in 1945.

Chapter 22

From which one may note that contact with Headquarters is not indispensable for keeping up the morale of those who are doing the fighting.

To go back to France, even if only for a few hours, was a fundamental aim of all those who were stationed at Elvington; but unfortunately difficulties of transport rendered that aim virtually unachievable.

How was it, then, that P.O. Jules was able to take advantage of a special leave when he still hadn't finished his tour of operations? Why this special, unexpected, privilege? I cannot explain it.

Whatever the reasons, he left Elvington one fine morning with all the necessary papers. He intended to spend a day in London, long enough to collect a travel warrant. But alas he did not realise the sort of maze into which he was about to stray.

On arriving in the capital of England he went straight to Headquarters, hoping to find there a charitable soul who would give his case a fair wind.

He reported at the First Office, where a *Commandant* apologised for not being able to deal with his case: he said he was too busy with the personal biographical data forms, which everyone at Elvington had filled in at least three times.

In the Second Office he was told, under the seal of secrecy, that no one there knew anything about the matter. In the Third Office the *Colonel* was very pleased to have news of the Heavy Bomber *Groupes* and what they were doing. In the Fourth Office they said that they were beginning to get just a bit fed-up with people who thought of nothing but going to France. P.O. Jules still hadn't been able to find any competent person who would give him a ticket.

Not giving up hope, he went to other offices that didn't have numbers but which were none the less important for that. He went and knocked at the door of *Commandant* S... , whom he congratulated on his marriage, but he got nothing in return. Eventually he decided to go to the top man himself, received a very warm welcome and left with two autographed photographs but still without a travel warrant.

Disgusted, he decided to stay in London, which is without any doubt the only town in England in which one can have a reasonably good time. That evening he started out on a tour of the nightspots, and in one of them he met up with a Frenchman who, as we shall see, was of great help to him. After they had had a few drinks together they got round to exchanging confidences, and our officer on leave confided his troubles to him. You can imagine his surprise when he heard:

'What - you want to go to Paris? Nothing easier. Look - here's a pass and a travel warrant. Report at the airfield tomorrow. There'll be a seat kept for you for a month or so.'

P.O. Jules couldn't believe his ears. He celebrated this remarkable stroke of fortune with a drink.

This event took place on the third day of his leave. On the morning of the fourth day a happy man, radiantly joyful, boarded the aircraft for Paris. But alas, one should never count one's chickens before they are hatched. What happened was that a few moments before take-off a big, ugly man of very military appearance, muffled up in a canary-yellow scarf, boarded the aeroplane and our poor P.O. Jules found himself back on *terra firma* like a horse that has refused at a jump and bows its head when admonished by its jockey.

On the fifth day his seat was taken by a diplomat whose suitcase, crammed with coffee and other commodities of a like nature, testified to the importance of his mission. On the sixth day he was replaced on the aircraft by the luggage of a senior Headquarters officer. Finally, on the seventh day, having resolved to adopt a firm attitude, and having made that quite clear to a fresh usurper, he at once had a conciliatory reaction on the part of his interlocutor, so that two hours later he arrived in Paris.

It was a great joy to be back on his native soil after so many years, even if it was only for a short time. Soon after his arrival, however, he was pacing up and down the corridors of the Ministry in an attempt to reserve a return passage. And then started another cycle of offices and frustrations.

When he knocked on the door of the First Office he could hear someone inside talking about biographical data forms and, profiting from his experience, he didn't go in. In the Second Office they received him in a very friendly manner and encouraged him with these words:

'Don't worry. We'll soon find a job for you.'

In the Third Office they put this question to him:

'But, getting down to basics, do you really think that bombing Germany serves any real purpose?'

He couldn't think of anything to say in reply, and he left the office. In the Fourth Office, having considered his case most carefully, they reserved a place for him the following month.

He then decided to make full use of his leave, and he cleared off to the railway station. But, before getting on to the train, he had, like all soldiers on leave, to report to Military Security Control. There, of course, he had to undergo the traditional interrogation:

'Where have you come from?' asked a character with a moustache, whose reddening nose testified to the fact that he drank nothing but soda water.

'I've come from England,' replied P.O. Jules.

Imperturbable, the moustachioed gentleman pursued his questioning: 'Have you had any contacts with Germans?'

'Yes,' declared P.O. Jules.

The moustachioed one could not conceal a start of surprise. He knitted his eyebrows and went on:

'And what was the nature of those contacts?'

'Oh, generally they were rather warm.'

He of the moustache was starting to look increasingly disconcerted.

'*Monsieur*,' he said, 'you are the first person I have met who had confessed so easily.'

'*Monsieur*,' replied P.O. Jules, 'if one has the courage of one's convictions, one has it to the bitter end.'

The man with the moustache was at a loss. He pushed his *képi* to the back of his head.

'*Monsieur*,' he said, 'I think that your case is outside my competence. I'm going to get the officer in charge.'

A few moments later the officer in command arrived. P.O. Jules explained everything to him, and he got his travel papers. And so he arrived home, happy to meet once again those whom he loved, happy to experience once more the atmosphere of his childhood. There were memories of his youth at every bend in the road, at every door, at every stone.

That morning he was wandering aimlessly around when he met *Monsieur* Martin[20]. He was exactly as he had known him before, with the same long cavalry coat, the same bowler hat, the same impeccably starched collar and the same smile. Between them there had always been a certain degree of intimacy, the result of respect on one side and affection on the other. *Monsieur* Martin was a man from another age, who had retained the poetry of the past. Everyone in the area respected him, and that was all that he wanted.

P.O. Jules greeted him. *Monsieur* Martin recognised him at once and shook his hand warmly. They began to chat about this and that. Still in conversation, they came to the District Courts where, for more than thirty years, M. Martin had dispensed justice with the same conscience and the same goodwill. They went in together, and P.O. Jules stayed on to watch the session.

After a number of uninteresting cases, that of a notorious collaborator came up. Throughout evidence given by a succession of witnesses M. Martin did not say a word. His face did not betray emotion of any kind. Just possibly his smile became bitter and his look scornful, but one would have had to know him well to perceive it.

After the final witness had been heard M. Martin rose in a dignified manner.

'I request of the tribunal over which I preside that I might have permission to express an opinion.'

And then, without waiting for a reply, he walked towards the accused. His gait was firm, his head was high, his integrity could be seen in his face. He halted a few paces away from the accused and then, moving slowly closer to him, he said:

---

[20] The original anecdote, which is authentic, was told to the author by Major Daniels of the American Army. M. Martin was a judge in Louisiana, and he was of French origin. The story took place after the 1914/1918 war.

'*Monsieur*, I only know one way of dealing with people of your kind.'

And then, suiting his actions to his words, he gave him a formidable punch between the eyes. And then he walked back imperturbably to his chair, knocked three times on the table to impose silence, and in a voice that brooked no reply he announced:

'The court fines *Monsieur* Martin the sum of 2,000 francs for grievous bodily harm against a third person. Clerk of the Court, enter it in the record. Let the case against *Monsieur* X continue.'

That evening M. Martin and P.O. Jules walked home together. On the way *Monsieur* Martin, without once betraying a flicker of emotion, told P.O. Jules that his son had been killed in action, and he concluded with these words:

'The more one thinks about it, the more one realises that there is nothing more sad than a war, whether one wins it or loses it.'

A few days later P.O. Jules returned to England in an American aircraft.

Chapter 23

In which the reader is present when the crew comes back from an operation.

Once back at Elvington, P.O. Jules had resumed his yoke of misery. His operations had become more and more difficult, and the one that he had just completed on the day in question had been particularly rough.

On arrival at the briefing room he went straight to the table where the padre was serving tea laced with rum. The chaplain at Elvington, Father Meurisse, was remarkable for his dynamism.

Fig 42. *The Reverend Father Meurisse, Padre of Elvington Base.*

He had never failed to be present when the crews returned from an operation, and he had a friendly word for each crew as they came in. Describing him, P.O. Jules commented, 'He's a first class bloke.'

When, however, they come face to face they can't resist saying disagreeable things to each other.

It could be that on the night we are talking about P.O. Jules was even more prone than usual to the habit of invective.

'*Père Curé,*' he said to the chaplain, 'your rum resembles water more than it does an alcoholic drink.'

'Jules,' replied the chaplain, 'if someone has baptised the rum that's to stop it doing you any harm.'

'There is no doubt in my mind, *Père Curé,*' went on P.O. Jules, 'that you still can't understand what makes a good Christian. A good Christian is like rum, in that he only needs baptising once.'

After a short time, when his turn to be debriefed still hadn't come round, he began to grow impatient.

'*Père Curé,*' he said, '*c'est le cheese.*'[21]

'I know what's wrong,' responded the chaplain. 'You want another shot of rum.'

'*Non, merci,*' replied P.O. Jules, holding out his glass.

Then, as always happens if one waits long enough, his name rang out through the room. He went to one of the tables where an intelligence officer who had just finished debriefing another crew was waiting for him.

As he sat down next to his navigator he had to misfortune to knock over the bottle of ink.

'*Je suis desolé,*' he said.

This remark made the rest of his crew burst out laughing, but not the intelligence officer. To the uninitiated, a debriefing can seem somewhat bizarre. It comprises a series of questions, which the pilot answers as best he can.

P.O. Jules said that at night one can't see a great deal and he adopted – as he would be the first to admit – an evasive manner in his replies.

Fig 43. *Commandant de Font-Reaulx, senior intelligence officer of Elvington Base.*

---

21   See Chapter 4.

'Did you notice any particular fighter activity?' the intelligence officer asked.

'*Non*, nothing special,' replies P.O. Jules.

'And the flak?'

'As usual.'

'Accurate or inaccurate?'

'Quite accurate.'

'And did you see the target?'

'*Oui*.'

'Do you think the bombing was accurate?'

'Certainly. We were there...'

'Thank you.'

'Not at all,' concluded P.O. Jules. 'Next time I'll try to be more careful with the bottle of ink.'

To be an intelligence officer one has to be something of a psychologist. There are those crews who never see anything, those who have unfortunate experiences every time, those who never see the funny side of things, and those who are always on the lookout for it. The task of the intelligence officer is to be able to juggle with characters like this, and it isn't as easy as it looks.

He has to try to understand the state of over-excitement in these men, who have been breathing oxygen for six hours or more and who are only thinking about one thing – they have come back from one more trip. And it is worth pointing out with some certainty that the intelligence officers at Elvington didn't come out of it too badly. As they were leaving, and P.O. Jules was whistling a romantic Jean Sablon song, '*Allez lui dire que je l'aime,*[22] his navigator said to him, 'Jules, you're singing it wrong.'

---

22 'Go tell her that I love her.'

'So what?, replied the latter. 'What's it to you?. I'm like *Jean de la Lune*. I have a good ear for music, and if perhaps it doesn't sound quite right to you, that's because I'm trying to harmonise.'

When they got back to the mess he sat down at a table opposite to his friend Popaul. He started to talk about the operation.

'*Mon vieux Popaul*', he said, 'we have fallen among a band of robots. Some of them are real, some of them are false.'

'That's OK,' replied Popaul, 'I've met them myself. It's six o'clock in the morning. Let's go and get a bit of kip.

'We're on again tomorrow.'

Chapter 24

From which the reader may form an idea of what a bombing mission to the Ruhr means.

This evening, the fourth of November, the target for 703 four-engined aircraft of Bomber Command, Lancasters and Halifaxes, is a synthetic fuel plant and a railway centre near to Bochum, which lies in the heart of the Ruhr. It is planned that the bombing will be carried out by successive waves of bombers, each comprising about a hundred, three of which will pass through the target in three minutes. The sixteen aircraft of the *Groupe Guyenne* that are taking part in the operation comprise part of the final wave, the one that will come into contact with the enemy night fighters if misfortune dictates that they succeed in intercepting the stream.

After take-off, at a height of about three hundred feet, the aircraft enters into the clag. It is almost dark. Patches of fog are spread out on the ground. Already, difficulties are piling up. There are some days – and this is one of them – when a pilot doesn't say the usual, 'I'll be OK' Today there is the feeling that the mission is going to be harder than usual.

P.O. Jules, his eyes riveted on his instruments, has climbed though 8,000 feet of cloud, and now he is flying near to his comrades, their red, green and white lights mingling with the stars. He begins to think. He thinks of all those whom he loves and whom he might never see again. For a few moments he calls up all his memories, and perhaps a prayer comes to his lips. And perhaps, too, he feels his heart beat a little faster then normal. Is it emotion, anguish or fear? He couldn't say, and in any case it is of no importance. Or could it be that he is trying to forget reality? His navigator, however, immersed in his calculations, doesn't forget reality. He calls up his pilot and says:

'Hello Jules. I think we're running a bit late. You can start to climb now.'

The Flight Engineer sets 2,400 revs. It is the maximum permissible setting for climb. 10,000, 12,000, 15,000 feet. The oxygen is switched on, the oxygen that dries your throat and burns your lungs. In the meanwhile, all the aircraft have switched off their navigation lights, and in the aircraft the crews check that the windows are blacked out. No light may be permitted to show outside. That is what night flying is

Fig 44. The instrument panel of the Halifax.

Straight ahead, all the flying instruments, the throttles, mixture controls and air-screw pitch controls. At the pilot's feet, in front of the control column, the magnetic compass can be seen.

On the right, the opening giving access to the forward positions (radio operator, navigator and bomb-aimer).

The flight engineer sat with his back to the pilot, with the engineering instrument panel in front of him. In practice, the flight engineer would be standing at the side of the pilot, ready to help him if necessary. He would also observe the sky to the right, with a view to avoiding collisions - alas, all too frequent!

like in wartime. By night everything takes on abnormal proportions. You are fighting against an enemy you can't see, and perhaps the worst enemy of all is the darkness.

For hours on end you look out, you search the sky, you try to penetrate the shadows, but you can see nothing. And then, suddenly, there is a great light: two aircraft have collided, and the navigator enters into his log, '1902 hours. Large explosion, two aircraft crash in the sea.' Then once more he immerses himself in his calculations, and a few moments later he calls up P.O. Jules:

'Hello Jules. We're two minutes behind time now. You'll have to increase speed.'

'*Non, c'est impossible.* I'm flying at maximum power. But it doesn't matter – we'll catch up when we level out.'

16,000, 17,000, 18,000 feet, and still two minutes behind time!

'Engineer,' says P.O. Jules, 'are the engines running OK?'

'OK for the moment,'.

Now they have reached Holland, enemy territory, the first reactions of the flak and the searchlights. The great saraband is beginning. I shall not attempt to describe it: to visualise it you have to have lived through it. In any event, it's no problem when things are going smoothly. But the engineer announces:

'The port-inner's overheating. The temperature is one-twenty degrees. You'll have to throttle back.' Nerves become a little more tense. In order to lose as little time as possible, P.O. Jules devotes all his attention to his flying.

The port-inner engine is throttled back to 1,600 revs., and they are now running three-and-a-half minutes behind time: it will be impossible to reach the target on ETA. They will have to go on alone, with all the risks that that implies. The navigator says to P.O. Jules,

'Perhaps we'd better turn back.'

The regulations would allow them to do so, but P.O. Jules decides to press on. They have fallen four minutes behind time when the engineer reports.

'The starboard-inner's overheating. We'll have to throttle it back as well.'

Two engines are running at full revs, two others are on reduced power, but what does that matter – the target can be seen in the distance, illuminated by the first incendiaries. About a hundred searchlights are barring the way, and that barrier will have to be crossed, dodging, turning, diving until they are on the other side, still four minutes late and with the feeling of being all alone against the world. At last the target approaches. Bursts of fire, black puffs of smoke illuminated by the flames, with the clutter of searchlights sweeping the sky. Straight ahead, course 110 degrees. The aircraft moves forward towards the fires, the flak and the beams of the searchlights. Course 110 degrees, straight ahead. It is a glimpse of the Apocalypse. Straight ahead, course 110 degrees. P.O. Jules looks at his instruments, then at the sky. There are 750 aircraft on the target, and he cannot see one of them. Course 110 degrees, straight ahead. 'Stand by, pilot - bombs going. Bombs gone!' Still another thirty seconds straight ahead for the photographs to be taken. Thirty seconds that seem like centuries, and then P.O. Jules starts to turn.

To his right now he glances down at the town, its streets marked out with fire. Just a swift glance, because he still has to watch the sky and try to penetrate the darkness. Searchlights light up, shells rise, and on the ground the fires flicker.

There is a smell – a strong smell of fighters. 'Look out, gunners,' and at that very moment, just ahead, two aircraft fall from the sky and crash to the ground in flames. P.O. Jules and his crew are no longer thinking about being late, or about their engines. Their only concern is to look after themselves, and they begin by taking evasive action. To one side of them an aeroplane is picked up by about fifty searchlights and goes down immediately. It is a spectacle both majestic and savage. They alter heading, fly corkscrews, change height. They do their utmost to defend themselves, to defend themselves against an enemy

Fig 45. Les Groupes Lourds français bombardant la Ruhr (The French Heavy Bomber Groups bombing the Ruhr) by Paul Lengellé, aviation artist.

they can't always see. P.O. Jules dives. Dives, keeps on diving. Now he is flying just above the clouds. And below him there is a flying bomb, or perhaps a jet fighter. He continues to take evasive action.

He carries on twisting and turning, and in this way he reaches Belgium, friendly territory. There only remain the dangers of enemy fighters and collision. Little by little the battle decreases in intensity. Little by little the sky seems to become less alive. Now everything has returned to calmness. P.O. Jules calls up his flight engineer, who has been standing beside him for the past hour scrutinising the darkness and ready to help him if necessary.

'That's that,' he says. 'You can go and see if all the bombs have gone.'

The battle is over. For more than two hours P.O. Jules has been glued to his controls, wide awake, ready to act in a tenth of a second, ready to carry out the manoeuvre that might save their lives. Now his muscles relax, his nerves calm down, his mind follows its own paths. It is the calm after the effort. The wireless op. comes up to him with a smile and gives him the thumbs-up. P.O. Jules shakes him by the hand. They have been flying together for five years now, motivated by the same spirit and the same mutual confidence. And since they have been in England this is the twenty-fourth time they have shaken hands in similar circumstances. The dangers they have been through together during five years of war have set the seal on their friendship.

The first part of the operation is finished. The second part is just beginning. Now it's a matter of getting back to base. The Met. Man forecast the arrival of a cold front at their ETA back at base, and now the nearer they get to the airfield the more the cloud-base lowers and the visibility diminishes. A few minutes out from Elvington P.O. Jules switches on his R/T. He hears the voices of his comrades:

'That's A...,' he says. 'That's B..., that's C...'

For more than five hours he has been fighting, isolated, lost in the immensity of the night, alone against the enemy, the elements, against the darkness, and it is a great pleasure to him, after his hard struggle, to be back with his friends, his comrades, again. P.O. Jules looks for them in the sky and he is happy when he finds that like him they too have come back home.

But as long as the engines are turning the mission is not over. For the time being P.O. Jules must watch the sky so as to avoid a fatal collision. Once more he says, 'Gunners, keep a good look-out.'

The aircraft is shaken by violent turbulence. On the ground a storm is raging, and suddenly a red Very cartridge bursts in the sky, a distress signal fired by the Elvington runway control personnel to let the crews know that something serious has happened and that the base is temporarily out of action. A few seconds later the landing ban is confirmed by the Control Tower. The pilots are informed by radio that they have to divert to the airfield at Pocklington, which is about twenty miles away from that at Elvington. An aircraft has just written off its undercarriage. The airfield is unusable. They will have to go and land at the other airfield. P.O. Jules sets the course given to him by his navigator. He knows that he will have to start all the landing procedures again and mingle with the fleet of aircraft that will be flying in the murk in the same direction as he is. He will need to redouble his vigilance to avoid collision, he will have to hold his aircraft steady against the squalls of wind. At last P.O. Jules touches down. Now the aircraft is taxying slowly along the perimeter track, guided by the ground mechanics directing it to its dispersal. At last he comes to a standstill. After a final burst of throttle the engines are switched off. P.O. Jules is exhausted, drained. There are times when one reaches the limits of human endeavour, and P.O. Jules is not far from that point. The controls still have to be blocked so that the storm can't damage them. For a few seconds P.O. Jules closes his eyes and breathes deeply. It's over. Not even yet, however, because they still have to do the long trip by bus from Pocklington to Elvington.

They have to go through debriefing again, and they learn that five aircraft out of the sixteen of the *Groupe Guyenne* that were on the operation haven't checked in. The following day they will be reported missing. And when they go for their traditional bacon and eggs, no one makes jokes, not even P.O. Jules.

The following morning, after a disturbed night's rest, P.O. Jules enters the mess. The atmosphere is sombre, more so than it has ever been before. No one can forget. Everyone remembers.

As he is accustomed to doing on difficult occasions, at about ten o'clock *Commandant* Puget rings up P.O. Jules and tells him to come and see him in his office. When he opens the door P.O Jules is struck by his chief's weary look and by his face, marked by the fatigue of a sleepless night spent waiting for news of the missing crews. Now there is no longer any hope. All there is to do is to work out the sad balance.

'Tell me how last night went,' asks *Commandant* Puget.

P.O. Jules describes the operation that he lived through, and he concludes his account:

'There is no doubt that the night fighters succeeded in intercepting the stream. As we were in the last wave we were their optimum target.'

There is nothing more to say, nothing more to add. The conversation comes to an end. The silence weighs down heavily on them. To bring it to an end, P.O. Jules speaks:

'Now, *mon Commandant*, you have the job of getting ready for the next operation and making out the list of the crews that will take part. Will you please put me on the list?'

Without waiting for a reply P.O. Jules gets up to go out. As he is about to close the door his glance meets that of his chief. In Puget's glance he seems to read something like, 'Thank you.[23]

Fig 46. *Commandant Puget*

---

23   The reader will no doubt understand why, in P.O. Jules' final citation, these words are included: 'At difficult moments he was a highly-regarded assistant to his Commanding Officer.'

Chapter 25

From which the reader will note that No. 346 Squadron, not completely forgotten, attracts the attention of certain personalities in London and in North Africa.

A short time after that particularly tragic night of Bochum, P.O. Jules looked back over the years that made up his life. It suddenly came to him that his crew was the only one to have survived intact through the six years of war. He recalled the path his life had followed. He remembered the days of the collapse, the days spent in North Africa when he felt that the moment would soon come when he should once more take up the overt struggle against the enemy, and then his arrival in England.

He pictured himself in the training camp, when it seemed to him that the day when he would see action would never arrive. And now that he had experienced this nightly saraband, this dance of hell, he tried to imagine and to hope for more peaceful times.

When he got to the mess and began to read his mail he discovered that the Finance Department had undertaken the delicate task of assisting him in this respect. They were reclaiming from him the sum of 425 francs for meals he had consumed, they said, two years previously.

P.O. Jules had imagined that, with the distance, the remoteness and the time that had elapsed, this idiotic debt would have been lost in the mists of forgetfulness. But he had still failed to realise that even across seas, oceans and hostile skies military accounting knew no frontiers and would always locate those who owed money. And that is why, on the day we are speaking about, P.O. Jules was disagreeably surprised to find that they were asking him to repay a sum of money which, although in itself trifling, was a considerable one to men who were waging war.

Like all the officers in the *Groupes Lourdes* he was quite clear about his financial situation, which he knew was not brilliant: at the end of the month, in particular, he knew it was desperate. He had therefore made a once-and-for-all decision to treat both financial problems and the Finance Department with some mistrust.

Mistrust, however, does not exclude politeness, and so he took up his best pen to reply to the Finance Department as follows:

'Today, the 458th day of the struggle of the French crews for an increase in pay.

> *Monsieur,*
>
> *I acknowledge the receipt of your letter of the 14th October 1944 reclaiming from me the modest sum of 425 francs.*
>
> *I am extremely grateful to you for the attention that you have devoted to me, but I fear I have to inform you that this sum, modest thought it might be, falls outside the meagre capabilities of my budget.*
>
> *As you will understand, I am very sorry.*
>
> *Your sincere but insolvent,*
>
> *P.O. Jules.'*

Right up to the very end of his operational tour P.O. Jules heard no more about this stupid matter. But many other happenings demonstrated to him the relentlessness of accountant officers when they were implementing reductions of greater or lesser magnitude in his pay.

All the pretexts were good. The inventive genius of the members of the Finance Department seemed to know no bounds. A few days later P.O. Jules was the victim of yet another unspeakable scheme. He was required to contribute to *'la dette du Général'* – the General's Debt. This notorious debt had been on the horizon for a considerable time. People had mentioned it again and again, but until now the Pay Section had not got as far as applying it.

The accountant officer had been watching the progress of operations carefully so that he could choose a propitious moment at which to bring stoppages into force. This opportunity arose when the aircrew had just received back-pay in respect of an increase in family allowance.

The head of the Finance Branch sent a letter to the accountant officer at Elvington, and in it he said that the time was right and that the deduction wouldn't be noticed.

They made the deduction, and P.O. Jules found himself as broke as ever. The various societies of which he was President and Founder Member went rapidly downhill. The Butchers of the Forest of Nieppe,

The Mutual Aid Society for the Protection of Pilots, even the Branch of the FFI, all were in danger of imminent bankruptcy.

But it would have taken more than that to break his morale.

'I am above such base contingencies,' he declared.

And, looking into his empty wallet, he felt growing within himself a sense of economics. So he made a balance sheet of his worries, and he found that money played only a very little part in it.

Chapter 26

An account of two consecutive raids on Cologne, from which it will become apparent to the reader that meteorology is anything but an exact science.

A very long time ago, a flying instructor said to P.O. Jules,

'Meteorologists – they know nothing. It's only old bastards like me who know anything about it, like music.'

And in the course of the subsequent conversation he quoted this fundamental axiom:

'If the sun rises, whether it's morning or evening, and you can see constellations of stars in the sky, you can relax – the weather will be bad the next day.'

At Elvington, in the field of meteorology, the most notable thing was the way in which clouds were classified. There were two types, either layer clouds or scattered clouds. But the met-man, ever prudent, took care to add.

'Sometimes layer clouds scatter, and sometimes scattered clouds join together to form layers.'

All types of cloud known to date were included in this classification, which had the advantage that it simplified the problem of predicting the cloud. Nevertheless, the Met. Man had to scribble all over his charts every evening to find a precise solution to the problem. On the evening in question it looked as if the situation was going to be unclear once again.

For rather more than two hours the Met. Man pored over his charts, assessing the risks of good weather and the chances of bad weather. He sweated blood, but he still couldn't say whether the weather was going to be good or bad. Briefing time arrived. And the more time passed, the more difficult the problem seemed, the more complicated the solution. At last, losing his patience, the Met. Man decided to take the bull by the horns and, taking a penny piece from his pocket, he tossed it into the air.

'Heads, layer cloud,' he said, 'tails, scattered clouds.'

The coin came down tails: layer clouds were out.

Impressed with the precision of this method, the Met. Man decided to carry on with his labours, and an hour later he arrived at briefing. There the crews, with characteristic attention, learned that the weather they would meet would be fine and clear. They left the Intelligence Section telling each other, 'At least, when we get there we'll have good visibility.'

But alas, that night all the forecasts proved to be wrong, and the weather was terrible.

This didn't surprise anyone except the Met. Man, and so he decided to follow a different procedure. The charts didn't tell him anything, and the penny was uninformative. After long reflection he decided to call on his knowledge of mathematics. He converted the problem into equations, and after he had filled twenty pages with factors he decided that the following day the weather would be exceptionally bad.

He had carried out his calculations by the light of a candle, which could not have improved their value or their precision. It is also worth noting that his results had been the same as those of other meteorologists, who had forecast that the weather tomorrow would be the same as that which had prevailed today. Increasingly happy and self-satisfied, the Met. Man went back to his room, where he slept the sleep of the just.

At briefing the next day the crews learned that they would encounter the worst possible weather and, to their great surprise, they saw on the projector screen clouds in the form of a great chimney, the like of which they had never seen before. They were given to understand that these were an intermediate stage between layer clouds and scattered clouds, and that over the target (Cologne once more) they would find the weather he was forecasting.

In the event the weather was beautiful, no clouds, no occlusions, no wind. Something had clearly gone wrong with the mathematics.

The Met. Man was somewhat disappointed by this. And therefore, after these two raids on Cologne, he tried to find a fresh solution. A little later he was overtaken by self-doubt and spoke with some degree of self-pity:

'It's quite clear to me that my winds are useless.'

From then on his weather forecasts always took an identical form:

'Layer clouds at all levels could well scatter rapidly. An occlusion resembling neither a cold front nor a warm front could indicate the arrival of a warm sector. Winds of the sirocco type will have spent some time at the North Pole.'

As for P.O. Jules, he expressed his opinion:

'Meteorology is like everything else – completely useless. It'll even tell you next that you can't go fishing.'

There was only one thing left for him to do: to retire to his room, sit by the stove and put his thoughts down in his diary. By the time he had finished it seemed to P.O. Jules that his gloom had vanished. In any event, here is the passage that he wrote on this particularly gloomy day:

'Winter days pass by, one after the other. September, October, November have all gone, and the Met. Man's work has become easier because occlusions follow on after cold fronts, which means bad weather, so the forecasters can be almost certain of not getting it wrong.

'Rain, fog and filth – do they have an influence on a person's character? It seems likely that they do, because this evening I feel as dismal as the weather. I'm tired out and as I am sitting at my little table with my hand on my forehead and my head bowed I'm trying to reflect and I'm trying to forget.

'But how am I to reflect, and how am I to forget?

'The sky is grey in my heart because too many of my comrades went out and didn't come back.

'The sky is grey in my heart, and I've got to do something about it. I have to do something about it in order to go on living, but that won't stop me being afraid. Some of us will tell you they're not afraid, but that's just not true.

'The sky is grey in my heart, and when I have to draw the route on my chart, to Leipzig, to Stuttgart, to Hanover, it is always with a feeling of hesitation, a certain apprehension.

'The sky is grey in my heart, but not so grey that I don't see the puffs of flak smoke that cluster round my aircraft, or the sighting shell that has just burst in front of me with an immense red flame. I call up the bomb aimer, afraid that he has just been killed, "Hello, bomb aimer – is everything OK?"

'The sky is grey in my heart. I hear the throbbing of the motors, the noise of the flak burst that has just shattered my windscreen. I pass my hand over my face. It is covered in blood. Splinters of glass blind me. I don't say anything.

'The sky is grey in my heart, and bursts of tracer sweep across the sky. Instinctively I lower my head. I take evasive action. All the dials of the flying instruments dance a frenzied saraband, and when the air gunner tells me, "The fighter has broken off – turn back on course!" I breathe more deeply.

'But the sky remains grey, and my heart remains sad. And is it possible for the sky to be anything but grey, or my heart to be anything but sad?

'Yes, because this morning, when I was on the way to the mess, I heard the first murmurs of Nature awakening, and as I breathe in the night air I tell myself, "Life is still sweet. You have to take risks to understand it."

'When I get to the mess I start to smile and to joke, and I forget my thoughts and my dreams, and I forget that in my heart the sky is grey and that my heart is sad.'

Chapter 27

The tale of a dog

That day the sky was more than grey. It was electric. It seemed as if the air was full of sparks, and you could sense it at briefing. There was a storm on the way. P.O. Jules looked at the *Colonel*, and he said, 'He's nervous.'

There was the feeling that something awful was going to happen. And in this heavy atmosphere something frightful did occur. It was one of those happenings that one usually classes as unpredictable. But before embarking on the sequence of events if is necessary to begin with a digression.

On the base at Elvington there are a number of dogs and, by the same token, an almost equal number of dog-owners. Is it, I wonder, by coincidence or design that all the dogs at Elvington are black and look like each other to the extent that one can never know just who the owner is? They were in the habit of frequenting the public areas and in particular the briefing room, and it was marvellous to see the interest they showed in the things that went on there.

And so, on the day we are now talking about, a dog had slipped into the assembly. There he sat quite calm, squatting on his hindquarters, his head raised and his ears pricked, following everything that was said. One might have felt quite confident that he would not show his displeasure by barking. But suddenly the unhappy creature stood up. He had probably seen something on the blackboard that had upset him. He advanced slowly, at a measured pace. The poor creature did not know that by so doing he was risking life and limb. And indeed, just when he got close to the blackboard for his interest and his curiosity to be satisfied, a lugubrious voice sounded:

'Will somebody please kill that dog for me?'

A vague murmur rang through the congregation as everyone repeated the sentence to those behind him.

Then a deathly silence ensued. There is nothing more deathly than a silence, and nothing more silent than death, and nothing affects one's nerve like a deathly silence. Was it the silence that caused *Madame* Pancake to burst into tears? I am unable to say, but the fact is that all of a sudden one could hear sobbing. *Madame* Pancake was weeping for the condemned dog, and she was on the point of fainting. The poor dog would never know that for a short moment his life hung on a thread and a tear. The death sentence was revoked, the dog was saved, and *Madame* Pancake's despair was turned into a radiant smile.

Other incidents, which it would take too long to recount, coloured this briefing. Crews were reminded that they were not to get their flying boots wet by walking in water or by sweating. Our navigator immediately took this order literally. He took off his boots and went about in slippers, stating after a short time that this wasn't a good solution, adding simply, 'Too much of anything does you harm'

But nevertheless the operation took place without any panic on the part of the crews.

Chapter 28

In which the reader learns how P.O. Jules passes the long winter evenings.

On the evening I am writing about I decided, instead of going to my own room, to pass a short time with P.O. Jules. I knocked at his door and went in. He was seated at his table, writing. I sat down on the bed and we began to chat.

The conversation turned to the subject of English hospitality, and he told me one or two stories of his adventures in England, particularly the time when he went for a spell of leave to the home of a lord. They had given a splendid dinner in his honour, with the lady of the house clad in an evening dress, with all the traditional formalities, an elderly Irish retainer in all his dignity wearing tails, a magnificent embroidered tablecloth, and a remarkable menu – but very little on the plates. P.O. Jules was greatly impressed, but the next day he sent a telegram to his friend Tony:

'Please recall me most urgently. Dying of boredom here. Risk severe diplomatic embarrassment if grounds for recall are insufficiently strong.'

And on the afternoon of the following day P.O. Jules packed his bags at high speed and went to London, where he spent the remainder of his leave.

But despite the fact that he told a number of amusing tales I had the feeling that something was troubling him, and I said, 'Jules, you're not on form.'

'You're right,' he replied, 'I'm feeling depressed. Look what I've just written,' and he handed me his diary. In it I read the following poem:

Why was it you, I ask, who had to die?
Why must it always be the best
Whom blind Fate calls? Yet sadness
Strikes most the friend who's left behind.

Why must I see it once again,
One final time? Was it not enough
That you should die? Why did I have to see
That fearful sight, inhuman and grotesque?

Can one watch unmoved and unafraid,
Burning dull, a hypnotising torch,
The debris of a plane whose flames conceal
Hopes forever stilled by random Fate.

And as I think of hours together spent,
And holidays, and talk of our return
To France, and all the plans – all pointless now -
For you, all gone in fire and blood.

For me the cold, cold days remain
As witness of a spirit lost:
Fears mingling with memories, with
Forgotten joys, the legacy of time.

And now the dark, grim Reaper gathers in
Our dreams, our hopes, our visions wide;
The gleaming home you said you'd build,
The flower-bright room, an infant's smile.

Is all now past? Must all now fade and die?
Must I despair? Dear God, just leave me now
Alone with him and with my faith:
But tell me that he has not died in vain.

When I had finished reading it I said to him, 'Jules, you're letting things get you down. You'll have to do something about it.'

And I tried to persuade him to come and drink a whisky with me in a little pub near to a level crossing on the road from Pocklington to York. It would take about fifteen minutes by bike. He decided to come.

When we went into the bar we met a number of our fellow-flyers, and immediately P.O. Jules entered into the spirit of things. What stories did he tell? Perhaps the one about the station-master, ones about deaf people, ones about people who stuttered, about adjutants and about generals – I can no longer remember. All that I do recall is that that evening his repertoire was in great demand. No one would have thought that the man who was entertaining everyone else had come there in an attempt to get rid of his depression.

At about midnight we separated at the doors of our rooms. As soon as he was in his room a ridiculous idea came into his head. He decided to check his position in the Northern Hemisphere. So he picked up his sextant and took a three-star fix. When he drew the three position lines on the chart he discovered that they put him several miles away from Elvington.

Greatly impressed by this result, he came and knocked on the door of my room, and after explaining what had happened he asked me whether we ought to perceive in this fact an unusual case of split personality. We talked the problem over for some considerable time, finally arriving at the simple solution that mathematical certainty could not be relied upon after whisky had been imbibed.

He went back to his room, put a shovelful of coal on the stove, and then whistled a sentimental, romantic tune, and when everything had become quiet once more I heard the wind in the trees again, the rain starting to fall and all the sadness of England in winter.

Chapter 29

From which the reader may see how things keep piling up.

On the day I'm going to talk about now, P.O. Jules seemed to be in good form.

'Only six more to go,' he said to me. I'll soon have them under my belt, my thirty-three operations, and I'm beginning to see daylight ahead. With a bit of luck everything will be over and done with by the end of January.'

'Have you ever thought of your chances of getting away with it?' I asked him.

'Yes, of course I have,' he answered. 'I've calculated the chances mathematically, I've consulted clairvoyants and I've studied the coffee dregs. All the results are exactly the same. I'm not going to make it. But as I base myself on the principle that to err is human, I reckon I've got all the trumps in my hand.'

And indeed, P.O. Jules had had very little trouble since arriving at Elvington. His confidence, furthermore, had grown from day to day, particularly since the Allies had gained air superiority. A large proportion of operations, indeed, were now being flown in the hours of daylight, so that you didn't have to fear night fighters or collisions. The only danger left was from flak, and in this connection P.O. Jules put his trust in his lucky star.

While waiting for briefing time in the big anteroom of the mess with his friend Joseph[24], they were partaking of a cup of tea. Tea, because it was forbidden to drink even the smallest glass of alcohol before operations. And, like everyone else, P.O. Jules observed this rule.

And while they were drinking their tea they talked about old memories that they shared.

---

24   *Lieutenant* Andre Gonthier, nicknamed 'Joseph', was shot down and killed in the course of a raid on Witten on the 19th of March 1945.

'Do you remember *Commandant* Dunablat?' asked P.O. Jules. 'A remarkable man. One day an inspector of equipment carried out an inspection of his unit and asked him this ridiculous question: "What current do you use here, *Commandant* – is it two-phase or triple phase?" The *Commandant* thought a few moments before replying "You know, it's more or less triple phase here."'

Joseph took hold of his tie with his hand and adjusted it. 'I'll tell you a true story,' he said.

While Joseph was telling his story the time for briefing arrived, and we left the mess at high speed.

Immediately we entered the big room we went straight to the large map fixed on the wall on which the target was shown in the centre of a big red blob: the red area represented flak.

'It's a real coal-miner's operation,' observed Dudu.

'No more little butcher's operations,' added P.O. Jules, 'and as usual the weather in England is bloody awful and it's fine over Germany.'

When briefing was over the classic routine ensued: pilots' meeting, final preparations, inspection of aircraft, taxi out, take off.

It is 1430 hours, and the aircraft is flying over England. As it is a daylight operation the navigator's task is rather less difficult. So every now and then Dudu goes and sits in the second pilot's seat, from where he can admire the immensity of the sky.

Now, with the end of their tour drawing near, P.O. Jules and Dudu have become much quieter. Phrases like, 'Why did we have to get mixed up in this nonsense?' and 'When will we be able to enjoy a Pernod 45 again?' are no longer to be heard on the intercom. The whole crew is quiet. Dudu and P.O. Jules look at each other from time to time. They smile and they raise their thumb, and that is all. The silence is only broken to give orders, alterations of course and important flight information,.

The aircraft has now passed successively over the North Sea, Belgium and the territory occupied by the army. Now the sky is serene.

In the distance can be seen an enormous black cloud, made up of flak bursts. They are so dense that they look for all the world like a thunder cloud.

Fig 47. "The Stream."

Unlike the Flying Fortresses of the USAAF, which used to operate flying as a group and drop their bombs when the formation leader gave them the order, in Bomber Command each aircraft was responsible for its own navigation. The bombs were aimed and released in a similarly individual way. All the aircraft in the formation would converge towards the objective as if in a funnel. The risks of collision were thus considerable. Vigilance on board therefore needed to be reinforced.

'I wonder,' thinks P.O. Jules, 'why they put a red area on the maps to show the flak zone, when in reality the zones are dark grey.'

The wireless operator has other ideas, and he breaks in on the silence with:

'I reckon they've been polishing the barrels of their guns and cleaning the breeches, and now they're trying to have a bit of fun.'

The deeper that the aircraft penetrates into enemy territory, so the more the cloud seems to lose its consistency, but the separate shell-bursts, like little black mushrooms, are exploding everywhere, filling the air like a macabre firework display.

While P.O. Jules is contemplating this Dante-like spectacle the target is coming up slowly, and as always the bomb aimer takes over the directional control:

'Steady as you go,' he says.

At that very same moment the aircraft rattles like a drum.

'We've been hit!' says P.O. Jules, 'but it's nothing.'

'Steady, steady!' says the bomb aimer.

The density of the anti-aircraft fire seems to be increasing. The aircraft is hit once more, this time by a shell that passes through the pilot's cockpit. P.O. Jules and his engineer flinch back automatically. Then they look at the instrument panel to see if everything is normal, while the bomb aimer, phlegmatic, continues to give his instructions

'Steady ... steady ... Bombs gone! 1, 2, 3, 4, ... 17, 18, 19, 21, 22 ... OK pilot, you can turn off now!'

So P.O. Jules starts his turn, at the same time climbing gently to escape from the zone of dense flak, which is still following him.

For more than half an hour the aircraft flies on amid the flak bursts, but at last they have crossed the front line and are on their way home again. The wireless operator listens in to the broadcasts that can be heard at set times and which give the latest weather situation. It is five o'clock in the afternoon when he warns P.O. Jules:

'Elvington is closed – no landings. Bad weather.'

A few minutes later he comes up again:

'We're diverted to Attlebridge.'

Attlebridge is an airfield in East Anglia, and the navigator gives P.O. Jules a course to get there.

The aircraft is flying above cloud. The navigator concentrates on his radar screen.

'You can start letting down now, Jules,' he says.

At 2,000 feet P.O. Jules stops his descent and levels out.

'Well start descending again five minutes before ETA,' he says.

Still using his radar, the navigator tells P.O. Jules to turn on to a heading of 300 degrees. Then, a few moments later:

'Five minutes to ETA. You can start letting down again.'

2,000 feet, 1,500 feet, 1,200 feet, and the ground is still not in sight. 700 feet, and the first lights begin to appear. At 500 feet P.O. Jules can make out an airfield below. He recognises it by the two illuminated letters 'AT', which tell him that he is safely overhead Attlebridge. He touches down at 2030 hours.

'That's another one in the bag,' says Dudu, as he gets into the lorry that will take the crew to debriefing, where an American officer immediately offers them a whisky. As there are only seven glasses, P.O. Jules asks for another one for the negress doll that serves as a crew mascot.

And when he has wet her lips with the precious liquid he swallows what is left in the glass. *Noblesse oblige.*

Debriefing is soon over and done with. P.O. Jules and his crew go to the Officers' Mess, where hospitality is offered to them and the other French crews who were unable to get back to Elvington.

How much whisky was consumed? P.O. Jules had no idea. At one o'clock in the morning he went to the chapel, where the altar had been concealed behind a curtain and straw mattresses had been spread out on the ground.

To conclude the evening's entertainment, *Commandant* Cattelat, nicknamed '*Le Général*' (which proves that not only colonels are promoted to general), gives a perilous display of somersaults. One of the American officers present attempts to imitate him. Alas for him, in the course of this exercise he strikes the ground rather heavily, which necessitates his immediate removal to Sick Quarters.

And so the evening comes to a close.

On arriving at his aircraft the following morning, P.O. Jules inspected it and noted that it had been riddled with shell fragments.

'They've turned us into a colander,' he said to his navigator. 'It's a real stroke of luck that no one was injured and that no vital part of the aircraft was hit.'

He landed at Elvington at 1000 hours the following morning. The ground crew counted ninety-two shrapnel holes.

"God, we were lucky,' says P.O. Jules once more.

'Let's not hold an inquest,' says Dudu. 'It's the result that counts.'

Chapter 30

From which the reader will note that in many ways Elvington resembles the Tower of Babel.

The next day P.O. Jules came to my room in search of a little warmth. He seemed to be in good humour. We started to talk about after the war and what we would do when we were demobilised. P.O. Jules was not short of schemes.

'Perhaps I'll go into business on the *Avenue de l'Opéra* selling ties under an umbrella,' he said to me, 'and then I'll be able to earn cash and watch the pretty Parisian girls at the same time.'

When I objected that that wasn't a job for an intellectual, he went on:

'Of course, if I had the talent I'd write books. I'm not short of subjects. In the technical field, for example, I would write a book entitled, "The art of being a Pilot, or How to Survive". Or else I could go in for politics. Then my title would be, "Gaullism under the Vichy Régime, and Vice-versa". That would be a fine historical subject to write about. On the other hand I could write about military subjects. "In the Shadow of our Great Leaders" would be a sure success. But alas,' he went on, 'my ideas flow better in my brain than they do from the end of my pen. I think I'd prefer to open a restaurant in a sunny part of the country where people would come to forget their worries, a long way away from grey skies and a long way away from the noise of towns.'

We enjoyed talking our plans for the future over in this way, but when it came down to brass tacks we always came back to the present and the little incidents of everyday life.

And P.O. Jules told me of the following quaint incident:

'This morning,' he said, 'when the *Colonel* went into a barrack room to carry out an inspection, an alert airman named Fernandez who was near the door was the first to see him, and he immediately gave the alarm, shouting out, '*À Elvington fixe!* At once all the room came to attention. But the *Colonel* could not fail to notice that the command was not one from the Drill Book and, what was more, that it wasn't one that was normally used at Elvington. So he asked Fernandez, "Where did you do your training?" "At Oran, *mon Colonel*,' replied the airman. "And did you learn to say '*À Elvington fixe*' at Oran?" "*Non*," replied the airman, "but we learned to say, "*À Oran fixe!*" ...'

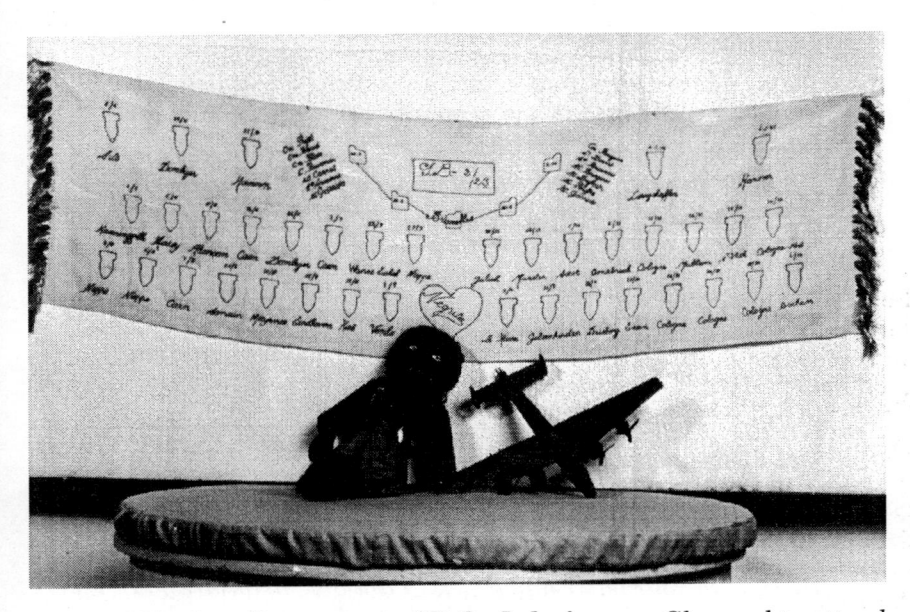

Fig 48. Négrita, the mascot of P.O. Jules' crew. She used to attend all briefings and follow every stage of the operation with great attention. She was the only member of the crew never to have felt apprehension or fear.

One of the difficulties with P.O. Jules was that one never knew whether he was speaking seriously or whether he was joking. This story could well have been true, because the ground personnel at Elvington were a curious mixture of Oran Spanish and Arabs, whose exploits in York did not suffer in the telling. With them everything was possible, and we ought not to let anything surprise us.

P.O. Jules followed their exploits without taking sides, impartially. He found particular interest in the story of a certain Mohamed ben Mohamed who, having conquered the heart of a nice English girl, became engaged to her.

But it was at this point that the drama began. In France you don't just get married more or less at will, as they do in England, particularly if you are in the forces. In addition, the young English lady was serving in the WAAF and so had to conform to the regulations of a hierarchical authority, who wrote the following letter to the Commanding Officer:

> *Dear Sir,*
>
> *I have in my unit a young lady, in whom I have some interest, and who is engaged to one of your subordinates, Mohamed ben Mohamed,*
>
> *I should be obliged if you would communicate to me your opinion on the prospects for a union of this nature. In particular I would like to know whether the airman in question has any antecedents of black blood.*
>
> *Signed, X.*

Love affairs are always difficult to control, above all when there is a question of mixed races and mixed blood.

A certain degree of reserve and discretion is to be recommended. The following is the reply sent by the Commanding Officer of Elvington:

> *Madame,*
>
> *In reply to your letter dated ......, I am able to assure you that the airman, Mohamed ben Mohamed, does not possess any black blood, being of pure Arab race.*
>
> *As you are aware, Arabs are not Catholics but Mohammedan, and the Moslem religion authorises polygamy. Consequently I am unable to give you any assurance that your protégée will*

be the first wife of Mohamed ben Mohamed, and even less that she will be the last one.

It follows that this marriage does not seem to me to be susceptible to the usual guarantees.

Signed, Y.

When I asked P.O. Jules how the story ended, he replied that he did not know whether the questions of race and blood had had any effect on *l'amour*. The officer who had discretionary responsibility for the matter had declined to give him any further information. And P.O. Jules finished by repeating this well-known phrase:

'Love is like art – it knows no national boundaries.'

Chapter 31

When the Pathfinders die at the time of the Breton Legends.

Today the *Groupes Guyenne* and *Tunisie* are on standby. P.O. Jules, whose name is on the Battle Order, waits patiently for the voice on the Tannoy to announce the time of main briefing. Now and then he goes over to the window. He looks at the low clouds that keep all colour from the foliage of the trees.

'The operation will be scrubbed,' he thinks.

Then he goes to his small table to read, to read again, or to write letters. Today he immerses himself in stories from old legends of Brittany. Reading them, he feels the same atmosphere that he associates with the county of Yorkshire, this countryside of hills and howling winds, of "Wuthering Heights".

In both of them he sees the same houses squatting on the land, the sky that is nearly always grey. In them he finds a deep sense of nostalgia, mingled with dreams and poetry. Above all he is fascinated by the description of the ancestral habits and customs, redolent of dignity, respect and shared values. For him the ties that bind masters and men provide an example. He appreciates the way they behave towards each other in the various aspects of their daily life, the way they wear their traditional costume when they visit each other. For him that is a mark of medieval civilisation.

Now and again he comes back to present reality, to the operation that they keep postponing, to the coming visit of an officer from headquarters in London that was announced yesterday.

For a long time P.O. Jules has entertained a certain reserve towards officers of this type, whom he considers largely responsible for the disaster we experienced in May and June 1940. He finds it hard to accept that these officers should visit Elvington clad in RAF battledress rather than in French uniform.

'One day,' he said to me on one occasion when one of them was paying a visit to Elvington, 'it'll be me who sets an example in the matter of uniform. I'll show them what's meant by Breton tradition. I'll go on an operation in full dress uniform.'

Today he decides that he will keep his promise. A few hours later, when he enters the big room where briefing is about to begin, the first person he meets is *Commandant* Puget, who is quite obviously somewhat surprised by the uniform he is wearing. When he comments on it to P.O. Jules, the latter replies,

'Beginning today, I have decided to make war in Number One uniform and white gloves.'

Then he goes and joins his crew. As the briefing continues he notes down the most important details in his notebook. This night the Krupp factories on the Ruhr are the target.

H-hour, when the bombing is scheduled to begin, is thirty minutes after midnight. The Master Bomber's callsign in 'Banana'.

Fig 49. Visit of French Air Minister (M. Charles Tillon), accompanied by C.A.S. (General Valin), Chef de Cabinet Militaire (General Piolet), Chef de Cabinet Civil(M. Jugeau) and Party, to RAF Station, Elvington, on 20th December 1944. YAM

The operation follows the usual rhythm: take-off, climb to altitude, keep on track, and so on.

At 0025 hours Dudu calls up the wireless operator:

'Switch over to the Master Bomber's frequency,' he says.

At 0027 hours there is a light crackling in the headphones.

At 0030 hours the voice of the Master Bomber can be heard for the first time:

'To all Main Force aircraft: wind velocity 300 degrees, 20 miles per hour. Continue aiming at the centre of yellow markers.'

The voice is calm, and there is no hint of emotion. It is an intense and solitary monologue from an elite crew, hand-picked from among the best. For more than ten minutes 'Banana One' issues succinct orders, demonstrating a rare mastery of his complex task. In order to monitor the situation on the ground he is flying at about 10,000 feet. From time to time he descends almost to ground level to drop more markers to replace those that have gone out. Then he climbs back to 10,000 feet

Fig 50. Visit of French Air Minister. YAM

and, throughout the whole twenty-minute duration of the attack, 'Banana' indulges in this very dangerous sport. Flying well below the other bombers, he is a prime target for the enemy gunners who, moreover, know how important his task is.

Despite the tension of the moment his voice remains calm and without the slightest degree of hesitation. From time to time he comments on the bombing or encourages the crews.

'Well done chaps! Carry on like that! You're doing a great job.'

It is a dark night, but not for long. Already the first incendiaries are raging in the distance and the sky itself seems to be on fire. Pale lights glow from the ground. P.O. Jules alters course slightly. The leading aircraft are marking his route, and he no longer needs his navigator to guide him. He gazes into the shadows, listening all the time to the voice of the Master Bomber.

But that night Banana One was destined not to see the end of the operation. A few seconds later he announces:

'Banana One; this is Banana One. Mayday, Mayday, Mayday. I have been hit. Take over Banana Two. Banana Two, take over.'

P.O. Jules, in common with all the actors in the Main Force, understands completely the drama that is being played out. He knows that in a few moments Banana One will crash into the ground. A violent spasm clutches at his heart. And then he hears Banana Two come in with the same calmness:

'This is Banana Two. All Main Force aircraft – continue to bomb the centre of the reds.'

P.O. Jules cannot avoid having great admiration for these above-average crews, who look death in the face and defy it. For his part Jules' navigator has already noted the facts and the time in his log, while the bomb aimer is making the final adjustments to his bombsight.

The gunners are scanning the sky. '*Attention*, pilot, aircraft at three o'clock.'

'OK,' replies P.O. Jules, I can see it.'

He looks down at the target, illuminated as it is by incendiaries. In his earphones the voice of Banana Two continues, just as imperturbable as that of Banana One was a few moments previously.

Fig 51. A Halifax shot down by flak over the target. The four engines are on fire.

'Now aim at the centre of the greens,' it says. Then, very suddenly, 'This is Banana Two, Mayday, Mayday, Mayday. I am going down, I am going down. All aircraft – do your best!'

A sinister silence follows this distress call, a silence even more terrifying than the call itself, a silence that takes you by the throat and presses on your gut. It is horrible, it is macabre. Men usually see death but don't hear it. P.O. Jules, who has heard, peers into the night to see it. He scans the heaven and then, suddenly, he sees an immense red glow. It is forty-three minutes past midnight.

'Dudu, note the time,' he tells his navigator.

Is the red glow from the Deputy Master Bomber, or from a Main Force aircraft hit by flak, or is it a violent explosion on the ground? For P.O. Jules and his crew the question will come to mind again and again, but without an answer. But rapidly the reality of the moment reasserts itself.

'Dudu', says P.O. Jules, 'switch on your radar. If the target markers go out you can take me in from your screen.'

'I don't think that will be necessary,' answers Dudu. 'The target's very close. The bombing run will begin any moment now.'

At 0047 hours the bomb aimer presses the bomb-release button, and a few seconds later P.O. Jules turns on to the heading that will take them on their way home. The enemy fighters have not succeeded in intercepting the stream, so the most difficult part is over. The intensity of the combat diminishes. The tension relaxes.

Why, then, do the minutes of anguish through which he has lived return to his mind? Why does he hear once again those dramatic phrases? Why do his ears ring with the memory of those fearful messages? Why do his eyes again see that Dante-esque spectacle? He would rather forget, rather not hear the distress calls, but he cannot help it. Then he asks himself – why must there be so many deaths, so much sacrifice? Everything seems senseless to him – the war and the men who wage it. Everything seems senseless to him, even the victory and the liberty that will come from the long sacrifice.

The remainder of the operation passes without incident. Back in the intelligence section he recounts the night's events as accurately as he can. Then he makes his way to the mess, eats the traditional bacon and eggs and leaves his crew and goes to try to find sleep,.

When he gets to his room he takes off his uniform, hangs it carefully in the wardrobe, and goes to his writing-table.

He relives every incident of this night. He recalls the tiniest details and the minutes that preceded the run over the target, when the sky was on fire and the multicoloured lights lit up the ground. But above all his memories turn to the two Pathfinders.

'This is Banana. This is Banana. Mayday, Mayday, Mayday.'

Like a sound that goes on forever he hears the words, hears them again and yet again. Then he sits down at the table. As he does every evening, he opens his notebook to record his impressions. But tonight he searches in vain for words that will translate his emotion and which would pay homage to those men, men not like others. He searches, but cannot find. So he simply writes:

'Tonight the two Master Bombers were shot down. Who can ever describe their courage?'

Then, remembering that he had done this operation in full-dress uniform, he adds,

'To live through such moments, to be there at the death of men like this, it is fitting to be in full-dress uniform.'

Just as in the Breton legends.

Fig 52. A French Officer's room (Seated is Capitaine Rousseau).

Chapter 32

From which the reader might sense that P.O. Jules' morale sometimes wavers.

It was December, and everything was combining to make us depressed. The German army had broken through in the Ardennes. When we had wanted to crush them with bombs, just as they had crushed us in 1940, the weather man was on their side again. Fog, which spread all over Europe, made accurate bombing impossible. And we watched the battle evolve, unable to do anything.

We spent the majority of our time looking for a corner in which we could keep warm. Coal was scarce, and the ration that was allocated to us was meagre in the extreme. In order to economise we would gather in one room, where we would make the stove roar. Long hours would pass there, in which we would talk about days gone by.

P.O. Jules no longer led the conversation. His tour of operations seemed to be getting on top of him. Was it fatigue, or nervous tension? Was it the gaps in our ranks left by comrades who had not come back? Or was it the long evenings with nothing to do that made him morose? The result was that his anecdotes became less frequent and that he would often leave us and shut himself up alone in his room. He played patience, or he wrote. This is one of the poems that he composed during this period:

ELVINGTON
Elvington,
Small English place, forsaken and apart,
Horizons fogged, whose grey pervades the heart:
And ceaseless winds that speak of days long gone,
And skies that speak of sadness, and no sun.
Where bombers fly and take into the night
Abandoned dreams of happiness and light.

Elvington,
Where lives depend on numbers random drawn,
And I have known the terror, hardly borne,
Of flames and fire, and searchlights reaching high,
While fighters sweep across a glowing sky,
And lonely in the night-time beats my heart,
To quell the terror, ere it start.

Elvington,
Where all seems sad to me, and grey,
Grey as the north, with death not far away,
Where we take to our bed as others rise
And nightmares fill our sleeping eyes;
And empty rooms, where once our comrades were,
Where daily head-counts breed despair.

Elvington,
Where once I would go happy to my room
And take my ease, nor think of doom,
And there forget the times when danger came,
And warm myself beside the friendly flame
And there forget the long black night
On oxygen, and lungs that gasp at height.

Elvington,
And comrades gone, and never to return
Who sleep in foreign fields, for whom we yearn,
Friends once with us; to you we vow
Your memory, your example now
To keep. You're with us yet.
We saw you go, and we shall not forget.

> *Elvington,*
> *Where all of us can truly say,*
> *'We did our job; we hope we did it well.'*
> *No pride, just hope: and hope we may,*
> *Hold our heads high, here where so many fell.*

As I read these lines I recalled the path followed by P.O. Jules since his first night raid, which was on the railway station at Alençon when, just after having bombed the target, he came within a hair's breadth of colliding with another aircraft, a few centimetres away from the collision that haunted each and every one of us.

Chapter 33

In which the reader is once more confronted with the risk of collision.

Of all the dangers that one could meet at any moment in the air, a collision was certainly the one that P.O. Jules feared the most. For him it was the most underhand, the most unpredictable, the most unstoppable, the one against which he was totally powerless.

From a number of combats with night fighters he had always emerged victorious. He had flown through flak barrages with confidence, even when the shell-bursts reverberated on his fuselage like a drumstick on a drumskin. He knew little fear. He trusted in his lucky star.

On the other hand he knew that there was nothing you could do against a collision, particularly when you were in the target area, when all the bombers are converging on the markers. Then, you are

Fig 53. 13/14 January 1945; Collision between the Halifax of Flying Officer Wilson and that of Capitaine Brachet.

Capitaine Brachet's Halifax crashed, while that of Flying Officer Wilson (No. 51 Squadron) managed to reach an airfield in South-East England. Looking at the above photograph one might well ask oneself how.

not flying on parallel headings. The density of the aircraft in the stream increases. They are less manoeuvrable with bomb doors open and on the point of releasing their bombs.

He remembers the first time he attacked the railway station at Alençon. Just after he had bombed, a Halifax crossed in front of him and came within a hair's breadth of him: the noise was still in his ears. And he would never forget the shock of the violent turbulence that rocked his machine.

And he also remembered a collision on the runway at Elvington, in which he lost his best friend.

He remembered all this. One day he wrote down his impressions in his diary. Here they are.

'A Collision:

A dark shape growing in the night, coming near too quickly, which you see too late, which you can't avoid.

An indescribable roar followed by sinister crunching noises, all amplified by the darkness.

A violent shock that shakes every part of the aircraft. Flames shoot from the engines and lick the main spar of the wing, which will break off in less than a minute.

An order that rings in the headphones – 'Jump, jump!'

A pilot struggling to the limits of human endeavour to hold his aircraft so that the crew can parachute out. A pilot, prisoner in his cockpit, who is destined inevitably to perish.

Hands in the darkness looking for the handles to the escape hatches, a trapdoor opening, the clips on your parachute harness that catch on the fuselage, a gaping hole, a thrust with the knees, the freezing air that lashes your face, the jerk to your shoulders as your parachute opens, the slow descent to the ground.

An aeroplane impacting with the ground in a crash of thunder, black-tinged flames reaching upwards hundreds of feet.

Comrades trapped in the inferno. Seconds that last for centuries.

All that – that is a mid-air collision.'

And for Brachet, a navigator in command of an aircraft[25], whose seat was close to the escape hatch and could therefore be the first to leave the machine, a collision meant above all six men to save, a pilot to help while the rest of the crew got out.

Then it was a disembodied cabin that crashed to earth, his last dwelling place, a charred coffin that he shared with his pilot and his rear gunner. A collision is all that – and worse.

Fig 54. Capitaine Brachet.

25 In the French Air Force, unlike the Royal Air Force, the senior ranking member of the crew was captain of aircraft.

Chapter 34

In which the reader is there when P.O. Jules flies his last operation.

Yes, P.O. Jules was suffering from nostalgia. He was living on his nerves, and he had the feeling that his nerves were at breaking point. He sensed that he was at the end of his tether. He now knew why the British set an operational tour at thirty-three missions. In nights of broken sleep he awoke to fighter attacks. He relived his combats, he shouted orders to the crew, and when the aircraft was hit he awoke with a start. He would wipe the sweat from his forehead, switch on the light, take up a book and try to think of something else.

His fatigue showed in his gaunt cheeks, in his sunken eyes and his weary bearing. He had to fight not only the enemy, but himself as well. He had to discipline himself, because he knew that he had to be in good shape to be able to fly his operations successfully. He had to see it out to the very end.

And as today was to be the final mission of his tour, and because his life hung on the throw of a dice, he looked back over the road he had followed.

While he was preparing his charts and his operational log he could not help thinking back to that night over Bochum on the 4th of November, from which thirty-five of his comrades from the Squadron did not return.

He saw himself, two months previously, standing at the table where *Lieutenant* Dabadie was playing bridge.

'You're a jammy bastard,' Flesch had said to 'Big Dab' when the game was finished. 'With your sort of luck you've got nothing to worry about. But the game's not over yet - we'll finish it tomorrow.'

Fig 55. *Lieutenant Dabadie, known as 'Big Dab'. One of the thirty-five missing on the night of the Bochum raid.*

While he was measuring courses and distances, P.O. Jules recalled every detail of that tragic night. Taking off, climbing up into the low cloud, reaching the Dutch coast. At 1939 hours precisely, in *Lieutenant* Dabadie's Halifax, D-Dog, the pilot, *Adjudant* Guise, announces,

'Bochum in sight. First green markers just beginning to go down.'

Lieutenant Pothuau, the bomb aimer, takes over the guidance of the aircraft. He is enclosed in the extreme front of the aircraft, encased in perspex, as if suspended in nothingness. Ahead of him the whole sky is lit up. White flashes from the anti-aircraft guns mark the ground below. Searchlight beams are all around. Shell bursts multiply. And D-Dog advances towards this inferno.

The first red markers appear at 1943 hours

'Left, left,' calls *Lieutenant* Pothuau, and then he adds, 'Just a bit further left.'

Then, a few moments later, in language unmistakable if not regulation, 'Fucking great – now dead ahead!'

A limpid night. From the ground, rockets climb spasmodically. Orange flames streak across the sky and then explode, bursting into three or four fragments and dropping burning downwards. Fiery balls zigzag in the darkness, exploding at regular intervals.

All of man's ingenuity in the art of warfare is unleashed. *Adjudant* Guise keeps his heading. Suddenly a burst of tracer shells surrounds the aircraft. In the flash as one of the shells bursts one of the gunners has time to recognise the Focke Wulf 190 that has taken them by surprise, but it has missed them.

'Christ! Gunners...!' shouts *Lieutenant* Pothuau.

'Quiet, Pothuau,' says *Lieutenant* Dabadie calmly. 'Direct the aircraft and shut up! Gunners – keep your eyes open and don't let us be taken by surprise!'

'Steady – steady!' from the bomb aimer. 'Bomb doors open.'

The bomb doors are opened. The aircraft is dancing, blown about by the slipstreams of other aircraft and by bursting shells. Searchlights probe the sky. One comes closer.

'Steady,' continues the bomb aimer. 'Stand by! Bombs gone!'

The time is 1945 hours. Within a quarter of an hour more than 700 crews will repeat that 'Bombs gone!'. And each time four tons of bombs will fall on Bochum.

A few moments later - 'Make a note of the time!' calls out *Adjudant* Guise.

'1947 hrs!'

An aircraft is going down. He has seen tracers, and he says, 'There are fighters around.'

Every member of the crew redoubles his concentration. Try as they might not to look at it, the town of Bochum draws the attention of the gunners. It is aflame from end to end. Streets stand out in black from a background of fire. Smoke is starting to spread, and there are more and more explosions on the ground. Suddenly there is a noise in the aircraft.

'Turn left, pilot. Five degrees port!'

And then, 'Straight ahead! Straight ahead!'

'We're on fire!' cries *Sergent Chef* Lelong.

'Guise, take over,' says *Lieutenant* Dabadie calmly.

But Guise doesn't reply. There's no doubt about it — he is badly wounded. The Ju 88 attacked them from below, and the port inner engine is aflame.

'Hello Guise!' repeats *Lieutenant* Dabadie. Still no reply. He stands up, opens the escape hatch. It opens, but it jams. Try as he might he cannot budge it. He can't get out through it. *Lieutenant* Pothuau and he are imprisoned, and the aircraft is still burning.

Sergent Chef Alavoine, the wireless operator, is by the side of the hatch. Alavoine looks round and sees the engineer, Lelong, fighting the flames in an attempt to get at his parachute and that of the pilot. Alavoine jumps. While this is happening the mid-upper gunner, Sergent Vautard, has descended from his turret. He opens the door. He too jumps.

But the rear gunner, Sergent Vega, cannot get out of his turret. D-Dog takes four living men and one dead one with her in her dive to the ground, where she explodes.

That evening's game of cards was destined never to end. Now, with these visions of horror still in his mind, P.O. Jules listens to the final briefing, navigation, the target and the hostile defences.

'It's our last trip,' he says to Dudu, his navigator. 'I feel as if I'm playing double or quits.'

The route that will take them to Hanover tonight passes Hamburg on the left, and on the way back the bombers will fly to the north of Münster and to the left of The Hague. It's a journey over enemy territory the whole time. Doubly anxious, P.O., Jules makes a note of the courses they have to fly, the distances, the weather. You never know: if the navigator should be wounded he would have to bring the aircraft back to England himself.

But why was P.O. Jules so worried that night? Why could he not rid himself of the memory of that night over Bochum?

As he climbs into the truck that will take him to his aircraft he thinks of *Lieutenant* Vlès, navigator and captain of aircraft, another one who didn't come back from the inferno above the Ruhr, another one shot down by fighters in circumstances befitting the heroic spirit he hid beneath his unprepossessing exterior.

Lieutenant Vlès was a hero, nothing more, nothing less. On that notorious Bochum evening he sets course just as the others do, he bombs as the others do. But suddenly there is a burst of tracer shells, and his port wing catches fire. The aircraft has been taken by surprise.

Adjudant Hannedouche, the pilot, immediately gives the order to abandon aircraft. *Lieutenant* Vlès stands up and opens the hatch. But the fire is fierce. Already the aircraft, its equilibrium lost, is out of control despite the efforts of the pilot. Steeper, steeper still, the Halifax dives. Inside they feel as if they are being pressed down to the floor. The navigator, close to the hatch, is the only one who could get out without difficulty. In a few seconds it will be too late. *Lieutenant* Vles could jump, but in the darkness he sees that the wireless operator, *Sergent Chef* Vlaminck, is in difficulties and cannot reach the opening. Vlès grabs hold of him and, with a strength he never knew he had, helps him part of the way to the escape hatch. But still Vlaminck cannot get out. It is as if he is being dragged backwards into the aircraft, and the seconds are passing. *Lieutenant* Vlès props himself against something and, with all his force, he pushes with his feet against the wireless operator's shoulders. At last Vlaminck finds himself in empty space, and he opens his parachute.

That took several seconds. *Lieutenant* Vlès knew that time was against him, but as captain of aircraft he did not wish to be the only one of his crew to survive.

In fact, *Sergent Chef* Vlaminck had hardly left the aircraft before it exploded. The pilot, who had remained in his seat to let his comrades bale out, found himself, not knowing how it had happened, suspended beneath his parachute and descending slowly through the darkness. The tail of the Halifax had become detached in the explosion: spinning, it hit the ground. As for *Lieutenant* Vlès, he had sacrificed himself voluntarily to save at least one of his men. Together with another four of them, he disappeared, a hero.

It is a vision of frightfulness. Lost in his memories, P.O. Jules has climbed mechanically into his aircraft, E-Easy. He has switched on, run up the engines, and positioned his machine at the end of the runway for take-off. A few moments later he is in the air.

On board, everything is running smoothly. By now darkness has fallen, but P.O. Jules is still thinking about that night of Bochum.

He thinks of his friend, *Capitaine* Béraud. After having passed over the target he too was caught by a burst of tracer shells that came at him from the left. At once *Capitaine* Béraud realises what has happened. He looks round. He sees his port inner engine on fire. In his normal voice, slow and calm, he gives the order, 'Put on parachutes.' And then, in drill-book fashion, as if he were carrying out an exercise, 'Jump. Jump. Jump!'

Capitaine Béraud knows that there is no time to spare. With an engine on fire a Halifax's wing breaks off in less than a second. The navigator, *Lieutenant* Valette, stands up. Cooped up in his cabin, absorbed in his calculations, he hasn't seen anything, and he asks: 'You think we should bale out immediately?'

'Jump at once! Jump!' shouts *Capitaine* Béraud.

The hatch is open. The navigator is the first to leave. *Adjudant* Manfroid, the rear gunner, bales out from his turret. It is the turn of *Lieutenant* Raffin, the bomb aimer, to jump. Does he think of what he's said so often – 'Béraud, if anyone has to stay behind, we'll stay behind together'?

Fig 56. The Navigator's harness.

On the harness can be seen the rings to which the parachute straps were clipped.

The mask, with its oxygen-pipe, was equipped with a microphone allowing telephonic communication within the aircraft. The pilot's microphone, in addition, allowed communication with the outside world.

The earphones were fixed to the helmet.

But Béraud isn't wounded. He will bale out, and they will meet again on the ground, he knows. Raffin jumps. The wireless operator and the mid-upper gunner also jump into the darkness.

Sergent Chef Imart has stayed behind to help the pilot, as is his duty as flight engineer. He has passed the pilot, Béraud, his parachute, which Béraud has taken and clutched in one hand, not wishing to lose control of the aircraft. He manages to hold the machine, which is beginning to pull away to one side. *Sergent Chef* Imart clips his parachute to his chest, goes to the escape hatch, turns round.

'Are you coming, captain?' he says.

'Jump! At once! I'm coming!' replies Béraud. The engineer jumps. His parachute opens. And as he is descending he seems to see an explosion on the air. Is it his aircraft? Sadly, it is. *Capitaine* Béraud disappears with it, and – a coincidence of friendship – Raffin is not found, even though his parachute had opened.

The two friends, the only members of their crew not to survive, are buried in the communal cemetery at Stommeln.

'If anyone has to stay behind, we'll stay behind together.[26]

While he is thinking of his friend Béraud. P.O. Jules' aircraft is flying over the North Sea on its way to Hanover. On board there is complete silence. Then the navigator announces:

'Hello, Jules. All navigation instruments u/s. We haven't got any radar or Distant Reading Compass or Air Position Indicator. What shall we do?'

'We'll press on,' replies P.O. Jules.

RAF regulations would allow him to turn round and abort the mission.

'What'll we do for navigation?' Dudu continues.

'We'll sort something out!' decided P.O. Jules.

Once more, complete silence. Intercom sets are switched off, so that there is not even a breath to be heard. Not even a crackle. No background noise. Not the slightest sound of life save for the throbbing of the engines. By this time the aircraft has reached its cruising altitude of 20,000 feet, and they will soon be crossing the German coast.

'Gunners – can you see any more friendly aircraft?'

'No, *Capitaine*, there's nothing to be seen.'

'Let's have a little more oxygen,' he says to the engineer.

'OK, pilot.'

P.O. Jules breathes the oxygen in deeply. It has the same effect on his body as coffee has. As he breathes in he can sense his reflexes growing sharper. Since he has been in England he has even learned how to breathe.

'Course 142,' says the navigator. 'When we pass Hamburg turn starboard on to a heading of 170.'

'Roger,' says P.O. Jules.

---

26   The three preceding anecdotes were written in collaboration with *Capitaine* Cochot.

But how is one supposed to make out Hamburg in this night, black as ink, when one cannot even tell the land from the sea? A few minutes later P.O. Jules sees the first flashes from the muzzles of the antiaircraft guns.

'Just crossing the enemy coast,' he informs the navigator.

'In five minutes alter course on to 179,' answers Dudu.

Now, far to the port side, there is a fury of shell bursts.

'Looks as if we're passing Hamburg!'

'Course 170 degrees,' says the navigator.

Using the magnetic compass alone, P.O. Jules turns on to the new heading. He doesn't want to stray from the flight plan route that they have worked out in advance. He steers the course even more precisely than he normally does. Minutes pass, each one taking them nearer to their target. In the terrible silence the minutes seem never-ending. P.O. Jules always demands complete silence on board, so that the gunners can pass their instructions immediately if the aircraft is attacked or damaged. But just now the silence is hypnotic. In order to break it he asks the navigator, 'What's our ETA?'

'In about twenty minutes.'

The entire crew keeps a lookout for other bombers taking part in the raid, but in the darkness they can't even see the horizon. Is P.O. Jules on track? Is the wind as forecast? Is the aeroplane drifting to either starboard or port?

No one knows. 'We'll sort it out!' Will P.O. Jules see the target? He knows that the whole operation is pointless unless the target is destroyed.

And still the minutes pass by in the silence. The night is calm.

'Green markers should be going down in three minutes,' says the navigator.

P.O. Jules continues to search the darkness. He no longer has time to think of *Capitaine* Baron, *Lieutenant* Hyenne and the others who died over Bochum. He mustn't miss the markers – and there, suddenly, just ahead, he sees a great white light.

'Bomb aimer!' he says, 'Get cracking! Target in sight.'

'OK, *mon Capitaine*.'

'Gunners, *attention*! Watch the sky. Don't watch what's happening on the ground!'

'Steady, steady!' calls the bomb aimer. 'Bomb doors open!'

Red markers are beginning to cascade downwards.

'Look out, pilot! Aircraft to port!' shouts the mid-upper. 'Can you make it out?'

P.O. Jules scans the sky,

'OK, I've got it!' he says.

It is a Halifax that is passing slowly on the port side. P.O. Jules keeps his eyes on it to avoid a collision.

'Engineer, keep a look-out to starboard.'

'Steady now!' the bomb aimer continues.

Green target indicators are now mingling with the reds. It is a veritable firework display. Searchlights sweep the skies, and in the beams antiaircraft shells can be seen bursting in clusters. The flak opens up as the first fires light up the sky. Very soon it will be as bright as day over Hanover.

'Steady ... steady! *Attention*! Bombs gone!' Wait for the photograph. There it goes! You can turn now,'

P.O. Jules begins his turn. 'What's the new course?' he asks his navigator.

'Head 272,' replies Dudu, 'and climb slowly to 22,000 feet.'

'Roger,' acknowledges P.O. Jules.

Fortune seems to be smiling on them. By following the simple entries on the flight plan, by relying solely on the forecast winds, they reached the target spot-on. Why shouldn't the journey home be trouble-free? And yet the navigator is uneasy. He knows that the route has been carefully chosen to avoid areas that are particularly heavily defended. The slightest error will take them off track and they will be caught in the whole network of enemy defences. But how can he avoid such errors when he has no means of checking his position?

Steering 272, P.O. Jules scans the sky and the ground, but the sky remains calm. The enemy fighters appear to have failed to intercept the bomber force. Only now and then do searchlights light up, search the sky for their prey, and switch off. The flak too seems to have lost its normal interest. And still the minutes pass by. And every minute that passes takes them closer to friendly territory.

And with the minutes, the miles pass too.

'It's always that little bit less to walk if I'm shot down,' thinks P.O. Jules. About half an hour after leaving the target behind, P.O. Jules sees, some distance on either side of his aircraft, two groups of searchlights and intense antiaircraft fire. He knows where he is. He knows every town near the route that he has to keep clear of.

'We should be about half way between Osnabrück and Münster,' he says. 'Dudu – check it on the map.'

The navigator comes back quickly: 'Spot on!' he says. 'We're bang on track.'

It certainly looks as if Lady Luck is on their side.

'Gunners, keep a look-out,' says P.O. Jules. 'This is a dicey area!'

And indeed, no sooner has he finished what he is saying that a searchlight switches on and catches him in its beam. He hasn't had time to take the slightest evasive action. He is completely dazzled by the light. For the past three hours the darkness has been making his pupils dilate, and now he has to close his eyes so that he won't be blinded. Then he opens them a little and tries to read his instruments.

'Light on full in the pilot's position!' he tells the engineer. 'Switch on your electric torch and point it at the instruments!'

P.O. Jules can just about make out the artificial horizon. 'Stand by!' he tells the crew, 'Hold tight!'

The evasive action comprises diving and climbing in succession, while at the same time making turns of more than forty-five degrees. Using both his hands and all his strength, P.O. Jules takes hold of the control column. He turns port, diving to the ground. Then brutally, his speed approaching 300 knots, he checks his aircraft, hurls it into a turn to starboard. He is lifted from his seat, but the seat belts hold him in place. Next to him the engineer is suspended is the air for several seconds, then drops heavily to the floor. The third time they carry out this manoeuvre the searchlight loses them.

All the crew had had a considerable fright. When a searchlight catches you in its beam the usual thing is for other lights to be switched on and pick you up, and then it is virtually impossible to get away. P.O. Jules has managed to escape before it was too late.

'OK Dudu,' he says to the navigator who, in the front of the aircraft, has been waiting impotently, 'they missed us! Turning back on course.'

That is P.O. Jules' final display of emotion.

The rest of the operation passes without incident. With the aid of one or two radio bearings they reach Elvington, where they touch down.

Their aircraft comes to a standstill at its dispersal.

Dudu approaches P. O. Jules. He shakes him by the hand, and he can think of only one thing to say: 'Thank you!'

Their tour of operations is completed.

Fig 57. Capitaine Notelle signing the log book after a flight.

Chapter 35

In which the reader rediscovers France at last.

And so the end of P.O. Jules' tour of operations had really arrived. At last he had succeeded in getting them behind him, those thirty-three missions. They had seemed a very long haul. Now that he counted them off, one by one, right up to the very end, it seemed to him that the months that he had just lived through had been nothing but a nightmare, that his life had now taken on a new rhythm, and that he was starting from scratch again.

During the three months that he stayed on at Elvington to complete his administrative formalities he would still hear the voice on the Tannoy:

'Navigators' briefing 1400 hours. Wireless operators' and bomb aimers' briefing 1500 hours. General briefing 1600 hours.'

But he knew that these orders didn't apply to him any more. He knew that he would no longer have to breathe the heavy atmosphere of the hours that went before an operation: he knew that he would no longer be prey to apprehensions, that he would no longer have to worry about being afraid or about the touch of death, that he was rid of the return flights in the fog and the dangers of collision that went with navigational difficulties. But he could not prevent himself thinking of all his comrades whose names were written on the blackboard in the main room of the control tower and who had to live through the terror from which he was now liberated. He tried to rid himself of these dark thoughts. He told himself that this recent past was of no more value than a memory that one tries to forget. He did not think in terms of gratitude. He was simply happy within himself. For the moment all he wanted to do was to return to his family and rediscover France, to leave Elvington, where he already felt as if he were a stranger.

When all the formalities of administration were behind him he fastened up his suitcases, caught the train to London and reported to the Air Ministry building in Queensway. Similar difficulties to those chronicled in an earlier chapter abounded when it was a matter of supplying him with a travel warrant to France. After many complications and numerous reportings and cancellations P.O. Jules succeeded in getting his ticket and in leaving London.

And so he left the capital of England with its habitual air of sadness and took the train for Newhaven, and from there the boat to France.

Standing on the deck at the bows of the ship he saw the French coast, and, overtaken by emotion, he felt a *frisson* inside himself. Perhaps a tear came to his eye, the eye of him who had never wept, and he turned his head away so as not to see the country for which he had been fighting for six years and for which he had suffered so much. He looked at the distant horizon, clear in the winter air. He tried to make out the smallest points, the smallest things. Then he watched the seagulls, the way they flew and twisted and turned, the way they caught fish, pulling up above them and then diving down like Stukas.

When he turned his eyes back to the coast again, it was quite near. It looked as if the war ruins were still smoking. After all his years of exile P.O. Jules thought about those who had stayed behind and suffered the occupation, the privations, the bombing and the cold. He compared his own fate, among the British people who had received him so well, and he imagined the many dramas and much misery hidden behind those ruined houses and devastated areas. He knew Dieppe from having been there on holiday before the war. He tried to reconcile his memories with the reality that was stretching out before his eyes, but in this mass of ruins he was unable to pick out any of the familiar sights of his youth.

'It's all so sad,' he said, turning to his navigator.

The following hours were taken up with the formalities of disembarking. Then they took their seats in the train. A few minutes after the train had started the bell of the dining car sounded.

'Have we got enough to buy a meal?' P.O. Jules asked his navigator.

'I've only got fifty francs left,' replied Dudu.

'Then perhaps I can offer you dinner,' said P.O. Jules, fumbling in his pocket.

Between them they succeeded in putting together six hundred francs. When they had settled the bill they found they still had enough left over to buy themselves a brandy, which was precisely what they did. When they reached Paris they still had enough for a *Métro* ticket. And that is how P.O. Jules found himself back in the French capital, where his new posting to the *Ministère de l'Air* awaited him. He became a headquarters officer, and he took up his place in his office on the third floor on the *Boulevard Victor*, quite genuinely without any preconceived ideas.

A few months later, when I had finished my own tour of operations, my first wish was to find my mother and my family again, from whom I had been separated for more than five years.

I could very easily imagine their worries, their anxieties, their anguish. How many sleepless nights must my mother have passed? How many times had she wept?

As the train took me northward I looked at the countryside, turning over these thoughts in my head. I could not wait to get home. As soon as the train had stopped I leapt out on to the platform, where my

Fig 58. *A 'Halifax' flying over the Pont Alexandre III in Paris at the end of the War !*

mother was waiting for me. What a great joy it was, what happiness, to see her again, to find her alive and well, to be alive myself.

When the first emotional moments had passed we began to talk. Question and answer mingled. We had so much to tell each other.

I was anxious to know how my mother had coped with my being away, and I asked her:

'During all these years, did you ever lose hope?'

'No,' replied my mother, 'I always listened to the news on the English radio.'

My astonishment must have shown on my face, because she went on: 'Everyone in France knew about *Colonel* Bourgain.'

With considerable surprise I told her that I wasn't a colonel, and never had been. There must, I said, be some mistake. In trying to come up with an answer I realised that she had simply confused our name with that of *Colonel* Bourgoin, the commanding officer of the Free French Parachute Corps, whose exploits on the field of battle were often newsworthy and were regularly the subject of reports on the BBC.

'There!' said my mother, somewhat illogically, when I had explained, 'You can always imagine certainties.'

After several days of deep happiness I returned to Paris, where the first thing I did was to go and see my friend P.O. Jules in his *sanctum sanctorum* in The Air Ministry. When I went in he was hidden behind an enormous pile of files. As soon as he caught sight of me he rushed towards me. We shook hands, and then he said, 'Sit down a few moments. Give me time to wash my hands and put my coat on, and I'll be with you.'

I sat down and began to leaf through a magazine. Sharing the same office with P.O. Jules was a *Commandant*, and he appeared to be very busy conducting a conversation with a sergeant, who was standing at attention in front of him. I didn't understand what was being talked about, but it seemed to be a matter of a pilot, half a pilot or a quarter of a pilot.

I didn't attach great importance to it, particularly as in the meanwhile P.O. Jules had finished getting ready and was ushering me to the door.

'If anyone should ask,' he said to the *Commandant*, 'perhaps you'd tell them I shall be out all day.'

We left the office. As soon as we were in the corridor he added:

'I'm going to take you to the Ministry Command Office.'

I was surprised that I should be invited to the holy of holies, but I was rapidly reassured because the Command Office was simply a small café nearby, where we were soon installed in front of a democratic *Beaujolais*.

When I had given him the news about old friends in England and the *Groupes Lourds*, the conversation turned to his current job. He explained to me the secrets of the conversation I had just vaguely overheard in his office a short time previously.

'Look,' he said, 'it's really quite simple. My colleague – who, incidentally, is a very charming man - 'is currently trying to work out a formula that will give him the total number of pilots in the Air Force.'

I retorted that that seemed improbable to me.

'Improbable, but true,' he went on. 'Within this formula there is a whole series of variables and unknowns, the principal ones of which are the number of public holidays, the numbers of days in the year (which varies with leap years), the present minimum availability of pilots, the number of days and nights on which flying can take place, etcetera, etcetera. The whole theory is based on extremely thorough statistical calculations. There is only one snag. That is, that the results never agree with reality. The last calculation gave us a total number of pilots in excess of the entire strength of the *Armée de l'Air*. Even that wouldn't be too bad, however, if you only got round figures. We find that we have got halves of pilots and quarters of pilots. Quite naturally we thought that we had made a mistake with the decimal point, but when we moved it one place to the right we can up with a ridiculous answer in the region of two million. So we've come to a dead end.'

I had listened quietly to this explanation, and I found myself asking myself to what extent one should believe such stories. I interrupted him a second time:

'That's very hard to work out,' I said, 'but we shouldn't be surprised at anything. By the way, I see from the uniform that you're wearing that you've changed some of your ideas.'

P.O. Jules was wearing battledress, the working uniform of RAF aircrew, whereas in England he had made it a point of honour never to go out except in French uniform. I added,

'What's more, dressed like that you have a very military look about you – of course, I used the French expression, *"air martial"*'.

'Yes – an Air Marshal in the Admin. Branch!' he replied.

And again he went on, and he gave me a few snippets of gossip from Headquarters.

Plunged into an ambience he had so often ridiculed, he seemed uncertain of himself. Quite clearly he was missing the atmosphere of an operational station, the extraordinary comradeship among those who went through the same dangers, but he didn't want to mention it to me. He was not born to live within four walls, and I had the feeling that he was impatient for it to come to an end.

At about midday he took me to lunch. I didn't know where he was going to take me. We took the *Métro*. When we got to the *Sèvres-Babylone* station he said to me:

'We'll get out here. I love the name of this station. It strikes me as having a certain poetic ring.' I replied that we were here to have lunch, not to write poetry.

'Does that mean,' he asked me, 'that poets don't need to eat well?'

We spent the rest of the day together, and at a late hour that evening we parted, promising that we would meet again at the first opportunity.

PART THREE

In Memoriam

'The finest memorial to those who died is the memory of those who still live.'

(André Malraux)

Section 1

The human and material losses in the French *Groupes Lourds*:

It is a longstanding principle of war that heavy losses can be accepted as long as there is the hope of results of substance. This adage applies particularly well to Bomber Command. As we have seen in the foregoing chapter aerial bombing had a decisive influence on the outcome of the war. The other side of the coin, as we shall now see, is that it was at the cost of heavy loss of life.

Human losses in the *Groupes Lourds*:

This inscription on our monument at Grandcamp-Maisy in the Calvados reads: 'One in two died.'

If one analyses the cause of aircraft losses one can compile the following table:

Cause	Number	Percentage
Fighters	16	44%
Flak	11	31%
Collision	3	8%
Crashed	5	14%
Vanished without trace	1	3%

The following comments apply to the table:

- Losses due to fighters were incurred during night operations, while losses due to flak were incurred by day.
- Although the figures are based on a smaller sample, they tally well with those of No. 4 Group, which are based on a much higher figure of losses.

Losses of *matériel*:

We must first of all make clear what we mean by the operational life of an aircraft. This is measured by the number of days elapsing from its delivery from the factory until it is lost.

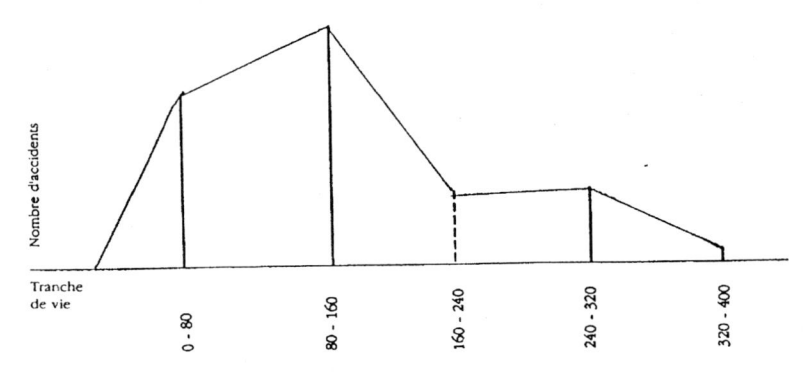

Fig 59. Number of losses: Operational life.

The analysis of losses to the French *Groupes Lourds* is shown by the graph below. The number of losses is shown against the length of operational life shown in figures: 0 to 80 days, 80 to 160 days etc.

The maximum on the Gauss curve is reached at the 140 days point or thereabouts, which means that the average operational life of a Halifax was four months and a half, corresponding to about nineteen operations.

One can understand why during the eleven months that the *Groupes Lourds* flew operations from Elvington ninety-six Halifaxes were delivered to Elvington to maintain the establishment of thirty-two operational aircraft at any one time.

In the list that follows the following details are given in sequence:
- The date of the incident.
- The names of members of the crew. The name of the captain of the aircraft is underlined. The names of those who died are followed by a cross.
- The circumstances of the loss.

Note: The names of the crew are given in the following order: Pilot, Navigator, Bomb-Aimer, Wireless Operator, Flight Engineer, Mid-Upper Gunner, Rear Gunner. Also listed are the Squadron, the serial number of the aircraft;factory where it was built, the period during which it left the factory;the operational life of the aircraft in days. Thanks to Colonel Plagnard and André Hautot for their callaboration in the writing of this chapter.

*Fig 60. **The insignia of the Groupes Lourds** (Heavy Groups), which comprised the Groupes Guyenne and Tunisie. The motif on this insignia is reproduced on the monuments at Elvington and Grandcamp-Maisy.*

Section 2

1. Members of Aircrew who became casualties on operations:

Target: Mimoyecques

6 July 1944

347 Sqn.	*Sous-Lieutenant* VARLET	+
LK 728	*Lieutenant* CHAPRON	+
Fairey Aviation	*Lieutenant* VIEULES	+
26.11.43 - 10.1.44	*Adjudant* CHARAUDEAU	+
215	*Adjudant* CHARLIER	+
	Adjudant ECKHARDT	+
	Sergent GODARD	+

Returning from an attack on the bunker at Mimoyecques that housed V3 long-range cannon aimed at London the aircraft crashed for unknown reasons at Thorne, Yorkshire, about thirty kilometres from the airfield at Elvington. The crew died in the ensuing fire. All were buried at the cemetery at Harrogate on the 11th July 1944.

Target: Les Hauts-Buissons.

12/13 July 1944

347 Sqn.	*Lieutenant* PASQUIER	+
NA 551	*Capitaine* GAUBER	+
Fairey Aviation	*Sous-Lieutenant* PETIOT	+
9.6 - 18.7.44	*Adjudant-Chef* VOGEL	+
26	*Adjudant* CUSIN	+
	Sergent-Chef VERDIER	+
	Sergent SERRA	+

On return from the operation and while on the circuit in very poor visibility, *Capitaine* Gaubert's aircraft was in collision with that of *Com-*

mandant Roy. It crashed and all the crew died in the ensuing fire. All were buried in Harrogate Cemetery on the 19th July 1944. *Commandant* Roy's machine developed intense vibrations and became difficult to control. The order to abandon aircraft having been given, the navigator and the rear gunner baled out. When one of the airscrews had been feathered the vibrations diminished. The order to abandon aircraft was withdrawn and it landed without further incident.

Target: Fromental
8 August 1944

347 Sqn.	Adjudant MILLET	+
NA 529	*Lieutenant* BALAS	+
Fairey Aviation	*Adjudant-Chef* MEYER	+
18.4 - 2. 6. 1944	*Sergent* DESRUMEAUX	+
69	*Adjudant* SIRE	+
	Sergent ACEZAT	+
	Adjudant FLAMANT	+

Hit by flak crossing the French coast, the aircraft went down in flames after having attacked the target, a V 1 site. *Adjudant-Chef* Meyer was able to leave the machine by parachute, but was machine-gunned and killed by the Germans during his descent. The other members of the crew were trapped in the aircraft, which crashed to the ground. All seven are buried at the cemetery at St. Omer under the direction of *Monseigneur l'Abbé* Nègre, almoner of military graves.

Fig 61. *The crew of Lieutenant Balas. Shot down by flak on crossing the French coast, 9th. August, 1944 - Halifax B/AMK*

Sergent   Sergent   Adjudant
Desrumeaux   Acezat   Flamand
(Wireless Operator) (Mid-Upper Gunner)(Rear-Gunner)

Adjudant   Adjudant-chef   Lieutenant   Adjudant
Sire   Meyer   Balas   Millet
(Flight engineer) (Bomb-Aimer) (Navigator)   (Pilot)

On the occasion of the fiftieth anniversary of the Liberation of the North of France, the Municipality of Lumbres, a little village situated a few kilometres from the old city of Saint-Omer, cared enough to honour its sons and daughters lost through deportation. They included the members of the crew of Lieutenant Balas, whose Halifax crashed on the territory of the borough on August 8th., 1944.

Target: Venlo
3 September 1944

347 Sqn.	*Adjudant* ROUILLAY	+
NA616	*Capitaine* MILLET	
Fairey Aviation	*Lieutenant* ALLEGRE	+
21.07 -17.09.1944	Sergent-Chef SOUILLARD	+
28	*Sergent* MOREAU	+
	Sergent VAYSSADE	
	Sergent-Chef WITZMANN	+

The aircraft was hit by flak over the target and the pilot and engineer, *Adjudant* Rouillay and *Sergent* Moreau respectively, were still in the aircraft when it crashed on the Franco-German border.

Lieutenant Allègre, *Sergent-Chef* Witzmann and *Sergent-Chef* Souillard were murdered on the ground by the Germans. All were buried at the cemetery at Wakum, north-east of Venlo.

This incident was the first of several in which the pilot and engineer remained at the controls of an aircraft in distress while the other members of the crew baled out.

Target: Octeville
10 September 1944

346 Sqn (Guyenne)	*Lieutenant-Colonel* VENOT	
NA585	*Lieutenant* GUILLOCHEAU	+
Fairey Aviation	*Adjudant* KIPFERLE	+
09.06 - 18.07.1944	*Sergent* LHOMOND	+
53	*Sergent-Chef* COUPEAU	+
	Sergent-Chef FINALE	+
	Sergent-Chef BIAGGI	+

On returning from the operation *Lieutenant-Colonel* Venot, the commanding officer of the *Groupe Guyenne*, carried out a normal circuit and came in to land. The moment his wheels touched the runway there was an enormous explosion. One of the bombs carried under the starboard wing, but not released at the time of bombing, had fallen off. The aircraft caught fire at once.

Despite the rapid arrival of the emergency services all the crew were burned to death with the exception of *Lieutenant-Colonel* Venot who, although seriously burned, succeeded in extricating himself from the brazier.

The six who died were buried at Harrogate cemetery on 14 September 1944.

***Fig 62.** CommandantVenot*

Target: Gelsenkirchen
11 September 1944

347 Sqn	*Lieutenant* BERTHET	+
NI 606	*Lieutenant* PATURLE	+
Fairey Aviation	*Capitaine* HILAIRE	+
21.07 - 17.09.1944	*Sergent-Chef* JENGER	+
46	*Adjudant* MADAULE	+
	Sergent-Chef EYRAUD	+
	Adjudant OGER	

The aircraft was hit by flak over the target. It exploded and crashed in Sterkrade. *Adjudant* OGER, the rear gunner, was the sole survivor. The six dead were buried in the cemetery in the north of Düsseldorf.

Figs 63 & 64. The crash of Colonel Venot's Halifax.

In the course of an operation on the Normandy front a bomb in the starboard wing failed to drop. When the aircraft landed it fell off shortly after touch-down and exploded, blowing the Halifax to pieces. Although he was severely injured, Colonel Venot miraculously managed to get clear of the burning machine. After several months in hospital he returned to Elvington to take over command in the place of Colonel Bailly.

Fig 65. *Lieutenant-Colonel Venot (right) with Air Commodore 'Gus' Walker and his son in the garden of the Air Commodore's house near York. On the left is the driver assigned to Lieutenant-Colonel Venot after his accident.*

[photo. from Louis Bourgain]

Target: Gelsenkirchen
11 September 1944

347 Sqn	*Adjudant* LIDON	
NA 515	*Lieutenant* LAC	
Fairey Aviation	*Sous-Lieutenant* ROTTE	+
28.04 - 02.06.1944	Sergent MORIN	
118	*Adjudant* PUTHIER	
	Sergent BENET	
	Sergent-Chef NONNENMACHER	

The aircraft was hit by flak over the target. The aircraft was badly damaged and the bomb-aimer, *Sous-Lieutenant* ROTTE, was killed on the bombing run. The crew succeeded in bringing the aircraft back to England in difficult conditions, landing at Woodbridge.

Sous-Lieutenant Rotte was buried in the local cemetery in Cambridge on 16 September. The Reverend Father Meurisse, the chaplain, officiated.

Target: Scholven
6 October 1944

346 Sqn	*Lieutenant* HABLOT
NA555	*Lieutenant* de SAINT MARC
Fairey Aviation	*Lieutenant* WUILLEMIN
09.06 - 18.07.1944	*Adjudant-Chef* PHILIPPE
107	*Sergent-Chef* PONS
	Sergent MANICK
	Sergent-Chef YVARS

On the way back to England after having bombed the target Lieutenant Hablot's Halifax was attacked by a German fighter. All the crew succeeded in escaping by parachute.

Lieutenant Hablot, *Sergent-Chef* Yvars (the rear gunner) and *Sergent* Manick (mid-upper gunner) were unharmed. The navigator, *Lieutenant* de Saint Marc, was wounded in the foot. *Adjudant-Chef* Phillipe was wounded in the shoulder. *Sergent-Chef* Pons was wounded in the eye and received shell splinters in the chest.

Lieutenant Wuillemin baled out uninjured. In the course of his descent, however, his parachute was hit by a number of cannon shells. He hit the ground heavily and was severely injured, his pelvis being fractured and his bladder perforated. The complete crew was reunited after the war.

Fig 66. *Général Hablot*

Target: Essen
23/24 October 1944

346 Sqn	*Commandant* SIMON	+
MZ 742	*Lieutenant* PELISSIER	+
English Electric	*Lieutenant* ZEILLER	+
04.06 - 22.06.1944	*Sergent-Chef* VIELLE	+
133	*Adjudant-Chef* BRIGALAND	+
	Sergent-Chef ROIRON	+
	Sergent FERNANDEZ	+
	Sergent-Chef FOURNIER	+

The aircraft piloted by *Commandant* Simon, officer commanding the First Flight of *Groupe Guyenne*, failed to return from this operation. The crew was at first declared 'Missing', subsequently amended to 'Lost without Trace'.

As a result of research carried out on debriefing reports of other aircraft taking part in the operation it seems probable that *Commandant* Simon's Halifax was in collision with another Halifax from the main force over the North Sea.

Sergent-Chef Fournier was making a familiarisation operation as Second Pilot. It is believed that his own crew was subsequently disbanded.

Target: Cologne
28 October 1944

347 Sqn	*Lieutenant* DELEUZE	
NA 519	*Lieutenant* COURVALIN	
Fairey Aviation	*Aspirant* VEZOLLE	
28.04 - 02.06.1944	*Sergent* CHABOUT	
158	*Sergent-Chef* JUSTE	
	Sergent MEAU	
	Sergent BASTIAN	

As night was falling the aircraft's engines began to malfunction. The pilot, *Lieutenant* Deleuze, succeeded in ditching the Halifax in the sea.

In a very short time the crew were rescued by the British Air-Sea Rescue Service, which once more demonstrated its remarkable efficiency.

Target: Düsseldorf
2/3 November 1944

346 Sqn	*Adjudant* MABILLE	+
LW 443	*Lieutenant* CONDE	+
English Electric	*Sous-Lieutenant* PETIT	+
29.11 - 22.12.1943	*Sergent-Chef* MEYER	+
312	*Sergent* SAYTOUR	+
	Sergent DEBROISE	
	Sergent SOURY LAVERGNE	

The Halifax of *Lieutenant* Condé and his crew, who were on their first operation, was attacked by a German night fighter soon after bombing. *Sergent* Soury-Lavergne, the rear gunner, baled out and succeeded in evading capture in spectacular fashion. He reached the American lines to the right of the Siegfried Line, crossing a minefield on the way. He was back at Elvington a few days later, on the 13th November 1944. *Sergent* Debroise, the mid-upper gunner, also succeeded in baling out. The five other members of the crew were killed.

4/5 November 1944. Target :Bochum

Of all the nights lived through by the *Groupes Lourds* that of the 4th/5th November 1944, in the course of which five crews of the *Groupe Guyenne* out of the fifteen operating were shot down by German night fighters, was certainly the most tragic.

Fig 67. Sergeant Guy Soury Lavergne

Target: Bochum
4/5 November 1944

346 Sqn.	*Sergent* ROCA	+
NA 549	*Lieutenant* HYENNE	+
Fairey Aviation	*Adjudant-Chef* CHABROUD	+
09.06 - 18.07.1944	*Sergent-Chef* MAXERAT	+
139	*Sergent-Chef* LAHERRERE	+
	Sergent MARTIN	+
	Sergent REYNAL	+

The aircraft of *Lieutenant* Hyenne was shot down at Dashausen. The seven members of the crew were killed. They were buried on 11 November 1944 in the civilian cemetery at the race-course at Dortmund, in the Ruhr.

Target: Bochum
4/5 November 1944

346 Sqn.	Adjudant HANNEDOUCHE	
NR 181	*Lieutenant* VLES	+
Fairey Aviation	*Sous-Lieutenant* LAMBERT	+
15.10 - 04.11.1944	*Sergent-Chef* VLAMINCK	+
13	*Sergent-Chef* BEAUVOIT	+
	Sergent-Chef LIMACHER	+
	Sergent-Chef OLIVE	+

Soon after having passed over the target *Lieutenant* Vlès' aircraft was attacked by a German night fighter. Severely damaged, it caught fire immediately and began to lose height. The pilot, *Adjudant* Hannedouche, gave the order to abandon aircraft. *Lieutenant* Vlès, the navigator, opened the front escape hatch. He was about to jump when, in the smoke that filled the fuselage, he saw his radio operator, *Sergent-Chef* Vlaminck, pressed against the side of the aircraft and unable to move. He did not hesitate, but went to him and succeeded in freeing him and dragging him to the escape hatch. Despite great difficulty he pushed him out into space. A few seconds later the aircraft exploded. The pilot, *Adjudant* Hannedouche, was thrown from the machine and found himself falling, attached to the straps of his parachute. *Sergent-Chef* Olive, the rear gunner, managed to bale out before the explosion but was killed on the ground by the Germans. The five other members of the crew died. *Sergent-Chef* Olive is buried in the cemetery at Burg. *Lieutenant* Vlès, *Sous-Lieutenant* Lambert, *Sergent-Chef* Beauvoit and *Sergent-Chef* Limacher are buried in the cemetery at Wermelskirchen.

Target: Bochum

4/5 November 1944

346 Sqn.	*Capitaine* BARON	+
NA121	*Lieutenant* TRUCHE	
English Electric	*Adjudant* VIGNERON	+
27.09 - 31.10.1944	*Adjudant-Chef* MIGNOT	
19	*Sergent-Chef* CORMIER	+
	Sergent-Chef PETITJEAN	
	Sergent BOURELLY	+
	Lieutenant-Colonel DAGAN	+

On the night of 4th/5th November 1944 the Halifax of *Capitaine* Baron was attacked on its way home by a German night fighter. Three members of the crew baled out and were safe and sound. The other four died in the aircraft, which crashed fifteen miles north-east of Vandelindoven. *Lieutenant-Colonel* Dagan, from French Headquarters in London, was flying on the mission in order to form personal impressions of the difficulties that applied to such operations. He was flying as second pilot. He too was killed in the course of the engagement. The five who died were buried in the cemetery at Norf.

Target: Bochum

4/5 November 1944

346 Sqn.	Adjudant GUISE	+
NA 546	*Lieutenant* DABADIE	+
Rootes Securities	*Sous-Lieutenant* POTHUAU	+

09.06 - 18.07.1944	Sergent-Chef ALAVOINE	
142	*Sergent-Chef* LELONG	+
	Sergent VAUTARD	
	Sergent VEGA	+

Lieutenant Dabadie's Halifax was attacked from below. The port-inner engine caught fire immediately. *Lieutenant* Dabadie called up the pilot, *Adjudant* Guise, who did not reply. It is probable that he was killed by the fighter's cannon fire. *Lieutenant* Dabadie then gave the order to abandon aircraft. He attempted to open the front escape hatch, but it jammed. *Lieutenant* Dabadie and the bomb aimer, *Lieutenant* Pothuau, were trapped in the front end of the fuselage. The wireless operator, *Sergent-Chef* Alavoine, went towards the hatch. *Lieutenant* Dabadie signalled to him to bale out, which he did after having cast a long glance towards the rear of the fuselage and seen the flight engineer, *Sergent-Chef* Lelong, attempting to clip on his parachute in thick smoke. During this time the mid-upper gunner, *Sergent* Vautard, had opened the rear hatch and jumped out. The aircraft crashed at Hückelhoven, twenty kilometres north-east of Cologne. There were only two survivors. *Lieutenant* Dabadie and *Adjudant* Guise are buried in the cemetery at Hückelhoven. The other three bodies were never found.

Target: Bochum

4/5 November 1944

346 Sqn.	*Capitaine* BERAUD	+
NA 558	*Lieutenant* VALETTE	
Fairey Aviation	*Lieutenant* RAFFIN	+
09.06 - 18.07.1944	*Adjudant* CLOAREC	
131	*Sergent-Chef* IMART	
	Sergent-Chef BELLON	
	Adjudant MANFROY	

On the same night the Halifax of *Capitaine* Beraud was hit by a burst of fire from a night fighter. The seven members of the crew succeeded in baling out, but unfortunately two did not survive. *Lieutenant* Raffin fell on high-tension cables and was electrocuted. *Capitaine* Beraud, for his part, came down not far away, his parachute canopy torn. The two had sworn that whatever might happen they would stay together. They are united in death in the communal cemetery at Stommein.

Target: Sterkrade
21/22 November 1944

346 Sqn.	*Lieutenant* FAUGES	+
NA 557	*Capitaine* LOEW	+
Fairey Aviation	*Sergent* GODEFROY	+
09.06 - 18.07.1944	*Sergent* BOUTILLIER	+
151	*Adjudant* THIERY	+
	Adjudant FLECK	+
	Adjudant LAFONT	+

In darkness, heading for the synthetic fuel refinery at Sterkrade, the Halifax of *Capitaine* Loew was in collision with a British bomber over Belgian territory. The two aircraft crashed to the ground together near Thynes.

All the members of the two crews were killed and are buried in the American Military Cemetery at Fosses, twenty-five kilometres east of Charleroi.

Target: Osnabrück
6/7 December 1944

347 Sqn.	*Capitaine* PERSON	+
NR 153	*Lieutenant* JOLY	
English Electric	*Lieutenant* BLOT	
26.09 - 15.10.1944	*Sous-Lieutenant* ADNET	+
52	*Sous-Lieutenant* BOURDEROTTE	
	Sergent-Chef CHEVALIER	
	Sergent-Chef GERARD	

Capitaine Person's Halifax was attacked by an enemy fighter after having bombed the target. All the crew, with the exception of

Capitaine Person, baled out. *Capitaine* Person was found dead in the aircraft at Wachendorf. *Sous-Lieutenant* Adnet underwent surgery but did not survive. Both the legs of *Sergent-Chef* Gerard had to be amputated. *Capitaine* Person and *Sous-Lieutenant* Adnet are buried in the cemetery at Lingen-Ems.

Target: Duisburg

17/18 December 1944

346 Sqn.	Adjudant RAMES
NA 561	*Capitaine* PETIT
Fairey Aviation	*Adjudant-Chef* DEZELLIS
09.06 -18.07.1944	*Sergent-Chef* MIMAUD
164	*Adjudant* BAUER
	Sergent VIDAL
	Sergent LE GUILLOU +

In the course of this operation the Halifax commanded by *Capitaine* Petit was severely damaged by flak and lost 15,000 feet in height. The order was given to abandon aircraft. *Adjudant* Dézellis baled out and was taken prisoner. *Sergent* Guillou also baled out, but his body was never found. On board the aircraft *Sergent* Vidal was slightly wounded, *Sergent-Chef* Mimaud very severely.

While *Capitaine* Petit gave first aid to the injured, *Adjudant* Rames managed to regain control of the aircraft. The order to abandon aircraft was rescinded. The crew managed to fly the severely damaged aircraft back to England and to land it safely.

Target: Essen-Mülheim

24 December 1944

347 Sqn.	*Sergent-Chef* BAILLON	+
MZ 489	*Lieutenant* LEROY	+
London Aircr.P	*Sous-Lieutenant* GAUTHERET	+
25.09 - 20.11.1944	*Adjudant* GRANIER	+
46	*Sergent-Chef* DURAN	
	Sergent GUEDEZ	
	Sergent EVEN	+

On reaching the Ruhr Valley the Halifax of *Lieutenant* Leroy was hit by flak. Despite the damage the crew decided to press on with the attack. They bombed the target, the aerodrome at Essen-Mülheim.

A short time later the aircraft was again badly hit. The order was given to abandon aircraft. The pilot, *Sergent-Chef* Baillon, remained at the controls to keep the aircraft in level flight while the other six members of the crew baled out one after the other. Sadly only two survived. The other four were murdered after reaching the ground.

Sergent-Chef Baillon died when the aircraft crashed. He was one of the many pilots who sacrificed themselves so that their crews might survive. They all died as unknown heroes. The five dead were buried in the North Düsseldorf cemetery.

Target: Ludwigshafen

2/3 January 1945

Fig 68.

Jacques Leclerq- came from near Nice,
Henry Martin - lived in Algeria
Pat Martin - (Nee Pattimore) ex Channel Islands
Francis Usai - Bouches du Rhone. Photo YAM

347 Sqn.	*Sergent* LECLERCQ	+
MZ 984	*Lieutenant* COTTARD	
Rootes Securities Ltd	*Adjudant* ADAOUST	
29.08 -30.09.1944	*Sergent-Chef* MOREL	
94	*Sergent* DUFAURE	
	Sergent USAI	
	Sergent-Chef AUBIET	

Lieutenant Cottard's Halifax was hit by American flak at Courcelles, in the Metz region. The pilot, *Sergent* Leclercq, died imprisoned in the aircraft as it crashed to the ground. He was nineteen years of age. This was another example of the pilot sacrificing himself while the remainder of the crew escaped.

Target: Hanover

5/6 January 1945

347 Sqn.	*Lieutenant* DELEUZE	
LL 557	*Lieutenant* COURVALIN	
Rootes Securities Ltd	*Aspirant* VEZOLLE	+
13.05 - 08.07.1944	*Sergent* CHABOUD	
176	*Sergent-Chef* JUSTE	
	Sergent MEAU	+
	Sergent BASTIAN	

On the way back to England the Halifax of *Lieutenant* Courvalin was attacked by a night fighter. A fire broke out and the order to abandon aircraft was given. The bomb aimer, navigator and wireless operator left the aircraft via the front escape hatch. The mid-upper gunner, *Sergent* Bastian, and the flight engineer, *Sergent-Chef* Juste, helped *Sergent* Meau to bale out, and then they themselves jumped. *Lieutenant* Deleuze, after making sure that all his crew had gone, switched in the automatic pilot and baled out himself.

The whole crew were taken prisoner with the exception of *Aspirant* Vezolle, who was shot on the ground on the pretext that he was attempting to escape, and *Sergent* Meau, killed by a civilian guard after having

Fig 69. Sergent-Chef Raymond Juste, flight engineer of the crew of Lieutenant Courvalin.

reached the ground. *Lieutenant* Deleuze and *Sergent* Bastian both succeeded in escaping in spectacular fashion.

Aspirant Vezolle was buried on the 10th of January 1945 in the Parish Cemetery of Ibbenbüren, twenty kilometres west of Osnabrück, and *Sergent* Meau was interred on 8 January 1945 in the Catholic Cemetery at Saerbeck, thirty kilometres south-west of Osnabrück.

Target: Saarbrücken
13/14 January 1945

347 Sqn.	*Adjudant* JOUZIER	+
LL 590	Lieutenant BRACHET	+
Rootes Securities Ltd	*Lieutenant* HABEZ	
08.07 - 29.08.1944	*Sergent* RIGADE	
151	*Adjudant* HUMBERT	
	Sergent MEMIN	
	Sergent-Chef MALTERRE	+

On the way back home *Lieutenant* Brachet's Halifax was in collision with a British four-engined bomber in the vicinity of Gisors. *Sergent-Chef* Malterre was killed immediately. *Adjudant* Jouzier, who had replaced *Lieutenant* Georgeon for reasons of health, and *Lieutenant* Brachet went down with the aircraft. The other members of the crew baled out safely. *Lieutenant* Brachet could have baled out, but he chose to help the pilot while the flight engineer escaped.

Fig 70. The crew of Capitaine Brachet.

From left to right : Sergent Rigade (wireless operator); Adjudant Humbert (flight engineer); Lieutenant Habez (bomb-aimer); Sergent-chef Malterre (rear gunner); Capitaine Brachet (navigator); Sergent Memin (mid-upper gunner); Adjudant Jouzier (pilot).

Fig 71. The Halifax III - MZ 465 - involved in the collision with Lieutenant Brachet's Halifax.

Fig 72. Flying Officer Wilson and some of his crew with the aircraft. Left to right: flight engineer, mid-upper gunner, pilot (Flying Officer Wilson), rear gunner, radio operator.

Target: Magdeburg
16/17 January 1945

347 Sqn.	*Capitaine* BRESSON	+
MZ 986	*Capitaine* DE SAUVEBEUF	
Rootes Securities Ltd	*Lieutenant* RONAT	
29.08 - 30.09.1944	*Adjudant* RABIER	
108	*Sergent* KANNENGIESSER	
	Sergent-Chef POILBOUT	+
	Sergent MARTIN	

Capitaine Bresson's Halifax was hit by flak when crossing the coast at Wesermünde and a large hole was seen by the flight engineer just in front of the aileron on the starboard side. The Halifax bombed the target and then turned west on to 270 degrees. *Capitaine* de Saufbeuf, the navigator, was just reporting that they would pass Hanover in three minutes when suddenly a shell exploded near them and there was a very loud noise. The pilot corkscrewed but a night fighter shot them down. *Capitaine* Bresson and *Sergent-Chef* Poilbout were unable to leave the aircraft and were in it when it crashed. The other five members of the crew survived. *Sergent* Kannengiesser was taken prisoner but managed to escape in brilliant fashion.

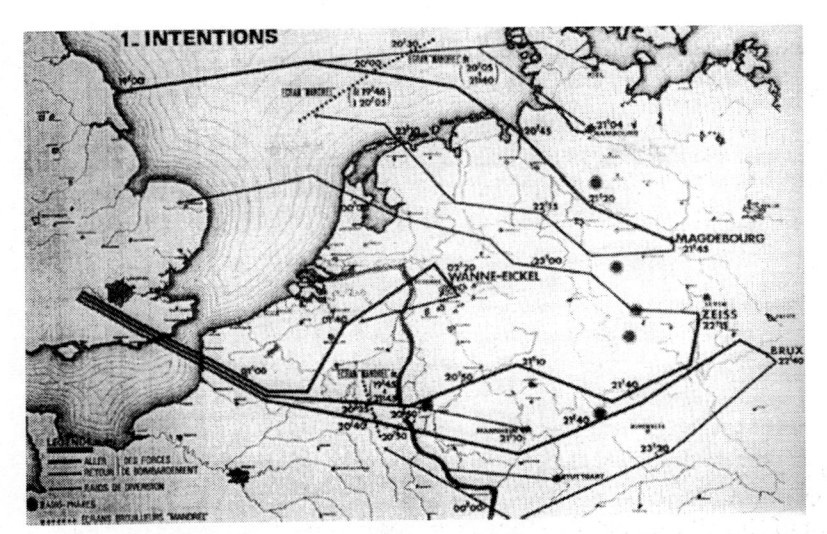

Fig 73. On the one map are shown the routes and timings of the various operations planned by Headquarters Bomber Command to support the main attack of the night.

Target: Magdeburg
16/17 January 1945

347 Sqn.	*Capitaine* MARIN	+
NA 572	*Lieutenant* FRANGOLACCI	
Fairey Aviation	*Lieutenant* MINVIELLE	
09.06 - 18.07.1944	Adjudant-Chef VUILLEMOT	+
188	*Adjudant* VILLENEUVE	+
	Sergent-Chef DARGENTON	+
	Sergent-Chef MEUNIER	

Fig 74. The crew of Capitaine Marin. From left to right : (standing): Sergent chef Pierre Dargenton, Sergeant-chef Robert Meunier, Adjudant Andre Villeneuve; (seated): Adjudant-chef Gabriel Vuillemot, Capitaine Xavier Marin, Lieutenant Roger Frangolacci, Lieutenant Jean Minvielle.

Capitaine Marin was a native of Tournan-en-Brie, and on the occasion of the fiftieth anniversary of Victory, the municipality wished to pay homage to its son and his crew by erecting a monument in the very heart of the community.

In reproducing the photographs of Capitaine Marin and Lieutenant Balas (shot down on 8th. August, 1944), I wished to associate myself with the efforts of the municipalities of Tournan-en-Brie and Lumbres, and in this way to thank them for what they have done in memory.

While on the bombing run *Capitaine* Marin's Halifax was seriously damaged by flak and he himself was killed in the pilot's seat. *Adjudant-Chef* Vuillemot baled out, but his body was never recovered. *Adjudant* Villeneuve and *Sergent-Chef* Dargenton were unable to leave the aircraft.

The other three members of the crew baled out safely. The machine crashed between Wülfingen and Poppenburg, fourteen kilometres west of Hildesheim.

Target: Gelsenkirchen
22/23 January 1945

347 Sqn.	*Lieutenant* PETUS	+
LL587	*Lieutenant* DESESSARD	
Rootes Securities Ltd	*Lieutenant* MIGNON	
08.07 - 29.08.1944	*Adjudant* COQUERON	
178	*Sergent* TRIBERT	+
	Sergent-Chef LINDEBERT	
	Adjudant RIVIERE	

On return from the operation *Lieutenant* Pétus' aircraft crashed in countryside near Grafton Underwood, south-west of Peterborough. *Lieutenant* Pétus and *Sergent* Tribert were killed.

Adjudant Coqueron, whose parachute failed to open, landed in a pile of snow, which broke his fall. Although his vertebrae were seriously damaged he succeeded, after months of rehabilitation, in living an almost normal life.

The remaining members of the crew did not suffer injury. The two who died were buried on the 26th of January 1945 in the cemetery at Harrogate.

Target: Goch
7/8 February 1945

347 Sqn.	Adjudant-Chef AULEN	+
NA 197	*Capitaine* STANISLAS	
Rootes Securities Ltd	*Sous-Lieutenant* ROGNANT	+
31.10 - 2.12.1944	*Sergent-Chef* BERDEAUX	+
10	*Sergent-Chef* PATRY	+
	Sergent BORDIER	+
	Sergent BORDELAIS	+

The Halifax of *Capitaine* Stanislas was hit by a burst of fire from a night fighter and exploded. Without having taken any conscious action *Capitaine* Stanislas found himself in mid-air hanging from the straps of his parachute. He was the only survivor.

The aircraft crashed in the village of Asten, twenty-five kilometres south-west of Eindhoven. *Adjudant-Chef* Aulen, *Sergent-Chef* Berdeaux and *Sergent* Bordelais were buried in the Woensel cemetery at Eindhoven.

Sous-Lieutenant Rognant, *Sergent-Chef* Patry and *Sergent* Bordier were buried in the French Military Cemetery at Kabelle (Holland).

Target: Goch

7/8 February 1945

347 Sqn.	*Sergent-Chef* BAGOT	+
NA 260	*Lieutenant* PELLIOT	+
Rootes Securities Ltd	*Lieutenant* ROLLET	
02.12.1944 - 30.01.1945	*Sergent-Chef* BRILLARD	
67	*Adjudant* MOLL	
	Sergent LE MITHOUARD	+
	Adjudant LOISELOT	

In the course of the operation *Lieutenant* Pelliot's Halifax was shot down by a night fighter before reaching the target. *Sergent-Chef* Bagot, *Lieutenant* Pelliot and *Sergent* Le Mithouard were killed. For this operation *Adjudant* Loiselot was flying in the place of *Sergent-Chef* Besnard for reasons of health.

Lieutenant Pelliot was buried at Woensel cemetery, Eindhoven.

The aircraft was still carrying bombs when it hit the ground, and it exploded. *Sergent-Chef* Bagot and *Sergent* Le Mithouard, who were still in the aircraft, were blown to pieces.

21/22 February 1945   Target:Worms

Preliminary note: German night fighters were particularly active in the target area on this night. Two aircraft from the *Groupe Guyenne* were shot down.

Target: Worms

346 Sqn.	Adjudant SOUCILLE	+
NA 547	*Commandant* BREARD	+
Fairey Aviation	*Sous-Lieutenant* FAUVET	+
09.06 - 18.07.1944	*Sergent-Chef* LEMAIRE	+
69	*Adjudant* AQUAVIVA	+
	Sergent-Chef CHIERICCI	+
	Sergent ZAVATERRO	+

The Halifax of *Commandant* Bréard, whose crew were on their thirty-first operation, was shot down nine kilometres from Worms.

All the members of the crew were killed and were buried in the cemetery of Klein-Bockenheim.

Target: Worms

21/22 February 1945

346 Sqn.	Sous-Lieutenant BAYLE	+
PN 179	*Lieutenant* JOUMAS	+
Fairey Aviation	*Sergent-Chef* Dugnat	+
16.10.44 - 17.02.45	*Sergent* BOURREAU	+
249	*Sergent* BARDE	+
	Sergent MARTROU	+
	Sergent ESQUILLAT	+

The Halifax of *Lieutenant* Joumas, whose crew were on their ninth operation, was shot down thirty kilometres south-west of Bad Kreuznach. All members of the crew were killed and were buried in the cemetery of Löllbach.

'Night of the Intruders', 3rd / 4th March 1945:

This night, called the 'Night of the Intruders' by the British and *Einsatz Gisela* by the Germans, was marked by the loss of three aircraft from the French *Groupes Lourds*. The intruders were German night fighters (Ju 88) which accompanied the British bombers on their way back to the British bases and attacked them at the moment when they were most vulnerable, that is when they were on the approach or as they were landing. They were fitted with heavy machine-guns firing along the axis of the aircraft and with vertically-firing cannon. They

Fig 75. The Ju 88, the most formidable of the German night fighters (but not this one . . .).

The aircraft in the photograph is equipped with two cannon firing almost vertically above (angle of incidence 80 degrees).

The Ju 88 would manoeuvre below the Halifax, which was 'blind' in that area. It could then draw near to the bomber with impunity and open fire a salvo of cannon shells at very close range. The blow it struck was fatal.

usually attacked from below, where the Halifax, which did not have a lower turret, was blind. In this way they could attack a bomber at very close range. Twenty aircraft were shot down this night, among them the three listed next:

Target: Kamen

3/4 March 1945

346 Sqn.	*Capitaine* NOTELLE
NR 229	*Lieutenant* MARTIN
English Electric	*Lieutenant* FLOUS
04.11 - 18.11.1944	*Sergent* SANTONI
117	*Sous-Lieutenant* BOUSSY
	Sergent NERI
	Sergent MALLIA

Fig 76. The débris of Capitaine Notelle's Halifax. During the night of 3rd / 4th March 1944, often referred to as the 'Night of the Intruders', German Junkers 88 night fighters crossed the North Sea to attack British bombers as they were landing. Three French Halifaxes were lost, among them that of Capitaine Notelle.

Looking at this photograph one cannot help but be surprised that the whole crew escaped almost unharmed.

On the way back from the target *Capitaine* Notelle's aircraft was attacked at low altitude and he decided to make a crash landing in open countryside. The seven members of the crew got out from the scattered wreckage of the aircraft. Miraculously five were unhurt, but the pilot was badly injured, as was the rear gunner, *Sergent* Mallia.

Fig 77. *The crew of Capitaine Notelle. From L to R.*

Capitaine Notelle(pilot), Sergent Santoni(radio),Sergent Neri(mid-upper gunner), Lieutenant Flous(bomb aimer), Lieutenant Martin(navigator), Sergent Mallia(rear gunner), Lieutenant Boissy(flight engineer) is not in the photograph:he probably took it. Note the different equipment each crew member was wearing.

Target: Kamen
3/4 March 1945

347 Sqn. *Sous-Lieutenant* TERRIEN   +
NR 235   *Sous-Lieutenant* MOSNIER
Fairey Aviation *Sous-Lieutenant* MICHELON
04.11 - 18.11.1944 *Sergent* DUGARDIN
115   *Adjudant* PUTHIER
          Sergent DELAROCHE
          Sergent DUNAN

Fig 78. Sergent Dugardin, wireless operator of Sous-Lieutenant Terrien's crew.

The aircraft was badly hit and caught fire immediately. *Sous-Lieutenant* Terrien gave the order to abandon aircraft, but he himself remained at the controls. He died, but he saved his six comrades.

Sous-Lieutenant Terrien was interred at the Harrogate cemetery on the 9th of March 1945.

Target: Kamen
3 /4 March 1945

347 Sqn.	*Lieutenant* LAUCOU	+
NA 680	*Aspirant* VIEL	
Fairey Aviation	*Sous-Lieutenant* GIROUD	
17.09 - 18.11.1944	*Sergent* POCHON	
136	*Sergent* LE MASSON	+
	Sergent HEMERY	
	Sergent CHARRIERE	

Fig 79. Capitaine Laucou. This was his first mission.

The same scenario applied to *Lieutenant* Laucou. While five members of his crew managed to bale out he and his flight engineer were trapped in the aircraft when it hit the ground. *Lieutenant* Laucou and *Sergent* Le Masson were buried at the Cambridge cemetery on 10 March 1945.

Target: Chemnitz.

5/6 March 1945

346 qn.	*Sous-Lieutenant* FONTIEX	+
MZ 738	*Lieutenant* ROUVEL	+
English Electric	*Sergent-Chef* SCHILLING	+
04.06 - 22.06.1944	*Sergent* HOUDELOT	+
239	*Sergent* LEROY	+
	Sergent GORRIAS	+
	Sergent FARNIER	+

Sous-Lieutenant Fontiex's crew were first reported missing, then 'lost without trace'. After the war Chemnitz was in the Russian Zone, and no information about the crew was received. Now that the Iron Curtain no longer exists, however, it is perhaps not too late for research to be carried out with the local authorities.

Target: Homberg (Palatinate)

14/15 March 1945

347 Sqn.	*Adjudant-Chef* VIDAL	
NA 512	*Lieutenant* GUENOIS	
Fairey Aviation	*Sous-Lieutenant* PICOT	
28.04 - 02.06.1944	*Sergent* CHANSON	
300	*Adjudant* PORTESSEAU	+
	Adjudant BRUNO	
	Sergent PIZEL	

On the way back home the aircraft, which had been badly hit by flak, force-landed in Belgium and caught fire. *Adjudant* Portesseau was flying in the place of *Adjudant-Chef* Gauthier, who had died of illness in England, and he was killed in the crash. He was buried at Neuville-en-Condraz, Belgium. *Adjudant-Chef* Vidal was seriously injured, but managed to land the aircraft at an American-occupied airfield a few kilometres from Brussels.

Target: Homberg (Palatinate)
14/15 March 1945

347 Sqn.	*Capitaine* BRUNET	+
MZ 909	*Sous-Lieutenant* FAUCHET	+
English Electric	*Aspirant* TROLARD	+
02.08 - 29.08.1944	*Sergent* MILLER	+
217	Sergent LUGARO	+
	Sergent DE LAUZUN	+
	Sergent GIRAUDON	+

On the return journey from the target the aircraft of *Capitaine* Brunet was shot down by a night fighter. All the members of the crew were killed. *Sergent* Lugaro survived, but he was murdered by the SS. (An autopsy was carried out by an American doctor, Max Berg). He was

Fig 80. *Presentation of the D.F.C. to Sous-Lieutenant Picot by Air Commodore Walker; Adjudant Vidal will receive the D.F.M. a few minutes later. photo. fom YAM Archives]*

buried in the American Cemetery at Grand Failly, eight-and-a-half kilometres north-west of Longuyon.

Target: Hagen (Ruhr)

15/16 March 1945

346 Sqn.	*Commandant* OSTRE	+
NA 681	*Capitaine* CHEVALIER	+
Fairey Aviation	*Lieutenant* CHEMIN	+
17.09 - 18.11.1944	*Adjudant* CHABRES	+
146	*Sergent-Chef* ESCIOLETTE	
	Sergent RAMOND	+
	Sergent-Chef TILLIERS	

On returning from the operation the aircraft crashed into hills to the north-east of Elvington. *Commandant* Ostre, *Capitaine* Chevalier, *Lieutenant* Chemin, *Adjudant* Chabres and *Sergent* Ramond died in the crash. The flight engineer, *Sergent-Chef* Esciolette, who had gone to the rear of the machine to check that there were no bombs still on board, and the rear gunner, *Sergent-Chef* Tilliers, escaped death. It is pointed out that that night the crew of *Commandant* Ostre were carrying out the final operation of their tour.

The five dead were buried in the cemetery at Harrogate on the 21st March 1945, the Chaplain, the Reverend Father Meurisse, officiating.

Target: Hagen (Ruhr)

15/16 March 1945

346 Sqn.	*Sergent* LOURDEAUX	+
NA 166	*Lieutenant* PONCET	
Rootes Securities Ltd	*Lieutenant* LAMONTAGNE	+
31.10 - 02.12.1944	*Sergent* BERNASCONI	
130	*Sergent* HAUTCOEUR	+
	Sergent DESPLACES	
	Sergent BRULET	+

The Halifax was shot down at Hasselt, Belgium, by a night fighter. The order to abandon aircraft was given. The pilot, *Sergent* Lourdeaux, feathered the airscrew on the starboard-outer engine, which was on fire, and activated the extinguisher. There was no result. Meanwhile the bomb-aimer, *Lieutenant* Lamontagne, baled out but his parachute did not open. *Sergent* Bernasconi jumped in his turn. At this point the aircraft banked hard to starboard, making it impossible to move within the fuselage. A few seconds later the aircraft exploded and disintegrated. The rear gunner, *Sergent* Desplaces, found himself suspended from his parachute. The navigator, *Lieutenant* Poncet, recovered consciousness stretched out on the ground. It was dark and he was surrounded by figures clad in dark clothes holding candles. Was this heaven or was it purgatory he wondered. In fact he was in the garden of a Belgian monastery.

The bodies of the other three members of the crew were found among the scattered debris of the aircraft, which covered an area of about a hectare. The four dead were buried in the cemetery at Hasselt on the 17th of March 1945.

Target: Hagen (Ruhr)

15/16 March 1945

346 Sqn	Sergent-Chef LACAZE	+
NR 287	*Lieutenant* DEPLUS	+
English Electric	*Aspirant* DU FRENOY	+
23.11 - 05.12.1944	*Sergent* CHARPENTIER	+
103	*Aspirant* GRIBOUVA	+
	Sergent TARTARIN	+
	Sergent TOUZART	+

When the aircraft returned from the operation there was very low cloud at Elvington. Ten aircraft landed normally. The eleventh, that of *Lieutenant* Deplus, reported by radio that the tail wheel could not be lowered. It was instructed to land at Carnaby, an airfield specially intended to cater for aircraft in distress. On the way to Carnaby the aircraft struck a hill at Scorton, five miles west of Helmsley, Yorkshire, for unknown reasons. There were no survivors. All the crew were buried at Harrogate on the 21st of March 1945. The Reverend Father Meurisse officiated.

Target: Witten
18/19 March 1945

346 Sqn.	*Lieutenant* GONTHIER	+
MZ 741	*Sous-Lieutenant* CAPDEVILLE	+
English Electric	*Sergent-Chef* DUSSAULT	+
04.06 - 23.06.1944	*Sergent-Chef* REYNAUD	
280	*Sergent-Chef* PATRIS	+
	Sergent HELLMUTCH	+
	Sergent SAINTSEVIN	+

On the way to the target the Halifax of *Lieutenant* Gonthier developed engine trouble. Regulations would have allowed him to turn back. As he had already been victim of trouble of this nature on a number of occasions, *Lieutenant* Gonthier decided that this time he would carry on with the operation. He dropped his bombs on the target.

Shortly after bombing, the aircraft was attacked by a night fighter, whose first burst of fire severely wounded the pilot, *Lieutenant* Gonthier, and set fire to a petrol tank in the port wing. *Sergent-Chef* Reynaud went to the controls to help his pilot to keep the aircraft flying straight, when a second burst of fire set the starboard wing on fire. The aircraft went into a spin and crashed at Nöllenberg.

The wireless operator was miraculously ejected from the machine and saved by his parachute, even although he had been severely wounded in the face by the second burst of fire. The aircraft came down close to him and, despite his injuries, he carefully pulled the bodies of his dead comrades from the remains of the Halifax and then set fire to the fuselage after destroying such secret instruments and documents as were still intact.

Sergent-Chef Reynaud was arrested soon afterwards but, although covered by a revolver, he shook off his captor by jumping into a deep ditch. He was rearrested soon afterwards and handed over to the Gestapo, where his refusal to talk earned him a fractured jaw. He was put into chains and handed over to the military authorities. He escaped again and spent eight days hidden in a forest, receiving food from a French worker.

The pain of his wounds, which had not received attention, his weakness due to his privations, and fatigue were his downfall, and he was captured a third time and sent to a prisoner-of-war camp. When he had got his strength back and a chance presented itself, he escaped once again, living hidden in a forest for three days, again being fed by a French worker, before finally being liberated in the victorious advance of the British Second Army.

The six dead are buried in the Catholic Cemetery at Beyenburg.

Target: Wangerooge

25 April 1945.

347 Sqn.	Sergent-Chef MERCIER	+
NP 921	*Capitaine* HAUTECOEUR	+
Handley Page Ld	Capitaine JACQUOT	+
11.12 - 21.12.1944	*Sergent-Chef* BARITEAU	+
131	*Sergent* MENNETRET	+
	Sergent FERRERO	+
	Sergent LEDUC	+

Soon after having bombed the target the Halifax of *Capitaine* Hautecoeur received a direct hit by a flak shell and was cut in two. The tail crashed to the ground and the front half crashed into the sea.

Capitaine Hautecoeur was the commander of the second flight of the *Groupe Tunisie*. He died in the course of the final operation flown by the French *Groupes Lourds*. He was a former pupil of the *École Polytechnique* and a man of impeccable reputation, and his loss was deeply felt by his parents, who could never come to terms with it. He was their only child.

Capitaine Hautecoeur, *Sergent-Chef* Bariteau, *Sergent* Ferrero and *Sergent* Leduc are buried on the beach on Wangerooge. The bodies of the three other members of the crew were never found and are presumed lost at sea.

2. Ground Personnel killed while preparing for an operation:

28 December 1944

Sq 347
NA 174 L8 Q
Rootes Securities Ltd
31.10 - 02.12.1944

Caporal STALENQ	+
Deuxième Classe ANTONIO	+
Deuxième Classe MAUPETIT	+
Deuxième Classe ANDREV	+
Deuxième Classe CONSENTINO	+
Deuxième Classe GIMENEZ	+
Deuxième Classe GOMEZ	+
Deuxième Classe JEANNELLE	+

At about 1430 hours on the 28th December 1944, while preparations were being made for an attack on Mönchengladbach, Halifax NA 174

Fig 81. Loading bombs in winter.

Climatic conditions in the winter of 1944-45 were often very rigorous. Nevertheless they never hindered operations on the ground or in the air.

was being loaded with bombs. Suddenly there was a massive explosion: a bomb had gone off, killing eight and injuring five.

The obsequies were observed at Harrogate Cemetery with the Reverend Father Meurisse, the Chaplain, officiating.

The accident also killed six British personnel.

3. Aircrew killed in training accidents in Great Britain:

Lossiemouth, 21 March 1944

20 O.T.U.	*Sergent-Chef*	CARDONA	+
Wellington III	*Lieutenant*	VANDENABELLE	+
X 3545	*Lieutenant*	LECOMTE	+
	Sergent-Chef	BILLOT	+
	Sergent-Chef	AMBULH	+
	Sergent	BRUNO	+

The aircraft, Wellington X 3545, had taken off from Leuchars at 2031 hours to return to Milltown.

Fig 82. *A Wellington bomber.*

The final message received by the wireless station at Wick was, 'Returning to base.' After that nothing more was heard. The reasons for the disappearance of the machine are unknown. An enquiry was mounted by the RAF but came to no conclusion.

A Catholic service was held in the Chapel in Milltown on 28 March 1944.

Fig 83. Lossiemouth - French staff 1945

Lossiemouth, 28 October 1944

20 O.T.U.   *Sergent-Chef*   COMTE   +

Wellington

XLP 672

While carrying out an inspection of the aircraft the pilot, *Sergent-Chef* Comte, was struck by one of the airscrews and killed. *Sergent-Chef* Comte was buried in a small graveyard near to the airfield at Lossiemouth.

Lossiemouth, 18 December 1944

20 O.T.U.   *Sergent*   FOURCADE   +

Wellington

XLP 546

During a cross-country flight, in very poor weather with cloud and icing, there was a misunderstanding on the intercom and *Sergent* Fourcade apparently thought that the order to abandon aircraft had been given. He baled out. The aircraft completed the exercise and returned to base. The body was never found.

Rufforth, 19/20 May 1944

1663 H.C.U.	*Sous-Lieutenant* CHOURNIOZ	+
Halifax DG 231	Lieutenant BECAM	
	Adjudant-Chef VIGNOLLES	+
	Adjudant WEBER	
	Adjudant-Chef MARCHI	+
	Sergent LEMOUSER	+
	Sergent-Chef RETORÉ	

During a cross-country at a height of 20,000 feet the port-outer engine of the Halifax caught fire. The order was given to abandon aircraft. The rear gunner, *Sergent-Chef* Retoré, baled out from his turret, while the wireless operator, *Adjudant* Weber, and the navigator, *Lieutenant* Becam, left by the forward escape hatch. The pilot, *Sous-Lieutenant* Chournioz, remained at the controls, where he was later found burnt to death. The flight engineer, *Adjudant-Chef* Marchi, the bomb-aimer, *Adjudant-Chef* Vignolles, and the mid-upper gunner, *Sergent* Lemouser, attempted to escape by the mid-fuselage hatch. Only *Adjudant-Chef* Marchi managed to get out of the aircraft, but his parachute caught on the aerial and did not deploy. His body was found one hundred metres from the aircraft. *Adjudant-Chef* Vignolles and *Sergent* Lemouser were found burned to death in the fuselage. The aircraft crashed at Haverfordwest in Pembrokeshire, Wales. The four dead were buried in the Allied Cemetery in Haverfordwest on the 23rd May 1944, the Reverend Father Meurisse, the Chaplain, officiating.

Rufforth, 8 November 1944

1663 H.C.U.	*Sergent* MAUROUX	+
Halifax DK 149	*Lieutenant* VIAL	+
	Adjudant TOIRON	+
	Sergent DIDIER-LAURENT	+
	Sergent CROLAS	+
	Sergent DELPECH	+
	Sergent TOURNON	+
	Sergent NOYEZ	+
	Sergent PINELLI	+

The aircraft was engaged in a fighter-affiliation exercise. Two mechanics, *Sergent Noyez* and *Sergent* Pinelli, were flying as passengers. A collision took place at 1524 hours. The aircraft came down six miles east of Pocklington, Yorkshire. It caught fire immediately and the nine men on board were killed.

Sergent Mauroux, a Protestant, was buried on Tuesday the 14th November 1944 at the RAF Cemetery at Brookwood, Surrey.

The other eight victims were buried on the 14th November in the Harrogate Cemetery. The Reverend Father Meurisse, the Chaplain, officiated.

Rufforth, 24 February 1945

1663 H.C.U.	*Sous-Lieutenant* GRIMAUD	+
Halifax PN 366	*Lieutenant* DEDIEU	+
	Aspirant ROQUE	+
	Sergent ROUGIER	+
	Sergent-Chef ARRACHE-QUESNE	+
	Sergent LAURENT	+
	Sergent-Chef BLASSIEAUX	+

The Halifax took off from Rufforth on a cross-country exercise on 24 February 1945. It crashed for unknown reasons at Cottesmore at 2200 hrs.

The seven members of the crew were killed.

They were buried on 2 March 1945 at the Cambridge Borough Cemetery, Newmarket Road. *Monseigneur l'Abbé* Masson officiated.

4.Crew members killed or injured on leaving Elvington for France.

Elvington, 29 October 1945

Sq. 347	*Sergent-Chef* ROQUE	
RG 561	*Sous-Lieutenant* WELLARD	+
	Sergent PRADES	+
	Sergent BAUD	
	Sergent GALEA	
	Sergent BOURGUND	
	Sergent BOISSAVIE	
	plus five passengers.	

Towards noon on 29 October 1945 No. 347 Squadron began its transfer from Elvington to Bordeaux-Mérignac in France. Halifax RG561 was the last but one to take off at 1156 hours. Only a short time afterwards, in very bad weather conditions, the aircraft was unable to maintain altitude and made a forced landing in a field at Escrick, fifteen miles from Elvington. German and Italian prisoners of war working in the field rushed up to rescue the crew from the fuselage. There were two killed and six injured: the injured were treated in the York Military Hospital.

The two dead, *Sous-Lieutenant* Wellard and *Sergent* Prades, were buried in Harrogate Cemetery on 2 November 1945 in the presence of an RAF Chaplain and the Reverend Canon Bentley of the Church of Saint Robert, Harrogate.

Alphabetical list of crews killed

Sergent	ACEZAT	
Sous-Lieutenant	ADNET	
Lieutenant	ALLEGRE	
Adjudant	AQUAVIVA	Jean
Adjudant-chef	AULEN	
Sergent-chef	BAGOT	
Sergent-chef	BAILLON	
Lieutenant	BALAS	
Sergent	BARDES	Etienne
Sergent-chef	BARITEAC	
Capitaine	BARON	Robert
Sous-Lieutenant	BAYLE	Pierre
Sergent-chef	BEAUVOIT	Norbert
Capitaine	BERAUD	Alphonse
Sergent-chef	BERDEAUX	
Lieutenant	BERTHET	
Sergent-chef	BIAGGI	Domminique
Sergent	BORDELAIS	
Sergent	BORDIER	
Sergent	BOURREAU	Guy
Sergent	BOURRELY	Louis
Sergent	BOUTILLIER	André
Capitaine	BRACHET	
Commandant	BREARD	Raoul
Capitaine	BRESSON	
Adjudant-chef	BRIGALAND	Roger
Sergent	BRULET	Georges
Capitaine	BRUNET	
Sons-lieutenant	CAPDEVILLE	Pierre
Adjudant	CHABRES	
Adjudant	CHABROUD	Jean
Lieutenant	CHAPRON	
Adjudant	CHAREAUDEAU	
Adjudant	CHARLIER	
Sergent	CHARPENTIER	James
Lieutenant	CHEMIN	
Capitaine	CHEVALIER	
Sergent-chef	CHIERICCI	Paul
Lieutenant	CONDE	Henri
Sergent-chef	CORMIER	Charles
Sergent-chef	COUPEAC	Marcel
Adjudant	CUSIN	André
Lieutenant	DABABIE	Maurice
Sergent-chef	DARGENTON	
Sergent	DELAUZUN	
Lieutenant	DEPLUS	Jacques
Sergent	DESRUMEAUX	
Aspirant	DUFRESNOY	François
Sergent-chef	DUGNAT	Georges
Sergent-chef	DUSSAUT	Alfred
Adjudant	EDCKART	
Sergent	ESQUILAT	André
Sergent	EVEN	
Sergent-chef	EYRARD	
Sergent	FARNIER	Rolland
Sous-lieutenant	FAUCHET	
Sergent-chef	FAUGES	André
Sons-lieutenant	FAUVET	Jacques
Sergent	FERNANDEZ	Gabriel
Sergent	FERRERO	
Sergent-chef	FINALE	Wilson
Adjudant	FLAMAND	

Adjudant	FLECK	André		Sergent	LECLERCQ	
Sons-lieutenant	FONTEIX	Abel		Sergent	LEDUC	
Sergent-chef	FOURNIER	Pierre		Sergent-chef	LELONG	Henri
Capitaine	GAUBERT	Jean		Sergent-chef	LEMAIRE	Jean
Sous-lieutenant	GAUTHERET			Sergent	LEMASSON	
Sergent	GIRAUDON			Sergent	LEMITHOUARD	
Sergent	GODARD			Lieutenant	LEROY	
Sergent	GODEFROY	Jean		Sergent	LEROY	Jean
Lieutenant	GONTHIER	André		Sergent	LHOMOND	Gabriel
Sergent	GORIAS	Jean		Sons-lieutenant	LIMACHER	Roger
Adjudant	GRANIER			Capitaine	LOEN	Claude
Adjudant	GRIBOUVA	Jean		Sergent	LOURDEAUX	Louis
Lieutenant	GUILLOCHEAU	Robert		Sergent	LUGARO	
Adjudant	GUISE	Raymond		Adjudant	MABILLE	Lucien
Sergent	HAUTCŒUR	François		Adjudant	MADAULE	
				Sergent-chef	MALTERRE	
Capitaine	HAUTECŒUR			Capitaine	MARIN	
Sergent	HELLMUTH	Roger		Sergent	MARTIN	Henri
Capitaine	HILAIRE			Sergent	MARTROU	Louis
Sergent	HOUDELOT	Bernard		Sergent-chef	MAXERAT	Louis
Lieutenant	HYENNE	Auguste		Sergent	MEAU	
Capitaine	JACQUOT			Sergent	MENNETRE	
Sergent-chef	JENGER			Sous-lieutenant	MERCIER	
Lieutenant	JOUMAS	Edonard		Adjudant-chef	MEYER	
Adjudant	JOUZIER			Sergent-chef	MEYER	Henri
Adjudant	KIPFERLE	Jules		Sergent	MILLER	
Sergent-chef	LACAZE	Gabriel		Adjudant	MILLET	
Adjudant	LAFFONT	François		Sergent	MOREAU	
Sergent-chef	LAHERRERE	JEAN		Sergent-chef	OLIVE	Henri
Sons-lieutenant	LAMBERT	Jean		Commandant	OSTRE	
Lieutenant	LAMONTAGNE	Henri		Lieutenant	PASQUIER	Raymond
Capitaine	LAUCOU			Sergent-chef	PATRICE	Guy
Sergent-chef	LE GUILLOU	Jean				

Sergent-chef	PATRY		Sergent	TOUZART	Pierre
Lieutenant	PATURLE		Sergent	TRIBERT	
Lieutenant	PELISSIER	Marcel	Aspirant	TROLLARD	
Capitaine	PELLIOT		Sous-lieutenant	VARLET	
Capitaine	PERSON		Adjudant-chef	VAUGEL	Roger
Sons-lieutenant	PETIOT	Emile	Sergent-chef	VEGA	Marcel
Sons-lieutenant	PETIT	André	Sergent-chef	VERDIER	Camille
Capitaine	PETUS		Sous-lieutenant	VEZOLLE	
Sergent-chef	POILBOUT		Sergent-chef	VIELLE	Paul
Adjudant	PORTESSEAU		Sous-lieutenant	VIEULES	
Sons-lieutenant	POTHUAU	Alfred	Adjudant	VIGNERON	Guy
Adjudant	RABIER		Adjudant	VILLENEUVE	
Lieutenant	RAFFIN	Pierre	Lieutenant	VLES	Jean
Sergent	RAMOND		Adjudant-chef	VUILLEMOT	
Sergent	REYNAL	Jean	Sergent	WITZMANN	
Sergent-chef	ROCA	Guy	Sergent	ZAVATERRO	Lucien
Sous-lieutenant	ROGNANT		Lieutenant	ZEILLER	Pierre
Sergent-chef	ROIRON	Robert			
Lieutenant	ROTTE				
Adjudant	ROUILLAY				
Lieutenant	ROUVEL	Jean			
Sergent	SAINT-JEVIN	Victor			
Sergent	SAYTOUR	François			
Sergent-chef	SCHILLING	Maurice			
Sergent	SERRA	René			
Commandant	SIMON	Jean			
Adjudant	SIRE				
Adjudant	SOUCILLE	Pierre			
Sergent-chef	SQUILLARD				
Sergent	TARTARIN	Georges			
Sous-lieutenant	TERRIEN				
Sergent	THIERRY	Georges			

PART FOUR

The Crews
15.4.1944 - 8.5.1945

Section One

The crews of *Groupe Guyenne*

Pil.	Lt-col. VENOT	Cne MARIAS		Cne LECLERE		Ss-lt MINARD	
Nav.	Lt GUILLOCHEAU	Lt VERROT		Asp. FAYARD		Lt DANNA	
Bom.	Ad. KIPFERLE	Asp. POUGNET		Ss-lt BERGEROO		Ad. PIROUTET	
Rad.	Sg. LHOMOND	Sg.-ch. DIAZ		Sg.-ch. MUNIER		Ad. LEPETIT	
Méc.	Sg.-ch. COUPEAU	Sg.-ch. LAFARGUES		Sg.-ch. POQUE		Sg.-ch. BOUGE	
M-S.	Sg.-ch. FINALE	Sg. FRESIER		Sg. SAINT-HILAIRE		Sg. DEMALAUSSENE	
M-A.	Sg.-ch. BIAGGI	Sg.-ch. BLANC		Adj.-ch. TASSERIE		Sg.-ch. BELLE	

Pil.	Cne BARON	Lt HABLOT		Ad. GUISE		Cne CALMEL	
Nav.	Lt TRUCHE	Lt de SAINT MARC		Lt DABADIE		Lt BERRARD	
Bom.	Ad. VIGNERON	Lt WUILLEMIN		Ss-lt POTHUAU		Ss-lt PARDOEN	
Rad.	Adj.-ch. MIGNOT	Adj.-ch. PHILIPPE		Sg.-ch. ALAVOINE		Sg.-ch. ALLIX	
Méc.	Sg.-ch. CORMIER	Sg.-ch. PONS		Sg.-ch. LELONG		Adj.-ch. ROUX	
M-S.	Sg.-ch. PETITJEAN	Sg. MANICK		Sg. VAUTARD		Sg. MECHALY	
M-A.	Sg. BOURELLY	Sg.-ch. YVARS		Sg. VEGA		Sg. LADET-CHASSAGNE	

Pil.	Cne BERAUD	Ad. CHAMPEAUX		Cdt SIMON		Cne BRION	
Nav.	Lt VALETTE	Cne BARBE		Lt PELISSIER		Lt BARTHELOT	
Bom.	Lt RAFFIN	Lt FAYE		Lt ZEILLER		Adj.-ch. DEMESMAY	
Rad.	Ad. CLOAREC	Ad. AGUER		Sg.-ch. VIELLE		Sgt DARRIBEHAUDE	
Méc.	Sg.-ch. IMART	Ad. GONDOLLE		Adj.-ch. BRIGALAND		Sg.-ch. RICHARD	
M-S.	Sg.-ch. BELLON	Sg. COCHOIS		Sg.-ch. ROIRON		Sg. FOURES	
M-A.	Ad. MANFROY	Sg. DELACLAVIERE		Sg. FERNANDEZ		Sg.-ch. GONNOT	

Pil.	Ad. VANTROYEN	Sg.-ch. BILLAULT		Ad. DELLUC		Cne ARAUD	
Nav.	Cne PLAGNARD	Cne THIERS		Lt VALENTIN		Lt GARDETTE	
Bom.	Ss-lt NOEL	Adj.-ch. MEYER		Sg.-ch. LE GOFF		Lt FOURNIER	
Rad.	Sg. HERVELIN	Sg.-ch. HERAULT		Ad. LEGUELLEC		Ad. BARDOT	
Méc.	Sg.-ch. HIBLOT	Ad. MATHEY		Ad. ENTRESANGLE		Sg.-ch. MONSEAU	
M-S.	Sg. ICHE	Sg. BADOSA		Sg.-ch. POLI		Sg. BRUNET	
M-A.	Sg.-ch. ALLAIN	Sg.-ch. RATIER		Sg. YCHE		Ad. MERLE	

Pil.	Adj.-ch. VASSEUR	Cne BOURGAIN		Lt PASQUIER		Cne THIRY	
Nav.	Cne GRIMALDI	Lt DUVERT		Cne GAUBERT		Cne GALLOIS	
Bom.	Lt COUILLEAU	Ad. BEAUVOIS		Ss-lt PETIOT		Lt ROUXEL	
Rad.	Sg. LEMOIGNE	Sg.-ch. DUFOUR		Adj.-ch. VOGEL		Ss-lt BLANC	
Méc.	Sg.-ch. LOUY	Sg.-ch. BOURGEOIS		Ad. CUSIN		Sg.-ch. GODOFFE	
M-S.	Sg. CONSTANTIN	Sg.-ch. GARRIDO		Sg.-ch. VERDIER		Sg. AUBOURG	
M-A.	Sg.-ch. VELASCO	Sg.-ch. RUFFIE		Sg. SERRA		Sg. TAYMOND	

Pil.	Ad. RAMES	Cne COCHO		Lt GROSNIER		Cdt PUGET	
Nav.	Cne PETIT	Cne BROCHARD		Lt RAVOTTI		Cne BREARD	
Bom.	Adj.-ch. DEZELLIS	Ss-lt ROMAND		Cne ROY		Cne BLAES	
Rad.	Sg.-ch. MIMAUD	Ss-lt CLUZEAU		Sg.-ch. DURAN		Ss-lt CARRAT	
Méc.	Ad. BAUER	Sg.-ch. JARDIN		Ad. KOPP		Lt ROUSSEAU	
M-S.	Sg. BILLAUD	Sg. DUBOURGEAL		Sg.-ch. KERGRENE		Sg. BRUNET	
M-A.	Sg. LEGUILLOU	Sg. SEMAIL		Ad. MOT		Sg. LASSERRE	

Pil.	Cne BOE	Sg.-ch. BUSNEL	Lt TROUETTE	Cne MARCHAL	
Nav.	Cdt. DEMAZURE	Lt VIALATTE	Lt LEGOUIC	Lt de PREVAL	
Bom.	Ss-lt RUELLAN	Lt SUTOUR	Lt DASPET	Ss-lt MUNIER	
Rad.	Sg.-ch. PLOYE	Sg.-ch. BONNAFOUS	Sg.-ch. FANTON	Sg. REBIERE	
Méc.	Ss-lt CARISTAN	Adj.-ch. CHOMY	Sg.-ch. CHEVALIER	Sg. MOLINIER	
M-S.	Sg. AZEMA	Sg. HELARY	Sg. GAZEL	Sg. FABRE	
M-A.	Sg. BRESSON	Sg. BAERT	Sg. BERTRAND	Sg.-ch. GODARD	

Pil.	Adj.-ch. PUGET	Ad. CROZIA	Ad. de LAISSARDIERE	Ss-lt GRIDELET	
Nav.	Lt FLESCH	Lt BECAM	Cdt. CATTELAT	Cne VEAUVY	
Bom.	Ad. AURIOL	Ad. LASSERRE	Lt DELCROS	Ad. BAL	
Rad.	Sg.-ch. BORS	Ad. WEBER	Lt MASSON	Sg. MAYEUX	
Méc.	Sg.-ch. MERIC	Sg.-ch. MONCELET	Sg. LALLEMENT	Sg.-ch. GRIFFE	
M-S.	Sg.-ch. JAFFREUX	Ad. COQUOT	Sg. GUICHEMERE	Sg. MASSON	
M-A.	Sg.-ch. SENLEBES	Sg.-ch. RETORE	Sg. COMAT	Sg. BARTH	

Pil.	Ad. HANNEDOUCHE	Ad. MABILLE	Sg.-ch. FAUGES	Ad. SOUCILLE	
Nav.	Lt VLES	Lt CONDE	Cne LOEW	Cdt. BREARD	
Bom.	Ss-lt LAMBERT	Ss-lt PETIT	Sg. GODEFROY	Ss-lt FAUVET	
Rad.	Sg.-ch. VLAMINCK	Sg.-ch. MEYER	Sg. BOUTILLIER	Sg.-ch. LEMAIRE	
Méc.	Sg.-ch. BEAUVOIT	Sg. SAYTOUR	Ad. THIERY	Ad. AQUAVIVA	
M-S.	Sg.-ch. LIMACHER	Sg. DEBROISE	Ad. FLECK	Sg.-ch. CHIERICCI	
M-A.	Sg.-ch. OLIVE	Sg. SOURY-LAVERGNE	Ad. LAFONT	Sg. ZAVATERRO	

Pil.	Sg. LOURDEAUX	Lt HUBERT	Cdt. BROHON	Sg. ROCA	
Nav.	Lt PONCET	Lt RIGAL	Lt PLUCHART	Lt HYENNE	
Bom.	Lt LAMONTAGNE	Ss-lt de GENNES	Lt PERSEVAL	Adj.-ch. CHABROUD	
Rad.	Sg. BERNASCONI	Sg.-ch. NICAISE	Sg. MOUREY	Sg.-ch. MAXERAT	
Méc.	Sg. HAUTCŒUR	Ad. GRIBOUVA	Sg.-ch. CARAYOL	Sg.-ch. LAHERRERE	
M-S.	Sg. DESPLACES	Sg. MATHIOT	Sg.-ch. GARDIOL	Sg. MARTIN	
M-A.	Sg. BRULET	Sg.-ch. BLEUZAT	Adj.-ch. POTET	Sg. REYNAL	

Pil.	Cne GOEPFERT	Ss-lt BAYLE	Lt GONTHIER	Cne BORNECQUE	
Nav.	Cne AUBERT	Lt JOUMAS	Ss-lt CAPDEVILLE	Lt LAFOND	
Bom.	Ad. TOLU	Sg.-ch. DUGNAT	Sg.-ch. DUSSAULT	Lt DELRIEU	
Rad.	Ad. SPRAUEL	Sg. BOURREAU	Sg.-ch. RAYNAUD	Sg.-ch. LEBEDEL	
Méc.	Adj.-ch. BONHOMME	Sg. BARDE	Sg.-ch. PATRIS	Sg.-ch. HEYVANG	
M-S.	Sg. LEROY	Sg. MARTROU	Sg. HELLMUTCH	Sg. CHEYNAL	
M-A.	Sg. LAFON	Sg. ESQUILLAT	Sg. SAINTSEVIN	Sg. SANSON	

Pil.	Cne NOTELLE	Cdt MARTIN	Lt IDRAC	Lt DELVOYE	
Nav.	Lt MARTIN	Lt GUEYDON	Cdt de VULPILLERES	Lt BALDASSARI	
Bom.	Lt FLOUS	Lt LAUTOUR	Ad. LARUE	Lt CAPPAROS	
Rad.	Sg. SANTONI	Sg. GUILLOU	Sg. GAVOYE	Sg.-ch. VIGNE	
Méc.	Ss-lt BOUSSY	Sg.-ch. VIDAL	Ad. TRACLET	Sg.-ch. MARAMBER	
M-S.	Sg. NERI	Sg. GALLET	Sg. BOUFFAND	Sg. GODEFERT	
M-A.	Sg. MALLIA	Sg. FEGER	Sg. ROUTHIER	Sg. GRAZIANI	

Pil.	Cne PLOTON	Lt GUIOMAR	Sg.-ch. JOMARD	S.L. BERTRANDE
Nav.	Lt POIROT	Cne MEMIN	Lt NEUFINCK	Lt FLURIN
Bom.	S.L. DEGISORS	Ss-lt BISMUTH	Lt DESPOSITO	Ss-lt BERNOLLE
Rad.	Sg. VERMEULEN	Ss-lt BAZIMON	Sg. MONNIER	Sg.-ch. DENAT
Méc.	Sg. SIMONETTI	Sg. VANPARYS	Sg. SAUVAGE	Sg. SAMARCELLI
M.-S.	Sg. VAUTRIN	Sg. RICHARD	Sg. PENDARIES	Sg. TOURON
M-A.	Sg. JUNQUA	Sg. QUENTIN	Sg. YVETOT	Sg. GLEDEL
Pil.	Ss-lt FONTEIX	Sg.-ch. LACAZE	Lt DUVILLARD	Lt HIEBEL
Nav.	Lt ROUVEL	Lt DEPLUS	Ss-lt GRUNBERG	Asp. DAUPHIN
Bom.	Sg.-ch. SCHILLING	Asp. DUFRENOY	Sg.-ch. ROHRWASSER	Sg. MATTEI
Rad.	Sg. HOUDELOT	Sg. CHARPENTIER	Sg.-ch. GIOUX	Sg. FREPPEL
Méc.	Sg. LEROY	Asp. GRIBOUVA	Sg. INGARGIOLA	Sg. PERRIN
M-S.	Sg. GORRIAS	Sg. TARTARIN	Sg. BOUBILAT	Sg. DOMAGE
M-A.	Sg. FARNIER	Sg. TOUZART	Sg.-ch. CLERGERIE	Sg. BOISSARD
Pil.	Lt KERBRAT	Sg.-ch. JOS	Sg.-ch. CHEVRIER	Lt CHOURROUT
Nav.	Asp. DUQUESNOY	Ss-lt MATHURIN	Ss-lt JOUSSELME	Asp. HERMAN
Bom.	Asp. PASQUINE	Sg. BOUQUETDESCHAUX	Ss-lt RENARD	Sg.-ch. QUINTANE
Rad.	Sg. BERNARD	Sg. DUGAST	Sg.-ch. PLAISANTIN	Sg. DIEZ
Méc.	Sg. LAMOTHE	Sg. PRADIER	Sg. VILLETTE	Sg. RESTOU
M-S.	Sg. LESCURE	Sg. HAUTOT	Sg. LEJEUNE	Sg. DUROUX
M-A.	Sg. FUND	Sg. DEUTSCH	Sg. BORTHOMIEU	Sg. POTET
Pil.	Sg. BONNET	Lt AUMONT	Ss-lt MARGAILLAN	Sg. ALBAREIL
Nav.	Ss-lt LASSUS	Ss-lt TRENTESLAUX	Ss-lt VERGE	Asp. LECOQ
Bom.	Sg. LUPISGICH	Asp. SERIS	Asp. SAUBRY	Sg. BEDARD
Rad.	Sg.-ch. DERBESSE	Sg. PROST	Sg. BARLOY	Sg. BOISDRON
Méc.	Sg. LATTES	Sg. DUBACH	Sg. PUIG	Sg. SARAFIAN
M-S.	Sg. BOURSET	Sg. BERTRAND	Sg. FLEURY	Sg. MARTIN
M-A.	Sg. BOUGEROL	Sg. VESQUE	Sg. BALASTEGUI	Sg. ARTIAQUE
Pil.	Lt LEFEBVRE			
Nav.	Asp. SCHMID			
Bom.	Sg.-ch. BOISJOU			
Rad.	Sg. REQUENNA			
Méc.	Sg. ESTIENNE			
M-S.	Sg. SCHUTRUMPF			
M-A.	Sg.-ch. LEHONT			

The name of the Captain of each aircraft is underlined.

Section Two

The crews of *Groupe Tunisie*

Pil.	Cdt OSTRE	Lt DELAUNAY	Cne DUTREY-LASSUS	Cne MARIN
Nav.	Cne CHEVALIER	Cdt LOQUETIS	Lt TROTET	Lt FRANGOLACCI
Bom.	Lt CHEMIN	Lt ULMER	Ss-lt HERROU	Lt MINVIELLE
Rad.	Ad. CHABRES	Ad. PUGNET	Sg. BOURGOGNON	Adj.-ch. VUILLEMOT
Méc.	Sg.-ch. SCIOLETTE	Ad. MAGNIOT	Sg.-ch. PARATORE	Ad. VILLENEUVE
M-S.	Sg. RAMOND	Sg. RUST	Sg. VAISSADE	Sg.-ch. DARGENTON
M-A.	Sg.-ch. TILLIER	Sg. XIRUEGA	Sg.-ch. De FELIGONDE	Sg.-ch. MEUNIER
Pil.	Cne PERSON	Cne BARRAULT	Lt PETUS	Ad. LECORNU
Nav.	Lt JOLY	Lt VALETTE	Lt DESESSARD	Lt PLUCHART
Bom.	Lt BLOT	Lt BERGEON	Lt MIGNON	Lt RIOU
Rad.	Ss-lt ADNET	Ad. BAFFICO	Ad. COQUERON	Sg. COLLARD
Méc.	Ss-lt BOURDEROTTE	Ad. LARONZE	Sg. TRIBERT	Ad. CAILLIER
M-S.	Sg.-ch. CHEVALIER	Sg.-ch. MONNET	Sg.-ch. LINDEBERG	Ad. LOISELOT
M-A.	Sg.-ch. GERARD	Ad. STEPHANOPOLI	Ad. RIVIERE	Sg. BENET
Pil.	Sg.-ch. LOTH	Ad. BISGAMBIGLIA	Ss-lt VARLET	Lt LAU
Nav.	Lt BIENAIME	Lt GIGUET	Lt CHAPRON	Cne SCHLEGEL
Bom.	Cne RUBY	Lt LE POITEVIN	Ss-lt VIEULES	Sg.-ch. DABITON
Rad.	Sg.-ch. LAGIER	Sg.-ch. PHILIPPON	Ad. CHARAUDEAU	Ad. LECLAIRE
Méc.	Ad. TIERCET	Ad. RIPERT	Ad. CHARLIER	Sg. BEGUET
M-S.	Sg.-ch. WOLF	Sg. MATTE	Ad. ECKHARDT	Sg.-ch. DI LELIO
M-A.	Ad. MOSNIER	Sg.-ch. SOULES	Sg. GODART	Ad. GIRAUDIN
Pil.	Cdt STOLTZ	Lt CANDELIER	Cne LAFAYE	Ss-lt GEORGEON
Nav.	Lt DUGIT-GROS	Cne VAUCHE	Lt CAPRON	Lt BRACHET
Bom.	Lt BENIT	Lt PEHUET	Ss-lt DONDELINGER	Lt HABEZ
Rad.	Ad. MOULIN	Ss-lt CLAIREFOND	Sg.-ch. HENRIOT	Sg. RIGADE
Méc.	Sg.-ch. VANICELE	Sg.-ch. LEFEBVRE	Ad. VAYRON	Ad. HUMBERT
M-S.	Sg. ROUILLARD	Sg.-ch. PRE	Sg. PATALANO	Sg. MEMIN
M-A.	Sg.-ch. SONZOGNO	Sg. D'ANDREA	Sg. REYNAUD	Sg.-ch. MALTERRE
Pil.	Ad. LIDON	Ad. ROUILLAY	Lt VERHILLE	Sg.-ch. BAILLON
Nav.	Lt LAC	Cne MILLET	Lt SUVERAN	Lt LEROY
Bom.	Ss-lt ROTTE	Lt ALLEGRE	Lt HENRY	Ss-lt GAUTHERET
Rad.	Sg. MORIN	Sg.-ch. SOUILLARD	Sg.-ch. BONNELALBAY	Ad. GRANIER
Méc.	Ad. PUTHIER	Sg. MOREAU	Ad. GORIUS	Sg.-ch. DURAN
M.S.	Sg. BENET	Sg. VAYSSADE	Sg.-ch. NYS	Sg. GUEDEZ
M.A.	Sg.-ch. NONNENMACHER	Sg.-ch. WITZMANN	Sg.-ch. MARTIN	Sg. EVEN
Pil.	Ad. MILLET	Lt-Cl. VIGOUROUX	Cne BONNET	Lt BERTHET
Nav.	Lt BALAS	Lt BOURGEOIS	Cne ALLEGRE	Lt PATURLE
Bom.	Adj.-ch. MEYER	Lt PERSINETTE	Ss-lt GLOAGUEN	Cne HILAIRE
Rad.	Sg. DESRUMEAUX	Sg. BOURDON	Ad. ECHEC	Sg.-ch. JENGER
Méc.	Ad. SIRE	Lt HABERT	Ad. MAFAYOUX	Ad. MADAULE
M-S.	Sg. ACEZAT	Sg.-ch. EGALITE	Adj.-ch. MANO	Sg.-ch. EYRAUD
M-A.	Ad. FLAMENT	Sg.-ch. BURLET	Sg. HOYEAU	Ad. OGER

Pil.	Lt HEGLY	Adj.-ch. AULEN	Sg. LECLERCQ	Sg.-ch. BAGOT	
Nav.	Lt SERVIERE	Cne STANISLAS	Lt COTTARD	Lt PELLIOT	
Bom.	Ss-lt TOUREL	Ss-lt ROGNANT	Ad. ADAOUST	Lt ROLLET	
Rad.	Sg.-ch. VAUTHIER	Sg.-ch. BERDEAUX	Sg.-ch. MOREL	Sg.-ch. BRILLARD	
Méc.	Adj.-ch. VILLARD	Sg.-ch. PATRY	Sg. DUFAURE	Ad. MOLL	
M-S.	Sg.-ch. JACQUEMIN	Sg. BORDIER	Sg. USAI	Sg. LE MITHOUARD	
M-A.	Sg.-ch. CHAMPAGNOL	Sg. BORDELAIS	Sg.-ch. AUBIET	Sg.-ch. BESNARD	
Pil.	Lt SANTI	Ss-lt PELLISSIER	Sg.-ch. PERSON	Adj.-ch. VIDAL	
Nav.	Cne NOIROT	Asp. POMPON	Cne SAUTEREY	Lt GUENOIS	
Bom.	Ss-lt BARROIS	Ss-lt SUSBIELLE	Sg.-ch. AZAN	Sg.-ch. BRUNET	
Rad.	Sg. CADEAU	Sg. RIBON	Sg. SEMBLANET	Sg. CHANSON	
Méc.	Sg. MAINGUEUX	Sg.-ch. GUEGUAN	Ad. TURINA	Adj.-ch. GAUTHIER	
M-S.	Sg. BUREL	Sg. HERRY	Sg. FERRIER	Ad. BRUNO	
M-A.	Sg. DESCOUSIS	Sg. ERLY	Sg. BOURGUIGNON	Sg. PIZEL	
Pil.	Ss-lt PINAUD	Cne BRESSON	Ss-lt TERRIEN	Ad. PELISSIER	
Nav.	Lt HACHETTE	Cne De SAUVEBEUF	Ss-lt MOSNIER	Cne VIRRIER	
Bom.	Lt LORIDAN	Lt RONAT	Ss-lt MICHELON	Ss-lt NICOLAS	
Rad.	Ad. LAGOUTTIERE	Ad. RABIER	Sg. DUGARDIN	Sg. DESCHAUX	
Méc.	Ad. ROY	Sg. KANNENGIESSER	Ad. LE GALL	Sg.-ch. HAIMERY	
M-S.	Sg.-ch. VIGNY	Sg.-ch. POILBOUT	Sg. DELAROCHE	Sg. MADALLA	
M-A.	Sg.-ch. BUIGNET	Sg. MARTIN	Sg. DUNAND	Sg. MAZILLE	
Pil.	Lt DELEUZE	Sg.-ch. DANIEL	Sg.-ch. MERCIER	Asp. FRICOUT	
Nav.	Lt COURVALIN	Cne JEAN	Cne HAUTECŒUR	Ss-lt MONTOUROY	
Bom.	Asp. VEZOLLE	Ss-lt ROBERT	Cne JACQUOT	Ss-lt VALENCIENNES	
Rad.	Sg. CHABOUD	Sg. HAAS	Sg.-ch. BARITEAU	Sg.-ch. JOYE	
Méc.	Sg.-ch. JUSTE	Sg.-ch. RICAUD	Sg. MENNETRET	Sg.-ch. LE LEVIER	
M-S.	Sg. MEAU	Sg. FAIVRE	Sg. FERRERO	Sg. PETIT	
M-A.	Sg. BASTIAN	Sg.-ch. THIBEAU	Sg. LEDUC	Sg. LASCOMBES	
Pil.	Ad. JOUZIER	Ss-lt QUENEL	Sg.-ch. RICAUD	Ad. UMBRECHT	
Nav.	Lt GERMAIN	Cne MULLER	Lt MARTIN	Cdt. DUFOUR de LATTRE	
Bom.	Adj.-ch. CIMINO	Adj.-ch. PLEINDOUX	Lt HUGOT	Cne REVERSAT	
Rad.	Sg.-ch. PIOLOT	Sg. BERTHOME	Sg.-ch. MELLURET	Adj.-ch. GRAND'EURY	
Méc.	Sg.-ch. CRETON	Sg. GEMOT	Sg.-ch. EMPTOZ-LACOTE	Sg.-ch. KLEIN	
M-S.	Sg. LONGHI	Sg.-ch. BECK	Sg. CLEMENT	Adj.-ch. LARDEAU	
M-A.	Sg. DRISCH	Sg. BEYER	Sg. CLIQUOT	Sg. LAREYNIE	
Pil.	Cne BRUNET	Lt LAUCOU	Ss-lt De MARLIAVE	Sg.-ch. CONTI	
Nav.	Ss-lt FAUCHET	Asp. VIEL	Lt MATHIEU	Lt MULCEY	
Bom.	Asp. TROLARD	Ss-lt GIROUD	Ss-lt DUBAYEE	Sg.-ch. REYNAUD	
Rad.	Sg. MILLER	Sg. POCHONT	Sg. HANUSSE	Sg. DOBSIK	
Méc.	Sg. LUGARO	Sg. LEMASSON	Sg. PRUVOT	Sg.-ch. NAKACHE	
M-S.	Sg. DELAUZUN	Sg. HEMERY	Sg. TORRES	Sg. FOURNIER	
M-A.	Sg. GIRAUDON	Sg. CHARRIERE	Sg. MEREAU	Sg. CARBONNE	

Pil.	Lt HYVON	Ss-lt De MIRAS	Sg.-ch. CHATAIN	Asp. HESNARD
Nav.	Ss-lt MOREL	Ss-lt BLANCHIN	Cne CORMERET	Asp. ITART-LONGUEVILLE
Bom.	Ss-lt BRIET	Sg.-ch. BRU	Sg. BERNIGAUD	Sg. BEAUFILS
Rad.	Sg. LEGAY	Sg. LETOUBLON	Sg.-ch. CACCIA	Sg. JACQUEMER
Méc.	Sg. LEROY	Sg. PICOT	Sg. ONKEL	Sg. BOMBARDIER
M-S.	Sg. PEIGNE	Sg. BERGES	Sg. LAGRANDE	Sg. BRODMANN
M-A.	Sg. FOUQUE	Sg. LOBELLE	Sg. AUNEAU	Sg. MIGLIANICO
Pil.	Cne ROUQUETTE	Asp. COUPVENT	Sg.-ch. PROVENSAL	Sg.-ch. TRAMOND
Nav.	Asp. MOLBERT	Ss-lt BOURGOIN	Asp. AUBAS	Ss-lt FAUQUETTE
Bom.	Asp. CONDROYER	Asp. DREVET	Sg.-ch. DOUSSET	Asp. LABETAA
Rad.	Sg. MEREAU	Sg.-ch. LENFANT	Sg. JOUBERT	Sg. FERRANDO
Méc.	Sg. BANCAREL	Sg. LAVOCAT	Sg. GHILINI	Sg. LORTAL
M-S.	Sg. ROQUEFORT	Sg. LAFFONT	Sg.-ch. PACE	Sg. MOLUSSON
M-A.	Sg. JACQUET	Sg. DIXIUS	Sg. GILIBERT	Sg. MONSILLON
Pil.	Sg.-ch. ROQUE	Lt ROBERT	Ss-lt VEYRE	Cne SERMET
Nav.	Ss-lt WELLARD	Ss-lt PILLOT	Lt CHARPIN	Asp. VIEL
Bom.	Sg. PRADES	Sg. BROUSSOUX	Sg. RECOING	Ss-lt GIROUD
Rad.	Sg. BAUD	Sg. BONCHAUD	Sg. MERLET	Sg. POCHONT
Méc.	Sg. GALEA	Sg. BERTRAN	Sg. MARESCAUX	Sg. MAINGUEUX
M-S.	Sg. BOURGUND	Sg. BOISSAVIE	Ss-lt MALARD	Sg. HAYMERY
M-A.	Sg. BOGAERT	Sg.-ch. LEYGONIE	Sg. RECHOU	Sg. CHARRIERE
Pil.	Sg.-ch. GRESELLE	Sg.-ch. VALAT	Asp. MOULIN	
Nav.	Asp. JOVER	Asp. ABOUCHEDID	Asp. ROGUE	
Bom.	Cne YUNG	Asp. MORIN	Sg. DUMUIDS	
Rad.	Sg. SGIETOWITCH	Sg. DUCIMETIERE	Sg. XIRAC	
Méc.	Sg. BRUGERE	Sg. DUHAMEL	Sg. MARIANI	
M-S.	Sg. NEMESI	Sg. JACQUIN	Sg.-ch. CAPDEVIELLE	
M-A.	Sg. RONCHETTI	Sg. SIMON	Sg. BARNEOUD	

The name of the Captain of each aircraft is underlined.

Section Three

Some of the crews who survived the war

Fig 84. The crew of Capitaine Barbe.

Fig 85. The crew of Capitaine Cocho

Lieutenant Minard, Lieutenant Danna, Sous-Lieutenant Lepetit

Sergent de Malaussene, Aspirant Piroutet,   Sergent-Chef Bouge,
Sergent-chef Belle

Fig 86. The crew of Lieutenant   Danna
Fig 87. Below, The crew of Capitaine Delvoye.

Fig 88. The crew of Commandant Demazure.

Fig 89. The crew of Capitaine Marchal.

Fig 90. *The crew of Commandant Marias.*

Fig 91. *The crew of Capitaine Memin.*

Fig 92. The crew of Capitaine Plagnard

Fig 93. The crew of "M for Mike". Top: Sergent Iche, Sergent Allain, Sergent Hiblot, Sergent Hervelin. Lower: Sous-Lieutenant Noel, Capitaine Plagnard, Adjutant Vantroyan

Fig 94. Crew of Capitaine Thiers. *Herault, Badoza, Ratier, Mathey Billault, Capitaine Thiers Meyer. (YAM)*

Fig 95. *The crew of Lieutenant Vialatte.*

Fig 96. *The crew of Lieutenant Vulpierres.*

Fig 97. *Commandant Hoquétis with The Bey of Tunis*

PART FIVE

The End of the War

The End of the War

When the war ended all the personnel at Elvington waited impatiently for the moment when they would return to France.

But activity at Elvington did not come to an end. On the one hand, the crews continued with training flights to keep in practice, just in case ... because we were still only in a period of armistice. And, in the same context, the Commander in Chief, Sir Arthur Harris, had authorised us to fly over Germany again, but this time in daylight and at low altitude in order, as he put it, to allow the crews to see for themselves the results of their bombing and, in addition, to show by their presence that they were ready to start again should the armistice be broken.

Fig 98.Loading bicycles into the bomb bay of a Halifax in preparation for the return to France

On the other hand we inherited a thankless task, which caused us to complain somewhat. The Americans had left behind stocks of small anti-personnel bombs with fuses set to explode at ground level. They sometimes even went off prematurely in the hands of the armourers, and the British were rather anxious to get rid of them. We received a large quantity, together with handling instructions, and were instructed to go and drop them in a clearly defined area of the North Sea.

At the same time we discreetly let it be known at Bomber Command Headquarters that we would like to take up contacts with France again, that official transport was scarce and that perhaps our Halifaxes might fulfil that function from time to time. A few days later a reply came back to us. Sir Arthur Harris himself had made the aerodrome at Cormeilles part of Bomber Command and had installed a small staff. He gave us permission to land there and to use our aircraft to ferry men going on leave. Needless to say we were very grateful, and that gratitude persists to this day. All the more so because neither the weight nor the stowing of the luggage posed any problem for the Halifax.

Fig 99. Farewell party. (YAM)

16 October 1945. The Ceremony at Harrogate Ceremony.

During the morning of 16 October 1945 a ceremony took place at the Harrogate Cemetery, in which reposed aircrew from the British Commonwealth and allied countries who died while serving with the RAF. In a separate area there was a line of fifty-nine French graves. Each grave was surmounted by a white cross inscribed with a name and a date and above it a three-coloured cockade, blue in the centre.

In the pale light of autumn the French flag was raised on the flagpole at the command of *Commandant* Puget. Two squads from Elvington were there. The first squad presented arms. The members of the second squad each carried a wreath of fresh flowers.

This ceremony was more than a symbol of homage to those buried in the Harrogate Cemetery, because it was also in memory of all those from the *Groupes Lourds* who had died for France and for Freedom in the skies of all Europe.

20 October 1945. The Ceremony marking the departure of the *Groupes Lourds*.

The Commander-in-Chief of Bomber Command, Air Chief Marshal Sir Norman Bottomley, arrived at Elvington on the 20th of October to take his leave from the *Groupes Lourds*. The *Groupe Guyenne* was leaving that very day and the *Groupe Tunisie* was scheduled to leave on the 29th of October. The crews of No. 347 Squadron, dressed in French uniform, and those of No. 346 Squadron, in battledress, paraded in front of the Flying Control building.

Air Chief Marshal Bottomley took the salute as they marched past and then made the following speech in French:

'As Chief of Bomber Command it falls to me to have the honour of bidding you "*Au Revoir*" on the occasion of your return to your own country after long exile. In one sense it is a sad duty for me, because we can only regret the parting of those who for so long have been our colleagues in moments of great peril. But like you yourselves we are happy that you are returning to your country covered in glory; because that marks the achievement of an aim long contemplated and sought after by you.

'In these words of farewell I wish to express to the *Groupes Tunisie* and *Guyenne*, which we know as 346 and 347 Squadrons, our profound appreciation for the heroic and generous spirit that has motivated your

Fig 100. *Final Parade. (YAM)*

units. You bravely underwent advanced courses in our schools, and you devoted yourself to the task of learning our methods, and in so doing you gained the admiration of all. Finally, you fought alongside us, flying from British bases from the beginning of the summer of 1944 onwards, carrying the war well forward into the enemy camp. I should like to stress here the debt that we and you owe to *Colonel* Bailly, your commander, who, together with his brave crews, has earned our admiration and our respect.

'I wish to add a word of appreciation to those of you who have worked on the ground to keep *Tunisie* and *Guyenne* in the air. Your work was indispensable, and you have the satisfaction of having maintained a high rate of efficiency.

'Now that bonds have been forged uniting our two air forces, we are happy to think – indeed to know – that the close cooperation between the *Forces Aériennes Françaises* and the RAF will continue into the future.

'Finally, we particularly remember for a moment those brave flyers who gave their lives for the Allied cause. They died for France, and not

Fig 101. March Past. Final Parade. (YAM).

Fig 102. Inspecting the Guard. Farewell Parade. YAM

only for France but also for all the Allied nations, for all those who suffered oppression and enemy aggression. We will never forget them. Their sacrifices and their names will for ever be a part of the history of the Royal Air Force.

We thank you from the bottom of our hearts. *AU REVOIR! VIVE LA FRANCE!*'

Fig 103. Waving Farewell to 'Groupes Lourds'. (YAM)

After the two *Groupes* had marched off, the *Guyenne* crews went to their aircraft. Then for the last time the aircraft taxied slowly on to the Elvington runway to take off for Bordeaux.

On the 29th October the *Groupe Tunisie* took off in its turn in wet and misty weather. Sadly one crew crashed soon after take-off, adding two more deaths to a list that was already long.

All the crews of the *Groupe Tunisie* were preparing to return to France. One after the other they took off, just as they had done so many times on operations. Their destination was Bordeaux Mérignac. Unhappily *Lieutenant* Wellard's Halifax crashed near a farm shortly after take-off.

Right up to the final moment sadness did not spare the *Groupes Lourds*.

Fig 104. 29 October 1945. The crash of the Halifax captained by Lieutenant Wellard. (YAM)

Fig 105 & 106. Returning home. *(YAM)*

- 250 -

Fig 107. *Flying over Renault factory, Paris, on return to France. YAM.*

Fig 108. *Halifax aircraft of 346 Squadron lined up on French airfield aifter leaving England after the end of the War. (YAM)*

26 November 1945. Bordeaux greets the *Groupes Lourds*.

On 26 November 1945 there took place in the *Place des Quinconces*, in the presence of Lord Stansgate, the British Air Minister, and *Monsieur* Charles Tillon, Minister of Armaments, the ceremony in which the people of Bordeaux officially greeted the *Groupes Lourds*.

After the troops had marched in review order past *Monsieur* Charles Tillon, who was accompanied by *Général* Bouscat, *Colonel* Cattelat read out citations for awards to the *Groupes Guyenne* and *Tunisie*. Then the Minister decorated their flags with the *Croix de Guerre* in recognition of their brilliant conduct.

An RAF Group Captain then read out a citation from the Commander of the Royal Air Force to *Colonel* Bailly and decorated him with the OBE[27].

The ceremony ended with the award of a number of decorations and the traditional military march-past.

As was right and proper, Bordeaux had honoured those who had contributed to Victory at the side of the Allies.

28th September 1957: The inauguration of the Elvington Memorial.

The Elvington Memorial is a tribute to the sacrifices of our dead and at the same time to the friendship that binds us to the British people. It is the very manifestation of our memories. However, as *Colonel* Delrieu relates in his book '*Feu du Ciel, Feu Vengeur*' ('Fire of Heaven, Avenging Fire'), this memorial marked the successful end of a long road of endeavour.

As early as the 11th February 1947 it was discussed at the meeting of the provisional committee of the *Amicale*. We had to wait more than ten years for the commemorative memorial to be completed and inaugurated. That required patience! It took a great deal of perseverance on the part of the members of the board of the Association to stir the British bureaucracy into action. Wearied by the war, *Colonel* Venot

---

[27] OBE – 'Order of the British Empire', a decoration awarded for outstanding services to the British community.

even suggested abandoning the idea altogether: it was then, in 1955, that *Colonel* Puget, recently appointed Air Attaché in London, took over the file.

Lieutenant-Colonel Venot, Officer Commanding Groupe Guyenne until 10th. September, 1944, then of the Base in the interim after the departure of Colonel Bailly.

Commandant Puget, Officer Commanding Groupe Guyenne after the departure of Colonel Venot, then of the Base, sharing the duties with Commandant Hoquetis, until the return to France.

Fig 109. Lieuteneant-Colonel Venot.

Figs 110. Commandant Puget

The action he took proved to be effective, because the memorial was inaugurated in the 28th of September 1957. At last – but what a lot of bumph!

Fig 111. The Groupes Lourds Memorial at Elvington, draped in the tricolour before its unveiling. YAM

Fig 112. *General Bailly*

A number of us, from both the Active List and the Reserve, attended the ceremony. Central were the *Colonels* Bailly, Venot and Puget, as well as British notabilities, among them our old friend Air Commodore Walker.

Fig 113. *Air Chief Marshall Sir Gus Walker*

A military ceremony, simple and moving – and short, too short, as is often the case. But the two aircraft put at our disposal were needed for other things. Ours returned to Paris-Le Bourget the same day.

Unveiled, the memorial symbolises a wing.

On a plinth of granite there is on the left a block in the shape of a truncated pyramid; attached to this block is a rectangular stone, wider but slimmer and a little less deep, across which appears, immortalised for posterity, the silhouette of a Halifax; above it, carved into the stone, are the two words '*GROUPES LOURDS*' in capital letters and forming a semi-circle. Mounted on the left-hand block is a bronze plaque on which is engraved a dedication in both French and English:

"*Here was stationed 1944-1945 Groupement de Bombardement No. 1 comprising French Squadrons 'Guyenne' and 'Tunisie' R.A.F. Sqns. 346 and 347. This monument recalls their battles and the sacrifice of their dead.*"

Fig 114. *Laying a wreath at the unveiled Elvington Memorial. (YAM)*

Fig 115. 'The Elvington Memorial

We had achieved our aim: the erecting of a memorial on a square of French soil at the side of the road from York to the village of Elvington a few hundred metres from the entrance to the airfield, an unbreakable link in the chain of Anglo/French friendship.

PART SIX

On Course......:

Chapter 36

In which the reader meets P.O. Jules again four years later.

A short time afterwards the war ended and we went our separate ways. The war had brought us together and made friends of us. Now peace had taken us to our own firesides and homes and distanced us from each other. Nevertheless we remained friends, because perhaps the only good side of war is the forging of the sort of friendships that it would be difficult to make otherwise.

I continued to exchange letters with him from time to time, and then one day it occurred to me that I might commit his stories to print. I devoted myself to the task and, when I had finished, I set out for the small village in the Alps where he had opened a restaurant. I gave him the manuscript and asked him what he thought of it. After reading it he said to me:

'But your book isn't finished: or, if it is, it finishes in the air.'

'That's correct,' I replied, 'but to tell you the truth I don't know how to end it. I've tried at least ten times. The harder I try to kill you off, the more you come back crippled but...'

'The harder you try to be nice,' he interrupted, 'the less you succeed. Why don't you simply tell the truth? Is it absolutely necessary to kill me off?'

'No, of course not,' I said, 'but it would be much easier that way. That would take care of a lot of things. You would be someone gone forever before whom everyone could bow their heads.'

I gave him a number of other reasons, but none of them convinced him. He simply answered:

'I don't give a damn for books. There's only one thing that counts, and that's to come through with both one's arms and both one's legs. I don't want to die, even in a book!'

No matter how I tried to insult his outrageous materialism, nothing would make him change his mind. The result was that I had to resign myself to the fact that P.O. Jules would not die.

But the problem of an ending remained unresolved, and I was still trying to find a solution to it when he said to me,

'But what the hell! Don't worry your head about an ending for your book. Night brings consolation, and I'm quite sure you'll find something to tell your readers to end with. Let's have dinner instead.'

The conversation through that meal was very animated. We came to the subject of our return to France, and he told me about his last trip to Paris.

'There I was,' he said, 'in our beautiful capital city, and I decided to take the opportunity to go to the Ministry and look up some old friends. So, when I had checked in at the holy of holies, I thought I would take advantage of being there to ask them about my personal position.

'I see,' I said. 'You wanted to see if there was any chance of getting your promotion to *Commandant.*'

'Precisely,' he said, 'but listen to the end of the story. When they had dug out my file and discovered that I had enough years' service, they asked me to fill in my application for promotion: three years' regular service in the rank of *Capitaine*, four years on the reserve, the war, Headquarters, I met all the requirements. It was marvellous – I would move up to the category of Senior Officer, me who until now had never been more than a junior. So I signed the form.

'Alas, after waiting for six months and not seeing my name on the list, I decided to find out how things were going. I therefore took advantage of another visit to Paris to contact the Administrative Officer of the Second Air Region, to which I was subordinate. Suddenly everything became clear:

' "It's impossible to promote you to *Commandant",* he told me. Somewhat taken aback, I asked why.

' "You're short of two periods of regular service," he informed me.

' "But I was a *Capitaine* for three years, and, what is more, during the war."

' "That doesn't count. You'd be in a much better position if you had two periods of regular service of thirty-six hours than with your three years of war."

' "But that's incredible!"

' "Incredible, but true," replied the administration officer. 'You come under the 1925 regulation as modified in 1936, and there is nothing I can do about it."

'Confronted by the might of regulations, I surrendered, but I still didn't consider myself defeated. "Would it be possible," I asked, "for me to do the two periods?" The response was quick:

' "Quite impossible. There's no provision laid down for bomber officers to do extra time. Only former fighter officers are allowed to do it."

'I tried to discuss it further, but all in vain, and although I'm not very quick on the uptake I soon came to understand that two periods of regular service of thirty-six hours are worth more than three years of daily danger. Whoever it was who said that war doesn't pay was absolutely right.'

During this conversation we had finished our dinner. Then P.O. Jules excused himself and went out, only to come back again a few minutes later with a very dusty bottle.

'This,' he said, 'is reserved for friends.'

We gossiped until a very late hour, and the following morning I left. As I was going I said to him, 'Au revoir, mon vieux Jules.'

'Salut et prosperité,' he replied.

Then my car began to descend the slope that goes down to Chambéry. I left behind my friend and my memories.

Reader, if you should ever pass that way, don't forget to call in at the *Relais P.O. Jules*.

There you will find a veteran of No. 346 Squadron. Don't try to get him to talk about what he did during the war. He never speaks about it. He will tell you that it's all ancient history and that he doesn't remember.

And if this book has been written, dear reader, it is so that you won't have to ask him, and so that the curtain may be drawn once and for all.

PART SEVEN

When the Past becomes the Present

When the Past becomes the Present

After so many years I had found my friend again. We recalled our common past. We philosophised about the real sense of the war, and all we were left with was its stupidity.

And then we each went our own way, happy to have seen each other one final time before the ultimate journey.

In Great Britain at the same time numerous individuals, both civilian and military, became aware of how memorabilia of Bomber Command had disappeared without trace in the course of the years. The vast majority of the airfields that had seen crews set off on the exploits far away had been closed down. The buildings were in ruins and overgrown with weeds. They noted that of the 6,651 Halifaxes that had been built during the Second World War there was not one remaining, except an example in its crashed state in the R.A.F. Museum in London. Not a single one that survived the War had escaped its fate at the hands of the breakers. One by one contemporary witnesses were disappearing, and soon there would be no one who could speak of what had happened with so many tears and bereavements, so much blood.

It was decided to restore one of the abandoned bases, and the airfield at Elvington was chosen to set up the Yorkshire Air Museum. In parallel the same spirit came to life in France. The *Amicale des Anciens des Groupes Lourds*'[28] was re-formed enthusiastically. To keep memories alive I, with the aid of a number of comrades, wrote two books. The first, 'Nights of Fire over Germany', tells of the combats experienced by the aircrews in the face of the many dangers with which they were confronted. The second, 'Victory after the Inferno' describes their missions and their targets and draws up a balance-sheet of their operations.

---

28 'The Association of Veterans of the Heavy Bomber Squadrons'

The creation of the Yorkshire Air Museum and the Memorial to the Allied Air Forces.

Throughout the period from the end of the war until 1982, failing memory and time had done their work. The vast majority of the airfields from which the bombers had taken off on their long nocturnal raids had fallen into disrepair. Their state of neglect became worse from day to day, their appearance more desolate and pitiable.

The veterans of the *Groupes Lourds* who made a pilgrimage to Elvington were overcome by what greeted them. As they approached the aerodrome the first building that they saw was the Control Tower, just as it had been before.

From a distance it looked at if it had not suffered the ravages of time. But when they came to it they could see just how much it had deteriorated. Rubble blocked the staircase and prevented them from reaching the big room on the first floor from which the duty operational personnel had controlled take-offs and landings. They climbed the safety ladder outside, which only gave access to the balcony, and from there they could see the countryside around and the buildings – the hangars, the barracks in which we had had our rooms, and the Nissen huts where briefings were held. As they looked at the spectacle of neglect they were overcome by sadness and bitterness. Each of them

Fig 116. "...*They saw the control tower, just as it had been before....*"

Fig 117. *"...the spectacle of neglect...."* (YAM)

could imagine that it would not be long before nothing would remain of what had encompassed their life during those years of war, where they had lived life so intensely.

This air of neglect was also resented by a large section of the local population and by many young aviation enthusiasts. All of them saw a need to do something about it. Some part of the past had to be retained at any price. From this beginning there was born the idea of restoring an airfield and attempting to reproduce the wartime operational atmosphere.

In this recreated world would be preserved memorabilia of former leaders who had graced the period. In that way history would be united with places, facts and men. To this first idea was later added that of participation by the allies, above all the French.

By its very being the Yorkshire Air Museum would be a memorial to the Allied Air Forces.

On the basis of these guidelines, it was a natural step for the airfield at Elvington to be selected. Six acres of ground surrounding the Control Tower became the property of the museum. Restoration work was carried out by the local authorities and a large number of volunteers. There is a new programme of work each year.

Since their early beginnings the museum and the memorial have continued to grow. Each year there are more visitors. Elvington Airfield has become a centre of attraction, to the extent that travel agents now include a visit there in their programmes. In this way future generations will be able to remember.

Fig 118. The restored Control Tower at Elvington. (YAM)

Fig 119. 'The Memorial to the Allied Air Forces. A Monument to Nos. 4 and 6 Groups. (Photograph Mike Wood, official photographer to the Yorkshire Air Museum'.)

Fig 120. List of the seventeen squadrons making up No. 4 Group: twelve British squadrons; one Canadian squadron; two Australian squadrons; two French squadrons.

- 268 -

Fig 121. The No. 77 Squadron Memorial.

*This memorial is located at the entrance to Elvington Airfield. In 1986 it was proposed to move our memorial, which was in the centre of the village, and place it alongside that to No. 77 Squadron. The people of Elvington formally opposed the sug**gestion**.*

The restoration of the Yorkshire Air Museum Halifax.

When the decision to create the Yorkshire Air Museum and the Memorial to the Allied Air Forces was taken in 1982, one of the first thoughts of the founders was to find one of the 6,000 Halifaxes that had been built during the Second World War. Their search, sadly, was in vain. There was not one single complete example still in existence in either France or Great Britain. That did not stop the British. They decided to reconstruct one using separate components obtained from anywhere and everywhere. From the wreckage of a Coastal Command aircraft that had force-landed in a Scottish marsh, they recovered part of the fuselage. This section was conveyed to Elvington by road. The four engines were provided and delivered by the French Air Force. The *Ailes Anciennes du Bourget* restored the tail-wheel from a Halifax shot down over France in 1944.

A YAM team led by Ian Robinson and apprentices from British Aerospace, from Brough near Hull, with help from various volunteers carried out the restoration work, which is now completed. For their part the French are happy to have been part of this undertaking. In it they see a symbol of the friendship that united us during the war and which still lives on today.

Fig 122. The YAM Halifax during restoration. YAM

Fig 123. The completed YorkshireAir Museum Halifax : *"Friday the 13th.." - With French veterans, after the Roll-Out ceremony on Friday, 13 September 1996.*

13/14 September 1985: the *Groupes Lourds* take part in the biennial No. 4 Group Reunion.

A year after the decision to go ahead with what was called 'the regrouping of the former *Groupes Lourds*', the pilgrimage to Elvington could take place at last. Louis Germain looked after the organisation of the visit together with Mrs. Semlyen, the Founder-President of the Yorkshire Air Museum, and Mr. Pontefract, its Treasurer. On the 13th of September the Ceremony of Remembrance was held. The French Air Attaché in Great Britain and the French Consul in Liverpool attended.

On the following day, the 14th of September, a religious service in honour of the dead of No. 4 Group, of which the *Groupes Tunisie* and *Guyenne* formed a part, was held in the prestigious surroundings of York Minster. As usual the ceremony was both simple and moving. The congregation joined heartily in the prayers and the hymns. There was no doubt, however, that the most moving moment came when Air Chief Marshal Sir Augustus Walker performed the ceremony of 'Turning the Page', which takes the form of turning a page in the volume that contains the names all members of No. 4 Group who died. Their names are inscribed in alphabetical order, independent of nationality. Throughout the year the register is kept in one of the side chapels of the Minster. At the mid-point of the service the book is solemnly carried to the Choir, where it is placed upon a desk, where the chosen dignitary turns the page. After the page has been turned the register is equally solemnly taken back to the side chapel. At this moment one would need to be made of wood not to feel choked with emotion.

Fig 124. Ceremony of Remembrance at the Memorial, September 1985. Left: Air Chief Marshal Sir Augustus Walker. Right: Général Jean Calmel.

For all those who took part this pilgrimage was a time of reunion, during which memories of the past were reawakened with much nostalgia.

Fig 125. Above, York Minster.

Fig 126. Right, 'The astronomical clock and the register of those who died, including those of No. 4 Group, Bomber Command'.

The Astronomical Clock in York Minster and the Register of the Dead of No. 4 Group

The Astronomical Clock, located in the north transept of York Minster, commemorates the sacrifices made by the aircrew of the Royal Air Force, the Commonwealth and the Allies who operated from bases in Yorkshire, Durham and Northumberland during the Second World War.

The Book of Remembrance and Honour contains the names of 18,000 officers, non-commissioned officers and airmen. They flew on bomber, fighter and reconnaissance duties. The majority of them belonged to the Royal Air Force, but 3,537 of the names were from the Royal Canadian Air Force, who were numerically large enough to make up an autonomous Group, the famous No. 6 (Canadian) Group.

Australians, South Africans and New Zealanders are included on the list. The book also commemorates the sacrifices made by allies from the Continent – Belgians, Dutch, French, Norwegians, Czechoslovaks and Poles – who were stationed in the area and who died in the war. Every three months a service is held at which a page is turned.

8th June 1988. The memorial at Grandcamp-Maisy.

From 1981 onwards a number of veterans of the *Groupes Lourds*, whom I will not name lest I should forget any of them, were frustrated to discover that nowhere in France was there a monument or a memorial paying tribute to the part they had played in the liberation of France. They realised that with the passage of time their ranks would thin out and soon there would be no one left who could tell of their sacrifice.

Admittedly their efforts were orientated towards the destruction of Nazi Germany, its ports, its railways, its factories. They reduced the industrial potential of the enemy. Who can estimate the contribution made by Bomber Command, and specifically by No. 4 Group, in the final victory? But the veterans also recalled their participation on the Normandy front and their operations in support of the Allied troops on the ground. And they remembered that on the night of the 5th/6th June 1944 they bombed German coastal batteries on the Atlantic Wall at Grandcamp-Maisy, not far from the *Pointe du Hoc* where the American Rangers covered themselves in glory in a combat that earned the admiration of the whole world. French aircrew were there on that memorable day, and it seemed only just to them that their presence should be acknowledged. In this way the idea of a memorial at Grandcamp-Maisy was conceived.

In 1987 and 1988 the will of the veterans of the *Groupes Lourds* and the unceasing effort of the Municipal Council of Grandcamp-Maisy and its Mayor, *Monsieur* Colin, succeeded in overcoming all difficulties. On 9 June 1988 the monument was inaugurated. The part played by the French crews and the sacrifice they made were engraved in stone for all time. Visitors or simply passers-by can now bow in thought and reflect that one out of every two died.

18 September 1988: Ceremony of Remembrance at the renovated Elvington memorial.

Fig 127. 'Memorial to the Groupes Guyenne and Tunisie. This is the text of the inscription carved on the monument: "French crews of the Groupes Lourds took part. They participated by day and night in the destruction of Nazi Germany. One in every two died.'

Since 1957 the condition of our memorial at Elvington had deteriorated slowly but surely as a result of bad weather and freezing fog. Regular maintenance work had been carried out, but it had not been enough. And so in June 1988 the Elvington Council, led by its Mayor, Mr. Jacques, decided to go ahead with renovation work.

In September 1988, on the occasion of the Ceremony of Remembrance, those taking part found themselves in front of a central monument that once more stood straight and which was surrounded by a newly planted hedge, with a lawn such as can only be found in England.

And so the monument had regained its original pristine condition. The people of Elvington are proud of it. It has become their own monument, honouring Frenchmen they have never forgotten, a memorial to an Anglo-French friendship sealed by blood and founded on reciprocal respect.

A monument unique in its simplicity.

The Fiftieth Anniversary of the Allied landings on the Normandy beaches, June 1944.

In 1984 the *Anciens des Groupes Lourds* got together again. Every two years, on the occasion of the anniversary of the Battle of Britain in mid-September, our Association takes part in the Reunion of No. 4 Group, which traditionally ends with a most moving religious service in the impressive surroundings of York Minster.

On the occasion of the Fiftieth Anniversary of the Allied landings on the Normandy beaches the civil authorities of the County of York, senior commanders of the Royal Air Force, members of the Committee of the Yorkshire Air Museum, the people of Elvington and their mayor decided to honour jointly the participation of the French *Groupes*

Fig 128. '...*In the bus were complete sets of aircrew equipment....*'

Lourds in operations, which to this day remains engraved in all their memories.

More than any sentence, more than any discourse, a simple telling of the facts will in itself be sufficient to demonstrate the spirit of friendship and cordiality that marked the whole occasion.

Fig 129. *From left to right: Sammecelli, Pierre; Bisner, René; Nicaise, Robert; Verbesse, Jean-Marie; Belle, Max; Bourgain, Louis; Hautot, André.*

To receive the aircraft carrying the French delegation the Royal Air Force had decided to bring the airfield at Elvington, disused since 1958, back into service. Air safety services – the fire service, radio aids, runway control - were put into place. When the aircraft arrived at eleven in the morning everything was ready for it.

The aircraft touched down without any difficulty. It rolled along the runway bearing 290 degrees, the same one used by the crews in 1944 and 1945. When we came to the end of the runway a ground mechanic gave us the signal to stop the engines. Mr. Derek Reed, the Secretary of the Yorkshire Air Museum, came to the door of our aeroplane. He wished us welcome and then led us to the 'bus', one of those 'good old' vehicles that carried us between the briefing room and the dispersals when operations were on.

In the bus were complete sets of aircrew equipment – flying suits, helmets, parachutes and harnesses, oxygen masks and so on.

We put them on, and it was in that gear that we arrived a few moments later on the hard-standing at the side of the Control Tower and near to the flagpole, at the top of which the British flag was flying. It was the moment of reunion, of hand-shaking, of greeting.....

Soon afterwards 'God Save the Queen' rang out, played by the Band of the Royal Air Force, while the Union Flag slowly descended the mast. Once down it was replaced by the French flag. In its turn the *Marseillaise* sounded, and the French flag was raised to the top of the mast.

It remained there throughout all the ceremonies. Elvington was once again the French base that it had been in 1944 and 1945, the only foreign enclave in England during the war[29].

For the two days that our visit lasted our delegation was the sinecure of all eyes, in the best of senses.

In that way we could tell that the memory of the French at Elvington still lives on, a symbol of the friendship that unites our two peoples.

The Yorkshire Air Forces Museum and the Memorial is situated at Elvington airfield near York. During the closing period of World War II, it was the home of the French heavy bomber squadrons, groupes Guyenne and Tunisie. Indeed it was our author's home then.

The strong French links remain to this day. The museum is a registered charity and is open throughout the year. There you will find the many things of interest a restored Halifax aircraft of the type flown by Jules and his comrades, a replica of a section of the French Officers' Mess, french artifacts and ephemera, symbolising this dynamic and unique French connection.

---

29   In those days the people around York called it 'Little France'.

Fig 130. Large scale model of Halifax. (YAM)

Fig 131. Colonel Goepfert and Mr. Ian Robinson, the Chairman of the Yorkshire Air Museum, at the unveiling of reproductions of two of the paintings from the Wartime French Officers' Mess - the Arc de Triomphe and Notre Dame.

Fig 132. Elvington Entente, *reproduced from a painting by Brian Gaunt which symbolises the enduring links between the French Air Force, past and present, and the Yorkshire Air Museum.*

PART EIGHT

Epilogue

Epilogue

October 1984.

It was cold, that autumn Sunday. The clouds pressed on the roofs of the houses and the tops of the trees. The bitter wind made haloes of mist on the window panes. On the low table in the sitting room a few flowers of different colours, carelessly thrown into a crystal vase, attracted the eye and stole the light. There were delicate but indefinable scents in the air. Above all, the sharp contrast between the chill of the road outside and the warmth of the room created a strange atmosphere of reverie and intimacy.

In this atmosphere of gentleness and melancholy I decided to set about sorting out a number of old books and papers, the sort of things that accumulate in the course of years. I started the task by going through some old photographs, reading again letters of other days. I found myself reliving the distant past, and then I suddenly came across a yellowed sheet of paper. It was a poem that P.O. Jules had dedicated to me, many years ago. Here it is:

To all my Comrades.

You who have known all there is to know,
Bombers leaving, second-precise,
The carousel that leads to tragic combat,
The infernal roar of engines in the night,
Dangers of the dark that hide and haunt –
You who have known it, what became of you?

You who have known all there is to know,
Raids ending in the shades of night
In a vast flame, a sudden burst and sinister,
T8787he tragic reckoning when some come back,
The sombre balance, inhuman and macabre
All those names, set out on blackboard cold –
You who have known it, what became of you?

You who have known all there is to know,
Weather dark and wet, and thick, thick cloud,
Cloud of sadness, in which you hide,
Where German fighters can't pursue;
And clear skies that dark furrows streak;
Nightmare skies that we would rather find
Than the soft clear light of starlight skies –
You who have known it, what became of you?

You who have known all there is to know,
The climate bleak of country north,
Countryside of fogs that blur the sight;
Returning in the morn to barrack cold.
The stove's flame, and the letter that you write,
The sleep you seek in midst of fears –
You who have known it, what became of you?

You who have known all this, and more besides,
What have you kept of all those years?
Perhaps just the smiling wink
Of a grinning gremlin, gently mocking,
Who watched over our fear-filled nights;
Perhaps only the half-lost glimpse
Of a night-time moth dancing in the moon,
The dance of a hope of passion warm,
Or perhaps a lyric dance
Of little goblins, laughing, mocking, gay,
Singing a forgotten bedside song –
You who have known it, what became of you??

And as for you, my gremlins, goblins, imps,
Who helped me live through nights of doubt –
Whisper to me now what they became:
They were my friends.

When I had read these lines again, it occurred to me that more than twenty years had slipped away since I had last seen P.O. Jules. Our fates had followed separate roads. Our paths had not crossed. Admittedly, we had exchanged letters from time to time. But neither of us had tried to see the other again. Why? No matter. On thinking it over I was gripped by an irresistible urge to see him again. I telephoned him and we fixed a meeting.

The following morning I set out on the road that would take me to the Savoyard village that P.O. Jules had moved to in retirement. It was a beautiful morning, and the countryside was radiant with light. I was happy, but at the same time I was uneasy, and my unease grew at every turning of the road. As time passed I asked myself what the atmosphere would be like when we met again. I had not the slightest doubt that he would welcome me with warmth. Yet I was afraid that all the years that had passed might, without our knowing it, have changed us profoundly. I was afraid that the wrinkles of accumulated worries on our foreheads might have altered the memories we had shared. Thoughts such as this occupied my mind to such a degree that the journey seemed short. Just before I reached my destination, a little unsure of the way, I stopped to ask a passer-by the way to my friend's *auberge*.

'It's just a bit higher up the mountain, by the side of the torrent,' he replied.

I continued along the road, which now wound upward through thick, bushy woodland. To still the emotion that assailed me I looked at the countryside, which changed at every turn. I was trying to analyse slight details when suddenly, at a bend in the road, the forest disappeared and gave way to the spectacular view of a small lake, its intense blue sparkling in the sunlight, a fresh breeze rippling its surface. All around dark rock-faces reached up to the sky, plumes of snow rising from their summits. Here and there on their flanks, like scars, were bare areas of deep red rock, almost russet in hue. The pale white expanses, the intense mass of the forest, the rocks streaked with lichen, the untouched escarpments, formed an extraordinary tableau, in which crystal waterfalls endowed the colours with a delicate harmony.

I went on. The road now ran alongside a torrent of foaming, dancing water. In this setting, imprinted with gentleness, I soon saw a small, red-roofed inn, its green shutters contrasting with the white of its walls. Once through the gate I passed along a gravel drive on which my tyres seemed to sing, as if they wanted to share the joy of our coming reunion. I stopped before the front door. I was hardly out of the car when I saw a man coming towards me. I recognised P.O. Jules. He recognised me as well. He came up to me with his well-remembered slow stride.

When he reached me he held out his arms, spread them wide and, without saying a word, embraced me firmly.

It was all as simple as that, yet I was more moved than I could have imagined. At the end of a road that led nowhere I had found my friend again, with the unbreakable bonds that join human beings when they are near the end of their powers. Time had passed, but nothing had changed.

When we had embraced I saw my friend furtively wipe away, with the back of his hand, a tear that glinted on his eyelid; and I knew that he was feeling the same emotion as I was. Taking me by the arm he led me to the entrance of the hotel. Once at the door he said to me,

'You are my guest,' and then, as if in an afterthought, 'I'll be with you in a moment – just give me a time for a small formality.'

He went behind a little reception counter just inside the entrance hall and came out with a small piece of cardboard, on which I could make out the word '*Complet*'.[30]

'In this way we wont be disturbed' he said, and he went on: 'The art of being a receptionist sometimes consists of not receiving.'

Having performed this preliminary operation, very important to him, he asked me if I would like to go and freshen up. 'After which,' he said, 'we'll be able to refresh our throats!'

Then he showed me to my room. When showing it to me he mentioned that it was the room reserved for VIPs. Then he left me.

While I was unpacking the bits and pieces I had brought with me I thought about this first contact, and I was happy to confirm that I hadn't been mistaken. I had found P.O. Jules as I remembered him,

---

30   '*Complet*' – the equivalent of 'Hotel Full'.

with the same look redolent of enthusiasm and friendliness. When he had embraced me I had rediscovered the kind of passionate exaltation that had always characterised him. As soon as I met him I knew that he had retained his love of living, serving and loving. I knew that we would talk for long hours about days gone by. I was in a hurry for our conversation to start. He was waiting for me, and I then had the opportunity to observe him more closely.

He had scarcely changed. He still had the same clear laugh, the same directness when he looked at you. Only a few wrinkles on his forehead and his silvery hair bore witness to the passing of the years. He wore, as always, a *blouson* drawn in at the waist, the dark-brown colour of which contrasted with the lighter brown herring-bone tweed of his trousers. He still had the same trick of scratching his head to 'stimulate his genius', as he said, which always became apparent when he used to expound his ever-original theories.

Medicine, for example, had always fascinated him. He had some very individual views on hygiene and diet, in which connection he had once given me a lecture on the virtues of good food and the merits of fats. He often compared the dark, preoccupied air of modern man, for whom a heart attack was lying in wait, with the much more attractive air of the *bon vivant* of former days, who took care to perpetuate the traditions of French gastronomy and who appreciated to the full the gifts of the Almighty. In this same way he had developed a profound and boundless admiration for the medieval monks who preserved and developed the science of viniculture.

He knew that old age did not only come to old men, which is why he tried to stay young. To implement this philosophy of relaxation, he had a series of formulae of which the reader will appreciate, just as I think I do, the high intellectual significance.

'In order not to die,' he used to say, 'one must find time to live.' And:

'A man of iron must always have a mind of steel.'

'An excess of worry is as pernicious as an excess of sauce'.

'The theory of relativity, as expounded most profoundly by Einstein, makes it possible to calculate values in four dimensions, except the time it takes to mature a Beaujolais.'

Sometimes, in discussions, he would develop revolutionary ideas in which paradox was elevated to the status of an institution. In addition, night-time was the most effective stimulant for his fertile imagination. So he used to call himself a 'noctambulist' and an anarchist, but he put it like this:

'I'm a night bird and a man of the *Grand Soir* at one and the same time.'

P.O. Jules came from a family of fishermen, and he loved to tell stories about the old salts among whom he had grown up as a child. He could talk knowledgeably about fishing grounds – Utsire, *La Grande Sole*, Dogger Bank. He had himself experienced the hardships of a fisherman's calling. He had lived with men with faces seamed by the salt, the wind and the fogs. He had often asked them to tell him about the campaigns they had fought in in the days of sailing ships.

From the contacts he had had with such old-time sailors, accustomed as they were to storms, danger and death, he had developed a profound faith. He believed in God, and he searched within his belief for some means of raising himself above the stupidity of war, accepting without recrimination its sacrifices and its injustices. But that did not prevent him mischievously criticising the chaplain by saying to him:

'Father, your Communion wine is not worth calling wine!'

Why did P.O. Jules become a flyer? Had he succumbed to the lure of infinite space? Did he yield to an irresistible urge? Was it simply a vocation or a result of a taste for adventure? I am unable to say with any degree of certainty. I do know however that for a long time he could not decide whether to make a career in the Navy or the Air Force. Throughout his entire youth he had dreamed about the sea. But his first experiences had disillusioned him. He had not discovered the atmosphere of the stories and the legends of his childhood. The poetry of brigs, schooners and dories had vanished. All he had seen was a world in confusion, dominated by industrialisation, in which the only thought was of profit. No doubt he had dismissed from his mind the storms when the elements, unconfined, battered against the hull, which groaned in unbearable suffering. No doubt he had reflected on the attractions of a calling in which one could overcome such forces. Nevertheless, looking up at the sky and reading avidly tales of the exploits of Mermoz, the Guillaumets, and many others, he came to admire the pioneers of a growing industry, where everything was yet to be done. The world of the sky beckoned him. Later he was to tell me that his joys had measured up to his hopes.

All his life had been an amalgam of contradictory ideals and realism, hope and despair, action and inaction, happiness and sadness, and we talked about it at length until well into the night.

I will not go back to his memories of the war. The reader has been able to absorb them already. Instead we might ask ourselves why a career that started under such favourable auspices was brutally interrupted, and what the reasons were that brought P.O. Jules to go into the hotel business, a calling for which he was completely untrained.

'It's very simple,' he told me, ' When the guns stopped shooting and wings were folded, I returned to my past. I was tired of being away from my own folk. And so I decided to stay in France, the country where it is said that you can always live well. I was posted to the Air Ministry, and I began a career in Administration. The war was over. I knew why and how we had been on the winning side. I had no desire to see war begin again, wherever it might be. It was then that I handed in my arms. I gathered together my meagre resources, and with the help of some comrades in England I took over the management of a hotel in Savoie.'

The page had been turned, and he had no regrets.

And so he gave up his Air Force career. But the hazards of existence did not allow him to forget it. The unusual way in which he ran his hotel earned for him the cognomen of *'Hôtelier pilote'*. And so he found himself in the position of being both a hotel manager who was a pilot, and a pilot who was a hotel manager.

It was a strange destiny.

The twelve strokes of midnight had sounded long before we went back to our rooms.

The following morning we parted.

Fig 13385. View through the Elvington Memorial. YAM

Dear Reader,

We hope you have enjoyed this book. During the course of your reading, you will have realised that the author, *Capitaine* Bourgain, **is** Pilot Officer Jules.

Many attempts have been made over the years to persuade the author, Louis Bourgain, to say how autobiographical the adventures of P.O. Jules were.

Just before this book went to the publishers, Louis Bourgain came across from France to York, despite ill-health, for an editorial meeting to discuss final details.

'Do you know who P.O. Jules is ?' he asked.

'Well, we've always wondered whether .... '

'C'est moi !' (It's me !)